Vivādaratnākara
of
Caṇḍeśvara
Thakkura

Vivādaratnākara of Caṇḍeśvara Ṭhakkura

PORTIONS
DEALING WITH
THE LAW OF
PARTITION
AND
INHERITENCE

Translated by

GOLAPCHANDRA SARKAR SASTRI
DIGAMVAR CHATTOPADHYAYA

Gian Publishing House
29/6 SHAKTI NAGAR • DELHI-110007 • INDIA

GIAN PUBLISHING HOUSE
PUBLISHERS OF BOOKS ON HUMAN CIVILIZATION
29/6 SHAKTI NAGAR, DELHI-110007

First Reprint in India, 1986

Printed at Goyal Offset Printers, Delhi-110035
and published by Smt. Gayatri Garg
for Gian Publishing House, Delhi-110007

TO

THE HONOURABLE

SIR FRANCIS WILLIAM MACLEAN, KT., M.A., Q.C., K.C.I.E.

CHIEF JUSTICE OF BENGAL

THIS BOOK

IS

WITH HIS LORDSHIP'S PERMISSION

RESPECTFULLY DEDICATED

BY HIS HUMBLE SERVANTS

THE EDITORS.

महामान्य श्रील श्रीयुक्त स्यार् फ्रान्सिस् उड्रलियम् म्याक्लीन्
नाइट्, एम् ए, कि उ सि, के सि आइ इ,
वङ्गश्रेष्ठधर्म्माधिकरणाध्यक्षमहोदयकरकमलेषु

भूतिव्राजैर्भुवनवलयं व्याप्य विद्योतमाने
साम्राज्येऽस्तं व्रजति तपनो नैव यस्या विशाले ।
सा सम्राज्ञी प्रतिनिधिवरं श्रेष्ठधर्म्माधिकारे
युक्तं सर्व्वैरभिमतगुणैः प्राहिणोद्भारते त्वाम् ॥ १ ॥

न्यस्तो भारस्त्वयि खलु तया योग्यपात्राग्रगण्ये
मीमांसायां सुनिपुणमतौ सूक्ष्मदृष्टौ प्रवीणे ।
यत् त्वं तन्वन्नविषमदृशा धर्म्मदण्डप्रभावं
तस्या एवोन्नयसि भुवने धर्म्मराज्यस्य कीर्त्तिम् ॥ २ ॥

शान्तं शीलं तव सुसदृशं सर्व्वथा सौम्यमूर्त्तेः
स्निग्धा वाचः सदयहृदयस्यानुरूपास्तवैव ।
शास्त्रज्ञानं तव च सदृशं तीक्ष्णगम्भीरबुद्धेः
शास्त्रज्ञानानुगुणमखिलं कर्म्म चैवानवद्यम् ॥ ३ ॥

त्रातुं दीनाननशनजनान् घोरदुर्भिक्षदग्धान्
नानाकृत्यैः कृतमपि सदा व्यापृतेन त्वया यत् ।
कारुण्यात्मन्नगणिततनूतापमश्रान्तयत्नैः
तत् ते कार्य्यं कमपि हि हृदो देवभावं व्यनक्ति ॥ ४ ॥

दण्ड्ये दण्डस्तव समुचितो जातिधर्म्माविशेषः
स्थैर्य्यं विघ्नेऽप्यतिगुरुतरे स्वीयकृत्येऽद्रितुल्यम् ।
विद्योत्साहः कृपणकरुणा भारतक्षेमचेष्टा
सर्व्वं तेऽस्मद्गृहलपितवज्जातमत्राचिरेण ॥ ५ ॥

धर्म्मशास्त्रमयो ग्रन्थो धर्म्माधिकरणेश ! ते ।
दीयते गृह्यतामेष भक्तिपुष्पाञ्जलिस्त्वया ॥ ६ ॥

PREFACE.

The Vivada-Ratnakara is one of the most comprehensive works on the substantive portion of Hindu Law, and is respected by the Mithila school as a most authoritative commentary. Having had to translate portions of it now and then, for reference in court in connection with matters left obscure in the authorities hitherto translated into English, we thought it desirable to have a translation of the Dáyabhága portion of the Book, that is, the portion dealing with partition and inheritance, in its entirety, and set about it more than two years ago, acting jointly in court when we were both free from other work. This is the reason that we have taken such a length of time in bringing out the present volume. We began our translation from the Edition of the original text published by the Asiatic Society of Bengal, but found it so unsatisfactory in several places and sometimes even wanting in the Rishi texts of which a commentary is given, that we were obliged to collate and compare the text with the original Samhitas and also with a manuscript copy of the Viváda-Ratnákara procured from the Library of the Calcutta Sanscrit College. Notwithstanding these precautions however, one mistake in Chapter XIX contained in the A. S. Edition escaped our notice and we have made the necessary correction in the *errata.* Although we have in many instances adopted the translation of the Rishi texts made by Mr. Colebrooke in his translations of the Mitákshará and the Dáyabhága* we have generally given our own rendering keeping as close to the original as we could.

---

* The book of that name by Jímútaváhana.

The presence of the original text side by side with the translation is of great advantage for testing the accuracy of the rendering and comprehending the full sense of the original. We have therefore added the original text after the translation. For the convenience of citation we have sub-divided each chapter into paragraphs numbered consecutively, each Rishi text with the commentary on it bearing a separate number, and for facility of reference we have made the Index as complete as we could. In short, we have tried to supply a want which we, in common with many others in the profession, have long felt.

HIGH COURT, CALCUTTA.
The 29th July, 1899.

G. S.
D. C.

INTRODUCTION.

CONTENTS OF THE INTRODUCTION.

ERRATA.

Page	ix.	Line	35,	*for*	dessension *read* dissonsion.
„	x.	„	9,	*for*	repentence *read* repentance.
„	xxiii.	„	39-40,	*for*	adminstrative *read* adminstration.
„	xxiv.	„	5,	*for*	previleges *read* privileges.
„	„	„	7,	*for*	reflection *read* infliction.
„	xxxvi.	„	33,	*for*	A *read* As.
„	xxxvii.	„	27,	*for*	vertually *read* virtually.
„	xxxviii.	„	17,	*for*	beas *read* bias.
„	XLV.	„	20,	*for*	con u- *read* condu-
„	„	„	21,	*for*	systemd *read* system.
„	„	„	30,	*for*	erroneos *read* erroneous.
„	XLvi.	„	7,	*for*	metaphorial *read* metaphorical.
„	XLvii.	„	26,	*for*	some times *read* sometimes.
„	XLviii.	„	13,	*for*	Univer-sity *read* University.
„	L.	„	37,	*for*	oceurence *read* occurrence.
„	Li.	„	16,	*for*	oceurence *read* occurrence.
„	„	„	35,	*for*	indifinite *read* indefinite.
„	Liii.	„	5,	*for*	idolatory *read* idolatry.

INTRODUCTION.

Chandesvara Thakkura.—The Vivåda-Ratnákara is a commentary on Hindu Law, purporting to be composed by the prime minister Chandesvara Thakkura son of the prime minister Víresvara Thakkura. There are some slokas at the commencement, and also some at the end, of the work, extolling the commentary and specially its author. But the account given by them of the author, is, as usual with Sanskrit writers, an exceedingly meagre one. He is described as the prime minister, but nothing is said about the king whom, or the state which, he served in that capacity. He is styled as the conqueror of the chiefs of Nepal. But the greatest importance has been attached to the performance by him, of the religious ceremony called *tulá-purusha*, as the year, the month and the place of its celebration have all been set forth. The distinctive feature of the ceremony consists in the distribution among the learned Bráhmanas, of one's own weight of gold, and explains its name *tulá-purusha* which means, "weighing the person." He is described to be also an able and skilful Judge, quite familiar with the rules for the construction of the sacred law, and to be an author who composed seven treatises, including the present one, on law and religious rites, all of which are styled with the generic name of Ratnákara, while each is distinguished by the name of the subject treated therein. Of them the present work on Vivåda (=dispute) or Substantive Law, is said to contain not only all that may be found in the Kalpadruma, the Párijáta, the Prakása, and the commentary of Haláyudha, but also much additional matter.

As to the time when, and the place where, the author flourished, information is furnished by the account of the time and place of the celebration of the aforesaid religious rite, which is said to have been performed on the bank of the river Bágvati in the month of Márga in the year 1236 of the Sáka era, corresponding to November-December, 1314 A. D. The river Bágvati rises in the Himalayas and falls into the Ganges of which it is a tributary, after passing through, the district now called Tirhoot, a corruption of the word Tíra-bhukti which literally means a place bounded by the banks of rivers, and is a name of the country well-known from ancient times as Mithila which is bounded on the east by the river Kosi, on the south by the Ganges, and on the west by the Gundak or Gandakí.

Mithila, seat of learning.—Mithila is celebrated as a seat of learning from ancient times. The Ain-i-Akbari says,—"Tirhut has from immemorial time, been a seat of Hindu learning," Vol ii. p. 152. It was the kingdom of the famous Rájarshi Janaka, the father of Sítá the heroine of the well-known epic poem of Válmiki. But it is not so much as a king, but as a great master of the science of theology and esoteric Hinduism or the Yoga consisting in the practice of communion of the human soul with the Supreme Being, that Janaka's name is wide spread in the Hindu Sástras.

In the Brihat A'ranyaka Upanishad the following account is given of the celebration of a solemn sacrifice by that royal saint, and of the display of theological learning by Yájnavalkya the promulgator of the well-known Institutes called after his name, of which the Mitákshará is a running commentary.

Royal saint Janaka, & Ya'jnavalkya.—The great king Janaka was celebrating at considerable expense a sacrifice, at which were assembled learned Bráhmanas of Kuru and Panchála. The king being desirous of ascertaining which of the Bráhmanas was the most learned in the scriptures and theology, appeared before the assembly of the Bráhmanas, and ordered a thousand cows with five gold coins attached to each horn of each cow to be set apart, and then addressing the learned Bráhmanas said, 'Whoever amongst you is most skilful in the theological science, may take these cows.' For some moments, silence prevailed among the assembled Bráhmanas, as none seemed ready to put forward a claim of superiority to all others, when Yájnavalkya who also was present there, directed his disciple Sámasravas to remove the cows to his house, and thus indicated his superiority to all the rest. His pupil drove the cows away, and thereupon the other Bráhmanas became indignant at what seemed to be his arrogant conduct. Then Asvala who was the priest of the King asked him, "Are you O Yájñavalkya! the most learned among us, in the science of the Supreme Being." He replied, "I bow to the most learned: I was only desirous of having the cows." Thereupon Asvala, and after him, some others amongst the learned Bráhmanas, did, one after another, put to him divers questions on various theological topics, which he answered; and by refuting their objections, he silenced them all successively. The rest did not venture to propose any more questions to Yájnavalkya. and when asked by him to do so, they remained silent. Thereupon he proposed to them the following question for solution—"From what cause, does mortal man rise afresh after death? It cannot be said that he was born once for all; for, he is born again; and I therefore ask you, what is it that produces him again?" The learned Bráhmanas who were thus interrogated being unable to answer this question yielded the victory to Yájnavalkya, who then solved the question at their request.

Subsequently the Monarch received religious instructions from that sage, who after inquiring of the King the doctrines he had learnt from various other theologians, examined him on them, and found that these had not been fully explained to him.

Institutes of Ya'jnavalkya.—The Institutes of Yájnavalkya show that it was in Mithilá that the sage communicated the laws to the saints who came to him for instruction. The following are the two slokas at the beginning of the work:—

योगीश्वरं याज्ञवल्क्यं संपूज्य मुनयोऽब्रुवन् ।
वर्णाश्रमेतराणां नो ब्रूहि धर्म्मान् अशेषतः ॥ १ ॥
मिथिलास्थः स योगीन्द्रः चणं ध्यात्वाब्रवीन् मुनीन् ।
यस्मिन् देशे मृगः कृष्णस्तस्मिन् धर्म्मान् निबोधत ॥ २ ॥

"The saints having bowed to Yájnavalkya the chief of Yogis or those engaged in the practice of communion with the Supreme Being, said, 'Tell us in their entirety the laws of the (four) tribes, of the (four) orders, and of others.' That lord of Yogis, who was residing in Mithilá, having meditated for a moment, addressed the saints, 'Listen to the laws of the country where there are (कृष्णसारः) black antelopes'."

As the Institutes of Yájnavalkya, form the foundation of the Mitákshará school, it may also be appropriately called the Mithilá School after the name of the place where the said sage flourished and taught.

Mithila, Nya'ya philosophy, and Nuddea.—Sákya Sinha the founder of Buddhism, and Kapila the originator of the Sánkhya system of philosophy, appear to have flourished in the ancient Mithilá country. The Nyáya system of philosophy, the study of which is said to have become necessary for the purpose of refuting the doctrines and arguments of the Buddhists, attained considerable growth in Mithilá, and the modern development of that system owed its origin, to the Pandits of this place, which had been the resort of students of the Nyáya philosophy from all parts of India, before Navadvípa or Nuddea in Bengal became the celebrated seat of Sanskrit learning, and more conspicuously, of the modern Nyáya which attained its perfection at the hands of the Pandits of that place. The Bengal Bráhmanas had to proceed to Mithilá for the completion of their study at the feet of its Pandits until the rise of Nuddea in the fifteenth century as a seat of learning founded by learned persons who had been pupils of Mithila Pandits, so that Nuddea may be deemed to be an offspring of Mithilá. The Pandits of Mithilá, however, did not like the idea of the establishment of a rival educational institution at any other place, and wanted to make Sanskrit education the monopoly of Mithilá. They did not trust to the legitimate means of acquisition by their descendants and successors of superiority in learning so as to maintain the position of Mithilá as the seat of learning, to be resorted to by students from all parts of India. They had recourse even to improper means for preventing their foreign pupils from setting themselves up as professors in their own country. The pupils were not permitted to take home any literary work, not even the manuscript copies they had themselves made for their own study. Tradition tells us that the founder of Nuddea as a seat of learning was endowed with a retentive memory of such an extraordinary character, that he on his return home reproduced all the works he had read in Mithilá, and thus obviated the difficulty created by the jealousy and envy of his preceptors labouring under an illiberal and narrow-minded sentiment of patriotism. Mithila has however continued all along to be a seat of learning down to the present day, but as regards the cultivation of the modern Nyáya system, the keen intellect of the Bengal Pandits has brought it to a perfection never before attained, and the fame of Nuddea has therefore surpassed Mithilá as the seat of that branch of learning.

Incompleteness of Sanskrit Works.—In this connection, may be mentioned a peculiar feature characterizing Sanskrit works on most subjects, whether on theology or law, on medicine or any other science,—namely, that their full meaning can not be realized by a reader on a mere perusal of them, although he may be so far advanced as to understand the language, unless the same be explained by a teacher who is himself versed in the traditional interpretation.

The reason may be that some of these had been composed before the discovery of writing, and were therefore necessarily condensed to enable the students to easily commit to memory the landmarks, as it were, of the ideas conveyed by the preceptor in his lectures to them, in the form of aphorisms. Or it may be that the works though composed after discovery of writing, partook of the same character as those just mentioned, for ensuring the facility with which the students might make manuscript copies of them for their own use and perusal, when printing or the art of multiplying copies with ease, was unknown. Or it may also be, that the learned persons reserved to themselves the privilege of imparting knowledge only to students chosen by themselves, by writing books in such a style that they could not be fully understood except with the aid of persons who are aware of the traditional interpretation handed down from preceptor to pupil in regular course of succession from the original author. Or it may likewise be that the subject was considered to be of such a character, that it should be communicated to none but those that were qualified for becoming the recipients of its knowledge.

Of this last class are works on theology or the science of the human soul, and the practice of *Yoga* or communion between the human soul and the Supreme Soul : for, संयोगो योग इत्युक्तो जीवात्मपरमात्मनो: । According to the Hindu view, religious education, like education in secular sciences, depends on the capacity and previous training and progress of individual students ; and persons not sufficiently advanced in spiritual training, are considered unfit for receiving instructions in the higher truths of religion, which are beyond their capacity to appreciate : different religious practices are therefore ordained for men of different characters, suitable to their respective capacities. The practice of the Yoga, which is conducive to the highest spiritual development of man, is intended only for those that have attained to a certain degree of spiritual progress ; and none ought to be initiated in this Yoga, unless he has come to regard the pleasures and pains of this world to be merely pleasures and pains of the flesh, and not of the soul.

All the Sastras on Yoga, setting forth its necessity for spiritual development, and exposing the hollow, unsubstantial and transitory character of worldly pleasures and pains, are studiously silent on the actual practice of Yoga which is prescribed as the only means of salvation, and accordingly we find the Bhagavat-Gitá which embodies the highest truths of religion and morality, taught in all the earlier works on scripture, and which sets forth in an exhaustive manner the training of mind necessary for Yoga, says as regards the actual practice itself that it must be learnt from a Guru or preceptor who knows it ; thus,

तद्विद्धि प्रणिपातेन परिप्रश्नेन सेवया ।
उपदेक्ष्यन्ति ते ज्ञानं ज्ञानिनस्तत्त्वदर्शिनः ॥ ४ । ३४ ।

"This (knowledge) you must learn (from the wise Teacher) by falling at the feet, by humble questioning, and by worship. The wise who are seers of truths will (if you are a fit recipient) instruct the wisdom to you."

And the wise Teacher would not initiate a person in the practice of *Yoga*, unless he be satisfied that his disciple's mind is prepared for Renunciation.

HINDU CODES

The Hindu Codes deal with man as a being of infinite existence. The complete codes of Manu and Yájnavalkya embody the legal as well as the religious and moral rules together, prescribing man's duties in the widest sense of the term, but more as a spiritual eternal being than as a member of society. This is illustrated by a consideration of the subjects dealt with in the said two codes. Of these that called after Manu is universally admitted to be entitled to the highest respect ; and Vrihaspati, himself a lawgiver, or more correctly, a law-compiler, explains the reason for the pre-eminence and superiority of Manu's code, in the following passage :—

मन्वर्थ-विपरीता या सा स्मृतिर्न प्रशस्यते ।
वेदार्थोपनिबन्धृत्वात् प्राधान्यं हि मनोः स्मृतं ॥

"That law which is contrary to Manu's meaning, cannot be accepted; for, Manu's superiority is ordained by reason of his recording the purport of the Revelation."

Code of Manu.—Manu's code is divided into twelve chapters: of them,—

1. The first chapter gives an account of the creation, the revelation of the code, the division of time, the four ages of the world, the evolution of the five elements, and the four castes and their general privileges and duties, and custom and law:

2. The second chapter deals with the sources of law, the sacred country, the initiatory or sacramental ceremonies, and more especially the *upanayana* or studentship ceremony, and the duties of the student, and his conduct and the respect due by him to his preceptors and elder relations and to the females of his preceptor's and parents' family, and to learned men:

3. The third chapter deals with marriage after the completion of studentship, its connection with caste, its eight forms, duties of the married couple, the duties of the householder or married man and his five great daily sacrifices, namely (1) the sacrifice to the Gods consisting of Homa and the like, (2) the sacrifice to the *pitris* or *manes* of ancestors consisting of libations of water, or of offering of *pindas* or oblations of food, (3) the sacrifice to the Rishis or propounders of the Sástras, consisting in their study, (4) the sacrifice to men, consisting in honouring guests and religious mendicants by offering of food &c., and in giving alms to beggars, and (5) the sacrifice to other living beings, consisting in the gift of food to animals, birds and the like, found in the locality:

4. The fourth chapter deals with the householder's means of subsistence, virtuous and sinful, and his duties and conduct, and is devoted to what may be termed economics and private morals:

5. The fifth chapter treats of different kinds of food that may be taken or abstained from, and especially of animal food, of pollution on birth or death of relatives, and of impurities of men and things caused by touch of impure matter, and of the religious improvement of women:

6. The sixth chapter describes the third and the fourth stages of life, prescribed for the twice-born classes, namely the life of a Vánaprastha or retirement to a forest, and the life of a Bhikshu or religious mendicancy, and the duties of persons adopting those orders of life:

7. The seventh chapter deals with the rights, privileges and duties of the King, who is deemed to be an incarnation of the eight Gods presiding the eight quarters of the universe; extols the supreme importance of punishment as the protector of society; gives direction regarding state policy, appointment of various officers, mode of taxation and so forth:

8 & 9. The eighth and the ninth chapters deal with Jurisprudence:

10. The tenth chapter deals with Caste System, and the means of livelihood of different castes in distress:

11. The eleventh chapter deals with expiation and atonement: and

12. The twelfth or last chapter deals with transmigration of souls, effect of man's own deeds on his condition and state of existence, and theology and liberation.

Yajnavalkya's Code.—The Institutes of Yájnavalkya deal with the very same subjects, and are divided into three Books, called the A'chára (religious and moral observances), the Vyavahára (jurisprudence), and the Práyaschitta (or expiation).

1. In the first Book after stating in sloka 8 that "of all acts such as sacrifices, ceremonial observances, repression of sensual desires, harmlessness, gifts, and the study of the Vedas, *átmajñána* or knowledge of the soul, derived by *yoga* or abstraction of intellectual faculties from external objects, is the best Dharma or duty of man,"—the sage describes the different sacramental ceremonies from conception to cremation. In connection with the ceremony of *upanayana* or the investiture with the sacred thread, the duties of *brahmacharya* or studentship the first stage of life, up to the *samávartana* or return from the preceptor's house, after the completion of studentship, are laid down. Next in order is the section on marriage which lays down the different kinds of marriage and details connected therewith, including the duties of husband and wife. The Sráddha ceremonies are then laid down in detail; and in enumerating the class of people fit to be invited to a Sráddha and those who are not to be invited, restrictions are laid down which if strictly carried out would find many a modern Sráddha without a single guest. The worship of Ganapati and his mother Ambiká with invocations for beauty and prosperity, and the propitiation of the planets by the *grahajága* or planet-appeasing-ceremony conclude the section on the general duties of householders. The duties of a house holder in the four different classes are then dealt with in detail

with reference to hygiene, etiquette, economy, moral restraint, and religious efficacy. Then follows an enumeration of things fit and unfit to be eaten, of things pure and impure, and of the means by which the latter are purified; of things proper to be given and accepted, and of persons by and from whom a gift can be accepted. The service of a sickman and the affording of relief to the fatigued are enjoined as duties of special merit.

The chapter on A'chára is concluded with a short dessertation on kings and their duties. The king must be of a noble family, truthful, pure, even-minded, righteous, modest, without a bad habit, and abhorrent of the wicked: he must be energetic and prompt in action, brave, talented, learned, skilled in the science of the soul, in the science of politics; and in that of agriculture, trade and other sources of wealth: he must be mindful of the past, and able to keep his secrets: he should appoint nobly descended ministers who are talented, steady and faultless: in every department he should employ clever, competent and blameless officers, well up in matters of receipt and disbursement: he should be forbearing to the Bráhmanas, candid to his friends, angry towards his enemies, and a father to his servants and subjects: he should protect his subjects from the oppression of cheats, thieves, vagabonds, depredators, and particularly the *Káyásthas* (or scribes and accountants, being generally favourite officers of the crown). If, being unprotected the subjects commit any sin, the king shares half of it: for he takes taxes. Those who receive bribes, he should deprive, of their wealth and banish. That king who enriches his exchequer by wronging his subjects, soon loses his fortune, and goes to ruin with his family. All that very duty of the king in protecting his own kingdom, devolves on him when becoming master of another kingdom. Customs, laws, and family usages which obtain in a country should be preserved when that country has been acquired by conquest.

After enumerating the four kinds of means to political ends, namely, (1) Peaceful negociation (2) Concession (3) Sowing dessension or *divido et impero*, and (4) War,—the holy Sage lays down,—"The accomplishment of an object is divided between *fate* (=*adrishta* or the invisible dual force being the resultant of a man's good and bad deeds in the past states of infinite existence) and exertion: some expect success from *fate*, some from accident, some from lapse of time, and some from effort: the wise however believe in the efficacy of a combination of all these."

2. The second Book is called Vyavahára or Litigation

or Jurisprudence, and is devoted to the rules of Judicature, substantive and adjective.

3. The third Book is devoted to impurities, sins and their penances, and the duties of those entering the third and the fourth orders of life. After dealing with the different periods of impurity from births and deaths of different persons, and also from contact with those that are impure, the holy Sage concludes by saying—"Time, fire, religious ceremonies, earth, wind, mind, knowledge, religious austerities, water, repentence and fasts,—all these are causes of purity. Charity is the purifier of those who do prohibited actions; velocity, that of a river; earth and water, those of unclean things; and *sannyása* (renunciation or entrance into the order of an ascetic) that of the twice-born. The recitation of the Veda is the purifier of those who know the Veda; forgiveness, that of the learned; water, that of the body; uttering of mantras, that of those whose sins are concealed; and truth, that of the mind. Religious austerities and self-knowledge are the purifiers of the soul; knowledge, that of the intellect: knowledge of God is deemed to be the pre-eminent purifier of the soul."

Then follows an enumeration of duties under distress, or means by which one can earn his livelihood in periods of distress, without incurring degradation.

Next comes a discourse on the duties of the third order of life, that of a *Vánaprastha* or hermit, which a twice-born man may adopt after completing the term of a householder. The duties of the fourth or last order of life mamely that of a *Yati* or ascetic are then enumerated. He only who has previously completed the term of the order of a householder or a hermit or both is entitled to enter this order after performing a sacrifice to Prajápati; he must have no property except his three sticks and his wooden pot, and be indifferent to all beings and to all regard for his senses; he must live by alms, purify his heart, and turn his mind towards the emancipation of his soul.

The holy sage lays down, however, that—"Asceticism does not consist in wearing its badges: for that (*i. e.*, the final purpose of asceticism) is attained even otherwise. (The ascetic) should never practise towards other men anything which would be disagreeable to himself, if practised by others towards him. Speaking truth, abstinence from craving and anger, modesty, cleanliness, discrimination, equanimity, sobriety, temperance and self-knowledge, these are declared (to constitute) the duties (of the order).

In connection with this topic, the Yogíswara introduces the subject of the evolution of the world with all its varieties from the universal soul or *Paramátmá*, and concludes with exhortations of the methods by which the highest end of human existence—*mukti* or final emancipation of the soul from the bond which unites it with the body, may be attained. The subject is extremely difficult and we reluctantly abstain from an attempt at giving a synopsis which would be scarcely intelligible to the uninitiated.

The *karma-vipáka* or the fruition of work, or the effect of deeds good and bad done in past states of existence, shewing what sin or transgression of social, religious and moral duties, leads to what form of existence,—is also dealt with in the same connection. Penances for the different sins primary and secondary are then laid down with a degree of discrimination and wisdom, that could be expected only from the great Prince of Ascetics, and the Institutes end with a commendation of a study of the same.

Vyavahara or Jurisprudence.

Thus, it is clear that the Hindu Codes deal with the rules of religious, moral, and legal obligations, prescribed for the observance of man as a spiritual being and also as a member of society.

The distinction however, between the rules of legal obligation on the one hand, and those of religious and moral obligation on the other, is a necessary one, and is based on an important principle which must have suggested itself from the very infancy of Jurisprudence.

For, legal rules generally prescribe relative duties, the violation of which necessarily involves injury to another person who is interested in seeking relief for the wrong done to him, and thus in enforcing obedience to the rules of this character.

Rules of religion and morality, prescribe duties, the performance of which is left to the conscience of persons, and cannot generally be legally enforced by an action at the instance of an individual member of society. These rules are absolute in character and concern a man's spiritual interest, and affect people individually, so that their observance or violation does not interfere with other people's secular or spiritual interest, so as to give them a cause of action, which is thus defined by Yájnavalkya,—

स्मृत्याचारव्यपेतेन मार्गेणाधर्षितः परैः ।
आवेदयति चेद्‌राज्ञे व्यवहारपदं हि तत् ॥ २ । ५ ॥

"If one injured by another or others in a way contrary to the law (Smriti) or custom, complains to the King, that is a cause of action." II. 5.

Although the arrangement of the subjects in the codes of Manu and Yájnavalkya, shows that the different kinds of rules were distinguished, still it would not be correct to suppose that that portion of these codes which deals with Jurisprudence embodies rules of legal obligation only, and does not contain rules of moral or religious obligation.

The division of these codes into chapters or books has reference to subjects, and not to the character of the rules: accordingly, rules relating to subjects that give rise to litigation are put together under the head called Vyavahára or litigation; but all of these rules do not appear to be of legal obligation. And from the nature of the codes in which the rules of all the different descriptions are mixed up together, a sharp and strict line of distinction cannot be expected.

In a similar way we find, that the subject of marriage has been dealt with under a head other than Vyavahára or litigation, that is to say, under the head called A'chára or customary rites, the rules relating to which are generally of moral obligation. Marriage is according to Hindu Law a sacramental ceremony and is therefore dealt with in a chapter which treats of all the sacramental or initiatory rites, although important legal incidents are annexed to, and important legal consequences follow from, the marital union, from a consideration of which it might be expected to be placed under the head of Vyavahára in the codes. It has been placed under the head of social customs, owing perhaps to the circumstance that the prohibited degrees and like incidents depend upon custom which differs in different localities and among different tribes, and are thus widely divergent; and also to the circumstance that litigation relating to it was rare in Hindu times.

Our Courts have therefore to differentiate the rules of moral and religious obligation from the legal rules, when these are found to be intermixed.

Adjective Law :—The chapter on Jurisprudence is divided into two parts, the first deals with the Adjective Law under the name Vyavahára-Mátriká meaning literally "the mother of litigation" ; and the second, the Substantive Law. The Vyavahára-Mátriká again is subdivided into two Sections called respectively General and Special. The first section of the Adjective Law deals with the constitution of the Court of Justice, and the Procedure relating to the institution of suits or complaints, reduction of the same into writing by the Court or its officer, the summoning of the defendant or accused, the personal appearance of the parties, the exemption from it, the verbal answer of the defendant or accused, and its reduction into writing, the issues, the proof, and the decree.

The second section deals with rules relating to counter claims and charges, taking surety of parties, penalty for false allegation by either party, expediting and delaying of hearing, discrediting demeanour of party or witness under examination, onus and its shifting ; fourfold means of proof, namely, (1) writing (2) possession (3) witness and (4) ordeal on failure of these ; priority among different transactions relating to the same matter or property ; title by prescription ; relative weight of title and possession ; decision of dispute (1) by relations, (2) by fellow tradesmen or fellow artizans, (3) by co-villagers or fellow-citizens and (4) by the King's Court ; disability to sue ; treasure-troves ; and restoration of stolen property to the owner, or payment of compensation to the owner from the king's treasury, when stolen property is not recovered.

The king's liability to pay the value of the stolen property to its owner, when the king's officers are unable to trace and recover the property, is a peculiar doctrine of Hindu Law, and is based on the principle that it is the duty of the King to protect the person and the property of his subjects, for performing which he takes taxes from them. The king's right to the taxes payable by subjects is coupled with the duty of protecting them from the internal and external enemies ; in fact, the taxes are deemed to be the renumeration of the king for the service to be rendered by him to his subjects by defending them from invasion by foreign enemies, and by protecting them from violation of their rights by their fellow-subjects. Thus Nárada says,—

अन्यप्रकारादुचितो भूमिः षड्भागसंज्ञितः ।
वलिः स तस्य विहितः प्रजापालनवेतनं ॥१७।४८॥

"The well-known revenue consisting of what is called the sixth share from (the produce of) land, and of the customary shares from other kinds (of income), is ordained for the king, as his salary for the protection of the subjects."

The king according to Hindu Law, is to be respected by his subjects as an incarnation of the Gods, but nevertheless he must think himself as a servant of his subjects, so much so that he is enjoined to make good the loss sustained by them owing to his failure to discharge his duty towards them.

Constitution of the King's Court.—The administration of justice is one of the chief functions of the king under the Hindu Law. The king is enjoined to preside personally in the court of justice; if he is unable to do so, he is to delegate this function to a learned Bráhmana or any other twice-born person endowed with the qualifications requisite for the discharge of that most important duty.

This was also the case in England in early times, and even now the King is the ultimate source of all judicial authority, and his personal presence in all the Courts is assumed, and the judges are deemed his representatives. Although this may be regarded as a legal fiction now, still in early times the adminstration of justice was, indeed, one of the functions of the English King, who himself sat on circuit so late as the reign of Edward IV., and even after regular tribunals were established, a reserve of judicial power still remained in the king and his council, in the exercise of which it was possible for the king to participate personally. The last *quasi* judicial act of an English king, was that by which James I. settled the dispute between the court of chancery and courts of common Law.

Jury system.—But it must not be supposed that the king or his representative was the sole judge under the Hindu Law. The king was directed to appoint learned, truthful, and impartial persons versed in law, not less than three nor more than seven in number, as *sabhyas* or Jurors or Assessors, and also to select some wealthy and unenvious tradesmen of good family, mild temper, mature age, and good conduct, to attend the court and assist him or his delegate in administering justice.

Thus it is clear that the idea that the Jury system is an institution which was unknown to the people of this country, and which has been introduced here for the first time, by the British people, is due to the ignorance of the ancient adjective law of the country, contained in the Hindu Codes.

It is almost impossible to ascertain the real state of things with respect to questions of fact depending solely on oral evidence of witnesses, when one set depose in one way, and they are contradicted by another set called by the opposite party, unless the trustworthiness, truthfulness and honesty, of the parties and witnesses can be ascertained with certainty. And it is difficult for a judge to do this unless he is assisted by Jurors or Assessors who are residents of the locality, from which the witnesses come, and which is the scene of the matter in dispute, and who as such are likely from their local knowledge to be able to discriminate between witnesses that are truthful and reliable, from those that are not.

The judges, who preside over our courts of justice, must necessarily feel considerable doubt and difficulty in most cases in which the evidence is only oral, and is conflicting and seeming to be equally balanced on both sides, and would, if that course were possible, refrain from passing any opinion whatever. But as their office requires that they must come to some conclusion one way or the other, they base it more on their own view of the probabilities of the cases as disclosed by the pleadings, than on a proper discrimination of the truthfulness or otherwise of the different witnesses. This creates a habit of mind weakening its faculty of judgment and judicial differentiation, and rendering it incapable of observation necessary for properly sifting the evidence: and accordingly the judge decides in his mind a case according to his own view of the probabilities, and then proceeds to deal with the oral evidence, and pronounces the testimony which supports that view to be credible, trustworthy, reliable or satisfactory, and that which is against that view to be of the contrary character. And it often happens that when the same case comes in appeal to be decided by another judge of the same habit of mind, the first court's judgment is reversed, because his own view of the case, derived from his preconceived notions about the probabilities arising from the allegations in the pleadings, is different: and he does not, in pronouncing his judgment feel any hesitation in believing the witnesses whose testimony supports his view, although they were disbelieved by the court of first instance, and also in giving a bad character to the witnesses whose depositions are against his view, in the same manner as the first court did, to the other set of witnesses: so that respectable gentlemen are generally averse to appear as witnesses before our courts. And although these judges are invested with the power of committing untruthful witnesses to the criminal court for being tried for perjury, yet they have not such confidence in the correctness of the views embodied in their own judgments, as to adopt that course against persons held by them to be perjurers. People do not feel that degree of respect for the decisions of our courts when they find that the judgment of the inferior court is often reversed by the superior court on questions of fact, and the view which ultimately prevails is really erroneous. This uncertainty of facts in our courts of justice, in addition to the well-known uncertainty of the law, appear to have been exercising a most demoralising effect on the people of this country, so that litigation has come to be regarded by a certain class of persons as a sort of judicial lottery, and false suits are often instituted, and become successful too.

Before returning from this digression one more remark may be made here in connection with this matter. The present system of adminstration of civil justice, according to which a suit is decided first by a court of original jurisdiction, then by a court of appeal, and lastly by a court of second appeal, is too expensive, vexatious, dilatory and harassing, and has proved to be unsatisfactory in many respects. The power of the High Courts in second appeals, to interfere with the decision of the Courts of appeal, is confined to errors of law only. But, if on a consideration of the facts, and the mode in which the evidence has been dealt with by the lower court it appears that justice has not been done, the judges, as a general rule, do not find it difficult to interfere; for, an error of law, consisting in the violation of a rule of the adjective law, may be easily found, though there may not be any error of the substantive law. There are, however, some judges who would require the pleader for the appellant to formulate the error of law on which he asks the court to interfere, before allowing him to go into the facts of the case; and should the pleader fail to do the same, they would dispose of the case without entering into the facts in detail, and without considering whether having regard to the mode in which the case has been decided by the court below, there has not been a failure of justice. This mode of disposing of second appeals is not approved by the majority of the judges who entertain and act upon the other view which was once expressed in court by Sir Richard Couch then Chief Justice of Bengal, who is universally acknowledged to be one of the greatest lawyers and an eminent judge, when a pleader for the appellant in a second appeal submitted to the court presided by his Lordship that on going through the papers on the record of the case, he found that there was no question of law, and therefore he did not wish to take up the time of the court by arguing the case. Thereupon his Lordship observed—"It is not for you to decide whether there is a question of law, place the facts before the court and read the judgment; it is for the court to say whether there has been an error of law". These are pregnant words: the judges are the repositories of the law, and they are presumed to be superior to lawyers as regards the knowledge of law; and they sit to administer justice, and not to dispose of cases.

Private or Arbitration Courts.—The King's Court, however, appears to have been generally approached by litigants, only as the court of last resort: ordinarily disputes were settled in most instances by the arbitration of (1) common relations when the parties were nearly related to each other, or (2) fellow tradesmen or fellow artizans, or (3) co-villagers or fellow citizens. In popular language these private or arbitration courts were called Pancháyets, meaning councils of five, and implying that the number of persons composing these courts must be five or not less than the same. The popular names of these courts were respectively, the Family Pancháyet, the Caste Pancháyet, and the Village Pancháyet. The Pancháyet of fellow tradesmen or fellow artizans is stated here as the Caste Pancháyet, because we find that the followers of each trade or art or occupation generally belong to a distinct caste. This may not have been so originally, but that is the state of things at present, and accounts for the very large number of modern castes.

The rank and grade of these courts were as follows: the Family Pancháyet was the lowest; superior to it was the Caste Pancháyet; and superior to the latter was the Village Pancháyet; and superior to them all was the King's Court. A party dissatisfied by the decision of any of these Pancháyets could come to the King's Court for a fresh trial. But a person was not bound to have the dispute settled by any of these arbitration courts in the first instance; for he was at liberty to complain to the King's Court at once. On the other hand the parties might choose to have a decision of the Family Pancháyet in the first instance; and then agree to appeal to the Caste Pancháyet for a fresh trial; and next to the Village Pancháyet; and lastly to the King's Court. But none could resort to these courts in the reverse order.

There cannot be any doubt that these arbitration courts would be best competent to decide correctly all questions of fact; and, therefore failure of justice in them would be least likely, provided the arbitrators were above corruption. Elderly persons who were known to be honest in life and religiously disposed were generally the members of these Pancháyets: they would therefore be above all suspicion, and enjoy the confidence of the people. Such courts would be most satisfactory, and it would be most conducive to the welfare of the people, if the old system could be revived and encouraged by the government, and litigants saved from the ruinous costs of modern litigation.

Substantive Law.—The constitution of the human mind appears to be the same everywhere: the growth and development of its faculties, the course of the progress of its thoughts through certain grooves, and the nature and character of its sentiments appear to be almost the same in all countries, under the same circumstances. A student of comparative jurisprudence will find that all the different systems of Law and many branches of it have passed through similar stages of development. One of these is the early classification under different heads of all kinds of legal disputes that were conceived to be possible in the then existing state of society, and the laying down of a limited number of forms of action corresponding to that classification; so that there was a form of action for each class of lawsuits according to that classification, and every suitor was required to bring his suit under one or other of these forms of actions. If, however, in the course of progress of society there came into existence new relations giving rise to new rights, duties and liabilities, never contemplated before, and if out of them arose a right to a new remedy to be enforced by a suit which could not come within one or other of the recognised forms of action under the classification, the difficulty in the way of the person wronged to obtain a remedy was almost insurmountable at first. The courts and lawyers in all countries are found to be technical and conservative, so that they would cling to unreasonable forms and technicalities rather than be guided by principles of equity. Until the iniquity of that course became prominently noticed as instances multiplied, and came to be regarded as a crying evil requiring a speedy remedy, the previous state of things continued, and then a change was introduced to do justice in those cases that were unprovided for by the existing system.

In Roman law the evil that sprung up from an early classification in the Twelve Tables was remedied by the Edict of the Prœtor Urbanus who introduced innovations in law and procedure on principles of equity.

In England also, the development of law and procedure passed through the same stages ; but the peculiarity of the English law consists in the fact that the classification of the law and the forms of procedure was made by the Common Law Courts, and not by any lawgiver. When the common law was in the course of its formation at the hands of the Judges, it was founded on principles of Equity and Justice. But in the course of time, and apparently at a very early time, its development became completed, and the system acquired the character of a *jus strictum*, in the same way as a positive and inflexible code prescribed by a Legislature, for administration by the courts. And the system of its procedure also became equally, if not more, strict, inelastic and inflexible. There was a classification of the civil wrongs, and for each species of them, there was a peculiar form of procedure in which a suitor was required to seek his remedy : and an injury was without redress, if it did not fall within some one of the recognised classes of wrongs, and consequently there was no appropriate form of remedy, called *writ* or *breve* for the same. There was at first an attempt made to remedy this evil by legislation, authorising the expansion of the recognised writs ; but it failed, as the statutory remedy proved inadequate. The inability of the Common Law Courts to grant relief in many cases of the above description, gave rise to the power of the Lord Chancellor as the keeper of the king's conscience, and led to the establishment of the Court of Chancery.

The history of the Hindu law also shows that it passed through the same stages of development. Wrongs were at first divided into eighteen classes ; and the same appears to be the number of the forms of action. Later on another class was added to obviate the difficulty created by the earlier classification, to which corresponded a new form of action. A short account of this subject may be given here, showing the scope and development of Hindu Jurisprudence.

Manu's classification of positive law.—In the Code of Manu rules of positive law are classified and discussed under eighteen different heads called Vyavahára-padas which were titles of law, as well as forms of judicial procedure corresponding to them. These eighteen titles of law or forms of Action as enumerated by Manu (viii, 4-7) are as follows :—

I. *Rinádána*, Recovery of debt.
II. *Nikshepa*, Deposit.
III. *Asvámi-vikraya*, Sale without ownership.
IV. *Sambhúya-samutthána*, Joint performance of work, or partnership.
V. *Dattápradánika*, Resumption or retraction of gift.
VI. *Betanádána*, Non-payment of wages or hire.
VII. *Samvid-vyatikrama*, Violation of agreement or a conventional rule affecting a class of persons.
VIII. *Kraya-vikrayánusaya*, Rescission of sale and purchase.
IX. *Swámi-pála-vivàda*, Disputes between master and servant tending cattle.
X. *Símá-vivàda*, Boundary dispute.
XI. *Vák-párushya*, Violence of words, or slander and abuse.
XII. *Danda-párushya*, Violence on person, or assault and battery.
XIII. *Steya*, Theft.
XIV. *Sáhasa*, Violent seizure of property, robbery.
XV. *Strí-Sangraha*, Seduction of maids and adultery.
XVI. *Strí-pum-dharma*, Duties of man and wife.
XVII. *Dáyabhága*, Partition and Inheritance.
XVIII. *Dyúta* and *A'hvaya*, Gambling with dice, and with animals.

Addition of a new title by Narada.—This appears to have been the earliest classification, and in the course of time it was found to be defective as the aforesaid classes of wrongs did not include many that were perhaps not thought of at the time, but came into existence subsequently. Accordingly we find **Nárada** adding a new title of law or class of wrongs under the name *Prakìrnaka* or Miscellaneous, which comprised many new matters throwing considerable light on the development of Hindu law. But the theory of the divine origin of law would not tolerate any change, and "the *fiction*" (stated by Sir Henry Maine,) "is that it remains what it always was", though the *fact* is that a change was introduced. Accordingly Nárada has kept unchanged, the number of the titles of law as propounded by Manu, *viz.* eighteen, by amalgamating into one, two titles in Manu's code, both of which relate to sexual relation, namely, the 15th and the 16th as shown above, thereby implying that Manu also laid down the same thing, though it has not been expressly stated in the text of the present redaction of his code.

Vivada-Ratnakara.—These eighteen titles of law are discussed by the Viváda-ratnákara in one hundred chapters. The following table shows the chapters in which the different titles have been dealt with, and the subjects discussed under each title.

I. The Recovery of debts.
   1. Different kinds of debts.
   2. Interest in general.
   3. Interest not stipulated by the debtor, but allowed by law.
   4. The limit of interest allowable upon different transactions.
   5 The prohibition of interest in certain transactions.
   6. (*a*) The subject of pledges, their redemption and foreclosure.
      (*b*) The validity of pledges.
   7. Sureties and their rights and liabilities.
   8. (*a*) The repayment of debts and the different degrees of liability of different heirs and successors, to pay different kinds of debts.
      (*b*) The recovery of debts and different means thereof.

II. 9. Deposit.

III. 10. Sale without ownership and claims to lost property.

IV. 11. Joint performance of work or Partnership.

V. 12. The resumption of gifts, that is to say, the law of the validity or otherwise of gifts and other alienations.

VI. 13. The breach of contracts of service.
   14. Emancipation from slavery.
   15. Slavery in reference to the classes and punishment for the violations of the rules connected therewith.
   16. The non-payment of wages of servants and workmen and generally the law of master and servant.

17. The law in respect of prostitutes and the law of hire for houses, carts &c :

VII. 18. The law in respect of herds of cattle or disputes between the owner and the keeper of cattle :

VIII. 19. The transgression of compacts, dealing with the maintenance of the usages and customs prevailing amongst societies, corporations, clans and the like :

IX 20. The rescission of contracts of sale :

21. The rescission of contracts of purchase.

X. 22. Boundary disputes, easements and public nuisances :

23. Bridges and dams.

24. The cultivation of lands left fallow and non-cultivation of lands taken for agricultural purposes.

25. The reservation of lands for cattle-grazing, and the preservation of crops from cattle trespass :

26. The fines leviable for unprivileged trespass by cattle on crops.

27. The exemption of certain cattle trespassing upon crops from the payment of fines :

XI. 28. Abuse and defamation :

29. Assault, and hurt ; cruelty to the animal and the vegetable kingdoms :

XII. 30. Theft.

31. The classification of thieves into primary and secondary classes : amongst the first primary class, that of open thieves, are included, quack-doctors, assessors taking bribes, cheats, fortune-tellers, prostitutes, artizans, forgers, false arbitrators, false witnesses, jugglers, tradesmen using false weights and measures, and amongst the second primary class, that of secret thieves, are included, thieves, robbers, highwaymen, kidnappers, cattle-lifters :

32. The punishment of "open" thieves and the levy of duties and taxes.

33. The punishment of the second primary class, that of secret thieves :

34. The employment of detectives for the search of thieves and the general rules to be observed by them :

35. The punishment of abettors of thieves, including those that supply them with food, fire, shelter

or weapons ; of receiver of stolen goods and of such police officers and others who being able to render help in case of robberies and the like, abstain from doing the same :

36. The difference in the punishment of thieves according to their castes and degrees of education :

37. The compensation of the person injured by theft, or robbery &c., from fines inflicted upon the officers in whose districts the offence . as committed or from the king's treasury in cases in which the stolen property is not recovered :

XIII. 38. Offences implying force and provides for the punishment of various heinous offences against person and property :

39. The investigation of murder cases and means of finding out murderers :

XIV. 40. Seduction and Adultery.

41. The punishment for adultery and rape.

42. The offence of the deflowering of virgins and its punishment :

43. The punishment of intercourse with prostitutes and unnatural offences :

XV. Duties of men and women :

44. The necessity of protecting women from temptations :

45. The means of so protecting them and their treatment under different circumstances :

46. The duties of women :

47. The duties and conduct of women whose husbands are absent :

48. The duties and rules of conduct for widows :

49. The appointment of women by their husbands or kinsmen for raising issue :

50. The subject of women who being previously married betake to other men :

XVI. 51 to 87. Dáyabhága or Partition and Inheritance.

XVII. 88. Gambling and prize-fighting :

89. The priorities of alienations :

XVIII. 9ə. Miscellaneous matters relating to the proper administrative of justice by the King and matters not dealt with before :

91. Ferries and fares for the same :
92, 93. Treasure-troves :
94, 95. The infliction of punishments :
96. Certain privileges of Bráhmanas :
97. Certain previleges of towns ; the punishment of suicides and the self-punishment of kings for improper reflection of punishment :
98. Measures applicable to fines :
99. Measures of weight and tables of money :
100. The collective names of societies of different classes.

Wrongs and crimes.—On a consideration of the subjects dealt with under the eighteen titles of law, it is apparent that many of them relate to matters that are now known by the name of crimes as distinguished from civil wrongs. But the principle of the modern distinction between criminal offences and civil wrongs, and the corresponding difference in the civil and the criminal procedures, was unknown to the Hindu law in the same way as to the other systems of ancient law.

With respect to the systems of early law in Europe, Sir Henry Maine observes* :—"All civilized systems agree in drawing a distinction between offences against the State or Community and offences against the Individual, and the two classes of injuries, thus kept apart, I may here, without pretending that the terms have always been employed consistently in jurisprudence, call crimes and wrongs, *crimina* and *delicta*. Now the penal law of ancient communities is not the law of crimes ; it is the law of wrongs, or, to use the English technical word, of Torts. The person injured proceeds against the wrong-doer by an ordinary civil action, and recovers compensation in the shape of money-damages if he succeeds." The learned Jurist then refers to the commentaries of Gaius and to the Twelve Tables, and goes on to say :—"Offences which we are accustomed to regard exclusively as *crimes* are exclusively treated as *torts*, and not theft only, but assault and violent robbery, are associated by the jurisconsult with trespass, libel and slander. All alike gave rise to an Obligation or *vinculum juris*, and were all requited by a payment of money."

Commercial principle unknown to Hindu law.—That a person feeling himself highly dishonoured by violence on his person or by adultery with his wife or by seduction of his maiden

* Ancient Law, Pages 369-370.

daughter, or the like, should be satisfied with a money compensation for the injury, is an idea which is utterly inconsistent with the spirit of chivalry and the keen sense of honour characterizing a nation at an early stage of development. The mercenary spirit which underlies this principle of money compensation appears to be opposed to the whole spirit of Hindu law, and we do not find the same recognised at any stage of its development. The strong and keen sentiment of vengeance roused by a wrong of this kind would be satisfied only by the condign punishment of the offender: and this is the only remedy contemplated by Hindu law. Accordingly we find that in cases of abuse and slander, assault and battery, and seduction and adultery, the person wronged lodged a complaint in the King's Court against the offender, an enquiry followed according to the same procedure as in civil suits, and on proof of the offence, fine or corporal punishment or both were inflicted on the guilty person according to the gravity of the wrong. This was the only redress the injured man sought to obtain from the king's court; the fine went to the Royal Exchequer, no part of it was paid to the complainant. In cases of theft and robbery also, the procedure was the same: but in these cases the injured party was entitled to the restitution of his property which was the subject-matter of his complaint. If the property could not be recovered, then the complainant was entitled to compensation, to the extent of its value, not however from the offenders, but from the king, as has already been mentioned in the preceding pages.

Wrongs against the King.—One class of wrongs dealt with under the title of law and procedure introduced by Nárada under the name Miscellaneous, consisted of offences relating to the king's revenue, namely, non-payment of the income-tax or evasion of payment of the duties on imports and exports. The tax payable by a subject consisted of a certain share of the produce of his land; a certain share of other descriptions of produce or increase of stock, such as honey, milk, young animals annually added to the flock of cattle-dealers, and the like; and a certain share of the profits of tradesmen; and the tax payable by artizans and labourers consisted of work done by them during certain number of days in the year, for the king, without receiving wages: so that taxation under Hindu law was based on the only rational principle, namely, that of payment by the subjects to the king of a share of their income. The prosecution for a fiscal offence was initiated by the king: and this form of litigation was called "Action dependent on the king," (नृपाश्रय:

व्यवहार:) and bears a distant resemblance to public prosecutions. But the analogy relates merely to the form; for, the idea of the king representing the state was wanting here. There were some other cases in which a suit could be commenced only at the instance of the king. One class of them illustrates the intermediate step between the *patria potestas* of the early law and the final abolition of it by the Mitakshará school recognising important rights of sons and wives against the father and husband respectively.

Patria potestas.—The joint-family system is still the normal condition of Hindu society and a cherished institution, but it is not the same at the present day as it was at its inception in ancient times. Society was at first composed of families as its units. Each family was within itself an independent state, and the early government of a nation seems to have been concerned with the common interests of the distinct but united states in the shape of families, and with the settlement of disputes between these different families: while within the family the *paterfamilias* was absolute monarch reigning over the *filiusfamilias* or dependent members of the family, over whom he exercised supreme authority including even the power of life and death. And in early law there was no remedy against the grossest abuse of his power by the *paterfamilias*. Accordingly in the early classification of law and procedure in Manu's Code there was no form of action for wrongs perpetrated by the *paterfamilias* on the *filiusfamilias*: no action lay by children and wives against their father and husband respectively, however grossly iniquitous and oppressive their conduct might have been.

The internal peace of a family was often disturbed by the effects of the usage of polygamy, which was generally prevalent in early times. Undue favour to some and undue harshness to others would give rise to bitterness of feeling that would end in insubordination and in infliction of severe punishments seeming to be capricious, iniquitous, harsh and cruel. Society would not long tolerate such abuse of the power possessed by a man over his wives and children: and the first step taken in that direction, was to include under the Miscellaneous title of law and procedure, an action by the king against the *paterfamilias* guilty of unnatural conduct towards a wife or a child. Although a son or a wife was not permitted to bring any action against the father or the husband respectively, yet the king could do so on their behalf, or for their benefit, if moved by information of the wrong perpetrated on them.

The condition of sons and wives was however considerably improved by a change of law regarding their capacity to hold property: and ultimately the sons were to a great extent emancipated by conferring on them proprietory right equal to that of the father in ancestral property, so that they could bring an action against the father under the title and form, called "Partition and Inheritance," for enforcing partition of the ancestral property, and thus withdraw themselves from the *patria potestas* which began to lose its pristine vigour by the king's interference for the benefit of the *filiusfamilias*.

Charge of incompleteness of Hindu Codes erroneous.—The Jurisprudence or positive law as dealt with in the Codes of the Sages appears to be complete and exhaustive and includes all the branches of law, suitable to the exigencies of Hindu society and actually prevalent therein; so that it cannot be said that the Codes were defective and left out of consideration any department of law.

Sir Henry Maine, however, maintains that these codes were incomplete; he observes:—"The codified or written law of the Hindus, then assumed to include their whole law, consisted of a large body of law regulating the relation of classes, especially in the matter of intermarriage; of a great body of family law, and a correspondingly extensive law of succession; and of a vast number of rules regulating the tenure of property by joint families, the effects on proprietory right of the division of those families, and the power of holding property independently of the family. There was some law of contract and some law of crime; but large departments of law were scantily represented, or not at all, and there was in particular a singular scarcity of rules relating specially to the tenure of land, and to the mutual rights of the various classes engaged in its cultivation. This last peculiarity was all the more striking, because the real wealth of the country is, and always has been, agricultural, and the religious and social customs of the people, even as recorded in the codified law, savour strongly of agriculture as their principal occupation." (Village Communities, 51)

One of the common errors to which we are generally liable is, that of supposing that the present state of things, with which we are familiar, and which seems very natural to us, has always been in existence. Another common error is often committed alike by jurists, legislators, judges and lawyers in British India, which may be called the Error of Translation, and owes its origin to the following circumstance. There are things and phenomena in this country, for which there are not exact and appropriate words in the English language. But these things and phenomena may be analogous and similar to certain ideas familiar to Englishmen, and the English words conveying those ideas are generally used to express the Indian things and phenomena ; and then the distinction between them is forgotten, and they are assumed to be identical, and their incidents are supposed to be the same.

It is in this way that we can account for the error, which a great jurist like Sir Henry Maine has been betrayed into. For there are not any words to be found in the Sanskrit language for expressing the relation of landlord and tenant, and the several essential elementary ideas forming component parts of that complex conception, namely, landlord, tenant, rent and tenure, each of which denotes one element and connotes the others, and all of which are necessary to be known for fully realizing that correlated conception. It is not possible that there was a branch of law actually prevalent in Hindu society, but no trace of it can be found either in the Codes or in the Commentaries thereon, nor any expression for its leading ideas in their highly developed language. The history of the present system of land tenures in this country will show that it is of recent origin ; and even under it, it is a mistake to suppose that the Ryots, or at any rate, the major portion of them who have obtained their lands in regular course of succession from their ancestors holding them from before the Permanent Settlement, or by purchase from such Ryots, are really Tenants in the English sense of the term, although it has of late become the practice to designate them by that term.

No land tenures before Permanent Settlement.—In India there were more lands than people to cultivate the same, and even at the time of the Permanent Settlement there were vast tracts of uncultivated land, side by side of the cultivated fields, not to speak of the jungles that exist even now. The theory of the Hindu law as to the origin of property in land is, that he who appropriated waste land by occupying or bringing it into cultivation, became the owner of the same. The waste land was the general property of the community, and the appropriation by a person of any parcel caused his property therein. The novel theory which is nowadays found to be often put forward, of the State being the landlord, is not supported by any principle of law or equity or sound reason. It is a hollow fiction to assert that the state represents the people, and is in that character entitled to all the unappropriated waste lands : in fact, no other principle except one based on the maxim, "Might is Right", can be assigned in support of that position. According to the Hindu law the King was entitled to a share of the produce yielded by cultivated land, ranging from one-twelfth to one-sixth, not as Rent but as Tax, not because he was the landlord, but because the owner of the land was his subject. This is abundantly proved by the Hindu Codes and commentaries on them, as well as by Sanskrit literature in general. The King was never deemed the proprietor of his territories. For the collection of the said land tax, there were different grades of officers, namely, the lord of a single village (ग्रामाध्यक्षः), the lord of ten villages, the lord of one hundred villages, and the lord of one thousand villages, or of a District, (सहस्रग्रामाध्यक्षः or देशाध्यक्षः). We may call them in the reverse order, by the familiar names, viz, the Collector of the District, the Assistant Collector, the Deputy Collector, and the Sub-Deputy Collector.

The Hindu system remained unaltered even after the conquest of India by the Mahomedans ; there was merely a change in the names of these officers, who were called Zemindars, Talukdars, Ijardars, and the like. The history of the fiscal arrangements by the Mahomedan rulers as well as by the East India Company, down to the time of the Decennial Settlement, shows that the Malguzars or Tax-Collectors, whether called Zemindars or Talukdars or Ijardars, were regarded as mere officers of Government having no proprietory interest in the land, of which the revenue they had to collect. Like every other occupation in India, this office of the tax-collector also, became practically hereditary in most instances. A transfer by sale or gift of this office did in a few instances take place. But succession by inheritance or transfer required the recognition and sanction of the ruling power which, oftener than not, was pleased to give the appointment to such successor, not as a matter of right, but as one of favour and state policy of convenience.

The East India Company did never claim any new or higher right in land than that possessed by the Hindu Kings under the codified law of the Hindus. On the contrary they invoked the aid of the Hindu law in asserting their right to impose revenue on land which was held free from revenue without a grant from the ruling power. The Preambles to the two Regulations of 1793 A. D., for re-assessing revenue upon invalid revenue-free lands, which according to the practice of those days, set forth in full the reasons and the objects of the Enactments, open with these words :—"By the ancient law of the country, the ruling power is entitled to a certain proportion of the produce of every beegah of land, unless it transfers its right thereto for a term, or in perpetuity."

Although it is asserted by some, and may be quite correct, that the East India Company became the *de facto* sovereign of Bengal, Behar, and Orissa either from the battle of Plassey, or that of Buxar, or the acquisition of the Dewany, yet the East India Company who as a trading body were in touch with the people, and were fully aware of their sentiments towards themselves as well as towards the Mahomedan puppets in their hands, did not think it politic to declare openly their real position in the eighteenth century. In concluding the Permanent Settlement and in making previously to it, the other settlements and fiscal arrangements of land-revenue since the Dewany, they did never profess or purport to act in the capacity of Sovereign ; but seemed to act only in the exercise of the authority delegated to them by the grant of the Dewany. And in everything they did, they endeavoured to convince the people that they were acting according to the ancient law and custom of the country, and with the object of promoting their welfare.

It would be erroneous to suppose that the Permanent Settlement was made by the East India Company as sovereign of the then Bengal Presidency. The truth is that it was a move in the direction of open assumption of sovereignty later on, it being intended as a means to that end. The Zemindars and Malguzars or the hereditary tax-collectors were men of position and considerable local influence : to enlist their sympathy, and to make them interested, in the establishment, stability, and continuance of the British rule was the political object of the Permanent Settlement. It was an act of the highest statesmanship, and has proved to be one of the rocks on which the foundation of the British Indian Empire rests. The Zemindars, and the holders of interests in land intermediate between those of the Zemindars and the Ryots, that is to say, the landed aristocracy and the middle class people of this country, who enjoy a portion of the King's share of the produce, by virtue of the Permanent Settlement, are from self-interest bound to be loyal to the British rule. Having secured by this self-sacrifice, the affection of the influential people of the country, and having waited for more than twelve years, the period sufficiently long in the estimation of the people of this country for acquisition of prescriptive title, by which time they became convinced of the good faith of the British Administration from its strictest adherence to all the promises made at the time of the Permanent Settlement in 1793, the East India Company did in 1806 openly assume the sovereignty of this country.

To a superficial reader the statements made in some of the Regulations of 1793, with respect to property in land, may appear to be contradictory: for instance, while Regulation I. of 1793 which embodies the terms of the Permanent Settlement, and may be called the *Magna Carta* of the landholders, describes the Zemindars as "actual proprietors of the land," the Preamble to Regulation II. of that year shows that the British Administration declared for the first time, the property in the soil to be vested in the landholders. The real explanation is to be sought in the fact that the East India Company did not think it politic that the Permanent Settlement Regulation should show that they were introducing an important innovation; while they did at the same time impress on the Zemindars the benefits conferred on them by the "British Administration," an expression indicating the same policy. The East India Company did undoubtedly create and confer a new interest in land on the Zemindars, but they did not intend to deprive the people of their proprietory right in the soil and transfer the same to the Zemindars: nor did they actually do it or profess to do the same.

By the Permanent Settlement the ruling power's right to the King's share of the produce yielded by all lands in defined tracts, was transferred to the hereditary tax-collectors on condition of their paying a fixed and unalterable amount of annual revenue to the Government: the total amount of the king's share to be realized according to the ancient law and usage by the Zemindars *minus* the fixed revenue payable to government formed the remuneration or profit constituting the interest of the Zemindars. This interest issuing out of land is called immoveable property, and all the incidents of real property are annexed to the same: the Zemindaris are declared heritable and transferable in part or whole, by sale, gift, mortgage, demise, or devise. Subordinate interests of different degrees, called in English by the names of tenures and undertenures, gradually arose from the exercise of this privilege of transfer, and in some places so many as a dozen intermediate interests of this description have by successive subletting been carved out of the Zemindar's interest.

The state of things that has arisen out of this fiscal arrangement, seems to be analogous and similar to the Feudal System introduced into England since the Norman conquest, which has in course of time become the only system there, by absorbing all the Allodial lands, the owners of which placed themselves voluntarily under the Barons by renouncing their rights and agreeing to hold their lands, as if received from these feudal lords by Subinfeudation, in consideration of the protection of life and property accorded by them in those troubled times. The said analogy led to the application of the English words "landlord," "tenant" "tenure" and "rent" to the analogous Indian things. The Zemindars and those whose interests are carved out of the Zemindar's interest bear a closer resemblance to the English land-owners. The English doctrine that the Sovereign is the fountain source of all rights in land may, without impropriety be predicated of them ; for, the Zemindars and the middlemen whose interests are intermediate between those of the Zemindars and the Ryots and are carved out of the Zemindar's interest, derive their rights in land directly or indirectly from the British Government.

But the same cannot be true of the people who and whose ancestors have been in actual occupation of the land from before the Permanent Settlement and who are the real proprietors of the soil. Accordingly we find that in many Regulations and Acts of the Legislature, Ryots are mentioned as distinct from Tenants, which word is applied to the middlemen who derive their interest immediately or mediately from the Zemindars.

A great deal of confusion and misconception have arisen from the use of technical English terms to designate these landed interests which are analogous to, but not identical with, the ideas expressed by them, and from the application of the principles of English law of Landlord and Tenant to cases relating to them upon the erroneous assumption that they are identical. Sometimes the permanent Taluks called tenures are deemed leasehold interests, and sometimes they are held complete transfers by the Zemindars of their interest, subject to a rent-charge, without reversion.

Thus it is clear that what seems to be a system of Land-Tenures came into existence as an effect of the Permanent Settlement; and the expression राजप्रजासम्बन्ध which is nowadays used to convey "the relation of landlord and tenant," but which means "the relation of king and subject," embodies the fundamental principle of this department of law, and furnishes the key to the indigenous and true conception on the subject.

Importance of study of Hindu Jurisprudence.—The study of the principles of all the branches of Hindu law appears to be of very great importance not only to the students of Comparative Jurisprudence, but also to those who have to do with the administration of justice in India, that is to say, the Judges, the Lawyers, and the Legislators. There are large gaps and interspaces in the law of this country, which our courts of justice are required to fill up by the application of the principles of equity, justice and good conscience, when cases arise for decision, for which there is no positive rule. The law of a country embodies the history of a nation's development, and reflects the character of the people; and knowledge of the law of the people of this country, will enable the Judges and the Legislators to form a correct view of what is the proper rule to lay down when they are called upon to legislate; and such knowledge is equally valuable to lawyers who have to advise the judges as to what would be conducive to the promotion of the welfare and well-being of the people.

A compilation of the principles of the Hindu Jurisprudence in its entirety, as contained in the Codes and explained in the commentaries of the different schools, showing the gradual changes and development of its different branches, would indeed be a work of great value in many respects. The Judges do sometimes invoke the aid of even the Roman law, while the ancient law of the country is practically beyond their reach.

Character of Vivada-Ratnakara.—The author composed two treatises on law: in one, called Vyavahára-Ratnákara, he dealt with the Adjective law; and in the other, of which the present work forms a part, and which is called the Viváda-Ratnákara, he discussed the substantive law.

The peculiar feature of the present work is, that it cites almost all the texts from all the Codes compiled by the different Rishis or Sages, bearing on a particular subject, and puts them in such order that the various rules of law appear from the texts themselves in their logical sequence, requiring very little extraneous aid in the shape of explanatory comments which, as a general rule, are accordingly very short in this work.

It has already been shown that this commentary was compiled by a minister of justice quite familiar with the customs and usages of the people, and with the sources of the law in the original, and also experienced in the practical administration of justice, being himself a Judge under a Hindu king. A work on Jurisprudence by an author of this description is expected to embody the law actually enforced at the time: the mode of treatment of the different subjects, and their division and subdivision prove the author to have been a practical lawyer.

But commentaries in so far as they deal with the mode of partition among the sons of a man by his wives of different castes, and among the primary and subsidiary sons of twelve kinds, are characterized by some writers as speculative. The reason assigned by them for this view is, that Intermarriage between the different castes, and the Affiliation of secondary sons other than the Dattaka or "Given son," are included in the list of practices that should be avoided in this *Kali* age, propounded by some of the Upa-puránas that were thrust into prominence by some writers of the Mahomedan period.

It is therefore assumed that these comparatively recent works are more authoritative than the Smritis, the universally admitted sources of Hindu law, so as to override them as regards these practices; and that the rules laid down in these modern works are imperative. But these assumptions cannot be supported by any sound reason.

Practices to be eschewed in Kali age.—Positive law does not come within the scope of the proper subjects of the Puránas, and they were never recognised by the Hindu Jurists as any authority in matters of positive law, far less the Upa-Puránas. The Puránas cannot override the law contained in the Smritis or Codes, which together with customs are declared to be the only sources of positive law, by the authoritative Codes themselves as well as by the leading commentaries regarded as paramount authority by our courts, and undoubtedly composed by writers in this very *Kali* age which admittedly commenced in the year 3102 B. C.; for, the present is the five thousand and first year of the *Kali* age according to the Hindu Sástras.

As the doctrine of certain practices being unnecessary to be observed in this *Kali* age though sanctioned and commanded by the Sástras, was comparatively recently introduced,—the Pandits who were appointed to advise the English judges on points of Hindu law and usages, somehow or other misled them by incorrectly representing the doctrine to be an authoritative and imperative one, which the judges were bound to act upon, although it was really intended by its propounders to be merely recommendatory and preceptive.

That these practices were merely what some comparatively modern writers thought to be such as *should* be eschewed in this age, appears clearly from what Jagannátha says after having elaborately dealt with the twelve descriptions of sons, and after having cited as authoritative the passages from the Upa-Purános, which lay down that sons other than the Aurasa and the Dattaka should not now be made,—namely, that he has nevertheless treated the subject of Affiliation in an exhaustive manner, for two reasons: first, to give an idea of the codified law on the subject in its entirety; and second, for the benefit of those who still follow the old law, not knowing or minding the above innovations.

As regards one of the practices, namely, that relating to Studentship for the study of the Vedas, it cannot but be admitted that all that was intended by these innovators is, that the rules of the Smritis relating to it are not obligatory in this *Kali* age; that is to say, the omission to study the Vedas is not to be followed by its inevitable consequence as laid down in the Smritis, viz. the reduction of the position of the person guilty of the omission from that of the twice-born to that of the Sudras. But it cannot be supposed that it would be illegal or irreligious on the part of a Bráhmana to lead the life of a student of the Vedas for a long time, as is required by the Smritis.

As for intermarriage, it has no doubt ceased to exist as an usage, not because it has been included in the list of the practices to be eschewed in the Kali age, but owing to other circumstances. Sometimes, however, intermarriage does take place when through ignorance, fraud and misrepresentation, a man of a superior caste is induced to marry a girl belonging to an inferior caste, and the real fact is discovered subsequently, and it may be, after the birth of children and after she has been recognised and treated as one of the same caste, and food prepared by her has been partaken of repeatedly by her husband and his relations. It depends entirely on the caste-people whether the husband is to be outcasted, or the discovery overlooked and suppressed by their consent. But the marriage cannot be pronounced invalid, there being no law against it.

As regards the twelve kinds of sons recognised by Hindu Law, the innovation sought to be introduced is, that sons other than the Aurasa and the Dattaka cannot be made in this Kali age.

With respect to this, it is worthy of special remark that the division of sons into twelve classes is rather a theoretical than a practical one. These sons may be practically divided into three classes only, namely, (1) sons by a man's married wife, (2) sons by his daughter, and (3) sons by adoption. Sons by a man's married wives are divided according to the classification of the Hindu Law, into five descriptions, namely, (1) the Aurasa or son procreated by a man himself on his lawfully married wife, (2) the Kshetraja or son begotten by a man on another person's lawfully wedded wife with that person's consent, (3) the Gúdhhaja or a son similarly produced but without the husband's consent, (4) the Sahodhhaja or pregnant bride's son and (5) the Paunarbhava or son begotten by a man himself on a re-married woman *i. e.* on his own wife not lawfully wedded. There cannot be the slightest doubt that all these five descriptions of sons do exist in Hindu Society, as they must in every society: for, if the husband, who by reason of impotency or other cause, allows his wife to be approached by another man, or who condones his wife who is approached by another without his consent, or who marries a pregnant bride, acknowledges as his own, sons born of these wives though not begotten by himself, all these sons must practically pass as his Aurasa sons, the distinction between them being merely of an academic character.

As regards the son of a twice-married woman, it is well-known that amongst lower classes widow-marriage has all along prevailed, and any doubt about its legality among the higher castes has been removed by legislation; so that this description of son has always existed and also exists now.

A regards the daughters' sons, becoming sons of their maternal grandfather by operation of law, the Kánina or maiden-born son does no longer exist, as Hindu girls are now disposed of in marriage before puberty. And as regards the Putriká-putra or Appointed daughter's son, he does exist in many parts of India, where the Mitákshará school prevails, more especially in northern India, except in Bengal proper where the Bengal school prevails and where the daughter's son as such becomes heir in preference to agnates in the ascending and the collateral lines. Whenever a daughter's son is affiliated, he must according to

Hindu Law be called Putriká-putra, although for the purpose of publishing and practically giving effect to the affiliation, some overt act as well as some ceremonies and the parents' consent, similar to those in the Dattaka adoption, are required, especially when there was no express ante-nuptial agreement appointing the daughter. The affiliation however takes place theoretically by operation of law, and not by act of adoption, although in loose language generally used even by lawyers all the subsidiary sons are called adopted sons, and their affiliation adoption.

Lastly, as regards sons by Adoption, the Apaviddha or deserted son is extremely rare; but the other four descriptions do exist even now in those places in which, and in those communities among whom, marriage, or investiture with the sacred thread, or higher age, does not offer any obstacle to affiliation. The Dattaka son does admittedly exist. The Kritrima also exists though it is supposed to exist in Mithila only. The Purchased son and the Self-given son also exist. It should be observed, that there is practically no difference between the Given son and the Purchased son, since the form of relinquishment and acceptance, takes place whether the transfer of parental dominion is made without, or for, a monetary consideration. And wherever a grown up man may be adopted in the Dattaka and the Kritrima forms, there cannot be any doubt that his assent must be necessary even when the parents are alive. For, the power of giving away a son in adoption is but a survival of the *patria potestas* which has been indirectly abolished by the Mitákshará school, as has already been shewn, and has vertually ceased to exist in both the schools. Hence it is impossible for parents to give away in adoption an adult son without his consent, and consequently, as a matter of fact his consent is practically all that is absolutely necessary in such cases, the consent of the parents being superfluous, and may be assumed to be always given when he is desirous and willing to be adopted.

The Kritrima and the Swayam-datta sons are practically the same, the only distiction between them being that in the former the offer for adoption comes from the adopter, and in the latter from the adoptee. Can there be any doubt that where grown up men may be adopted, these forms must subsist ?

All these four descriptions of sons are in fact recognised in Bombay, in the Punjab, and among the Jainas. The nice distinction between them is above the comprehension of the people who adhere to their old customs, and who fail to see any charm in a formal gift by the father or the mother, neither of whom possesses real dominion over an adult son.

The exigencies of particular communities require the adoption of adult persons, owing to the disability and the seclusion of women: for instance, among Gayawals of Gya where votaries have to worship the feet of a male priest of sufficient age and discretion to be able to officiate at the ceremony, and among Jainas who are tradesmen and money-lenders by occupation and who feel the necessity of an adult person in the family to take charge of its business, adoption of adult persons, in any of these forms, is prevalent.

It is however a matter of regret that the two special treatises on adoption which seem to have been written on purpose to invalidate or validate particular adoptions, should have been recognised as works of authority, without sufficient enquiry. The mode in which many of the topics have been discussed in the Dattaka-mimánsa discloses a beas in its writer whose conclusions appear to be foregone, and arguments special pleading. The book appears to have been written to invalidate the affiliation of a daughter's son whose age was more than five years, made by a widow, without performance of the Homa ceremony. The writer endeavours to establish that (1) a daughter's son cannot be affiliated as Putriká-putra, (2) he cannot be adopted as Dattaka among the twice-born castes, (3) a widow cannot adopt at all, (4) there cannot be affiliation unless the Homa ceremony be performed, and (3) unless the boy be of an age not exceeding five years.

The innovations under the name of कलिवर्ज्यानि or practices to be avoided in the *Kali age*, must have acquired their present authority, as Sir William Jones was misled into giving prominence to them by inserting at the end of his translation of Manu, an English version of the texts of the Upa-Puranas, one of which was palmed off on him, as Smriti or *passages of law.*

Daya-bhaga.—The portion of the Vivada-Ratnákara translated in this work is the title of law called Dáya-bhága which has been rendered by Colebrooke into "Partition of Heritage," and this version has been adopted by other writers. But the word "heritage" does not convey the full meaning of the word Dáya according to the Mitákshará school. For, under that school, Dáya is the property in which a relation's interest arises by reason only of his relationship to the owner; and it is twofold, as it may arise either during the owner's lifetime, or only on his affected by them, the law can be changed by Parliament. But the case of the Privy Council in its relation to India is very different. Very few of its members have much knowledge of India, and fewer still have ever been much in touch with the Indian peoples, and it would be very difficult to change either the Hindu or Mahomedan law as declared by the Privy Council by legislation. The Queen's Courts are under the obligation to administer Hindu law to Hindus, and Mahomedan law to Mahomedans, and any attempt by the legislature to change, what had been declared by the highest tribunal to be Hindu or Mahomedan law, unless it were to premise that the highest tribunal had been misled in some of its declarations as to such law, would look very like an infringement of the rights of the Indian peoples which were created by Statute in 1781, and have since been over and over again recognized and confirmed by Acts of Parliament, Acts of the Indian Legislatures, and the Charters of the Courts."—*Law Quarterly Review Vol. XV. p. 184.*

The Hindus would certainly be grateful, if the British Government can see its way to restore the law of their joint family, such as it was before its modification by the superior courts.

The misapprehension of law owing to error of translation of the text-books on it, has undoubtedly been attended with changes and modifications not suited to Hindu Society.

Failure of justice through errors of translation some times arises from the new practice introduced by the High Court of Calcutta, soon after its establishment, according to which the papers on the record in appeals from the Mofussil Courts are to be translated into English, and upon these translated materials the cases are heard and decided by the judges of that court. The High Court was formed by amalgamating the old Supreme Court and the Sudder Dewany Adawlat. The jurisdiction of the former was ordinarily confined to the town of Calcutta, and its language was English. But the latter exercised appellate jurisdiction over all courts in Bengal, Behar and Orissa excepting those in Calcutta, and though the language in which its proceedings were recorded was Persian, yet the language of the papers on the record was the language of the suitors. When a case was called on for hearing before the Sudder Court the original record was read in open court by the Peshkar to the Judges, in the presence of the Vakils of the parties, and upon that the argument of the pleaders turned and the decision of the court rested.

But the aforesaid practice gradually introduced by the High Court, effecting a radical change by making English the language of the court, has opened another door to miscarriage of justice owing to errors of translation into English, of the pleadings, the evidence and the documents which are in the vernacular languages of the people.

This change of practice seems to have been due to the policy entertained at the time by the authorities, of gradually Anglicizing the people in language ; accordingly we find that a few years before the High Court introduced this innovation, the Calcutta Univer- sity also had pursued the same policy by making English the medium of instruction in our Schools and Colleges. But the effect has proved most unsatisfactory, if not disastrous, in both the instances : for, while on the one hand the result has been miscarriage of justice in many cases, we have on the other hand, cramming, instead of sound education or healthy growth and development of the intellectual faculties.

The policy again is one which is destined to be unsuccessful ; for, a people that cherishes with pride the traditions of a world-old civilization, and whose vernacular tongues are the offspring of the classical language of their country, which has been pronounced by one who was so extensively acquainted with those of other ancient and modern nations, that his opinion is entitled to the greatest respect,—to be "of a wonderful structure more perfect than the Greek, more copious than the Latin, and more exquisitely refined than either,"—can never be expected to give up their own mother tongue and adopt that of the ruling race. On the contrary the effect of the spread of education under the fostering care and encouragement of the benign British Rule has been, that all the vernacular languages have made vast and wonderful strides of improvement in their literature. Knowledge of English is cultivated by the middle classes only, as a bread and butter science, being the *sine qua non* of service under the Government as well as the English traders and capitalists.

The only other ground on which this practice can be justified is that as the High Court here is now constituted, there are five Barrister judges who are ignorant of the language of the people. But this argument seems to be of doubtful force, when the other judges whose number is eight at the lowest, are acquainted with the language of the original record in most cases. These judges are either Civilians or natives of this country, who know the vernacular languages. There can be no doubt that these judges, like those of the Sudder Dewany Adawlat, are quite competent to understand the original record, and to decide cases without an English translation of the same. Hence the present practice is not absolutely necessary, and justice free from errors of translation may be administered in most cases, if not in all, by a proper constitution of the Benches.

There is another serious objection to the present practice of compelling the suitors to pay the costs of translation, which is sometimes enormous, and is often out of all proportion to the value of the property in dispute. This heavy tax levied by the High Court from the suitors on pain of denial of justice, cannot be supported by any equitable principle. The translation is made not for the benefit of the suitors, but for that of the judges. If the Government appoint judges who are unable to do their duty unless the record be translated into English, the costs should be paid by the Government and not by suitors who as subjects are entitled to have courts of justice for redress of civil injuries in a mode recognised in every civilized country. India is universally admitted to be a poor country, and it is therefore extremely hard on its people to make justice more costly here than in the richest countries.

How miscarriage of justice arises when a case turns on the construction of a document in a vernacular language, and the same is made through its English translation, is very clearly explained by Sir Comer Petheram in his first Article entitled "English Judges and Hindu Law" in the Law Quarterly Review, in these words :—

"A few years ago a question was argued before a bench of the Calcutta High Court as to the validity of a clause in a Bengalee Will. Except so far as the meaning of a document is always a question of law, no question of law arose. If the clause meant one thing, it was valid, if another it was void. The testator was a Bengalee Hindu, and the will was written in Bengalee. The Bench of the High Court was composed of an English Barrister and a Bengalee Hindu, who after having enjoyed one of the largest practices as a Vakil in Calcutta had been a Judge of the High Court for ten or twelve years. His native language was Bengalee. The Bengalee Judge sent for the original will, and, after a long and careful study of it, came to the conclusion that the English Court translation did not accurately represent the Bengalee document; and that the wishes of the testator as represented by the Bengalee words were such as could not be legally carried out by a will. The English Judge then asked another Indian Judge of the Calcutta High Court, who is also a Bengalee Hindu and a very experienced lawyer, whose native language is Bengalee, to examine the original will, and see if he agreed with the first Bengalee Judge as to its meaning. He did so, and expressed his entire agreement with his colleague. Upon the opinion of these two Bengalees as to the meaning of a document written in their own language, the Judgment of the bench was given and the clause declared void. The matter was appealed to the Privy Council, who reversed the Judgment of the High Court. They treated the English translation as the will, and construing it by the rules of construction which English Judges apply to English documents, they said that the testator did not by his Bengalee words mean what the Bengalee Judges thought he did."—*Law Quarterly Review Vol. XIV. p.* 392.

Instances are not rare in which a document is understood by natives in one way and by European Judges in a contrary way. Take for example, the following Will :—

"Being seriously ill, I execute this Will, providing as below for the preservation and management of my properties, moveable and immoveable, after my death.

"I. My three sons shall be entitled to enjoy all the moveable and immoveable properties left by me equally. Any one of the sons dying sonless, the surviving sons shall be entitled to all the properties equally."

This is the translation of a Bengali Will, upon which the High Court and the Privy Council held that under the rule laid down in Section 111 of the Succession Act, the contingent bequest in favour of the surviving sons in the event of any son dying sonless, cannot take effect unless the death of a son without leaving male issue happen before the death of the testator, because no time is mentioned in the Will for the occurence of the son's death.

But there cannot be the slightest doubt on the mind of any Bengali gentleman on reading the Will, that the testator intended that if any of his sons die sonless *after* his death, then that son's interest will pass to his surviving sons ; and this was the view maintained by the Bengali Subordinate Judge sitting in the original court.

That English rule of construction may be in perfect harmony with the intention which English testators convey by similar words. But it ought not to have been extended to Hindu Wills, for the following simple reason. As a general rule, Hindus make Wills either when they are confined to their deathbed or when somehow or other they believe their days to be numbered; hence the events contemplated by them are presumably those that are to happen after their death and not before, unless the contrary is expressed. Accordingly, the native judge held that the words "after my death" in the introductory clause of the Will, ought to be taken to govern the contingent bequest, and to satisfy the requirement of the Section; as otherwise the testator's intention would be defeated, and the bequest rendered unnecessary, as the same thing would take place under the Hindu Law. Besides, death is the most certain event in a man's life, only the time of its occurence is uncertain; hence, when a bequest is made contingent on the death of a legatee under certain circumstances, it appears to be quite natural to presume that the testator intended that the bequest is to take effect, should the contingency happen when the death actually occurs. This is the mode in which Hindus are found to think and express their intentions.

A few instances may be given here, as to how translations lead to error. Suppose in a case of disputed Will a Vakil examined as a witness says that the alleged testator had met him once and told him আমি একটা উইল করেছি আপনাকে সেটা দেখে দিতে হবে, and the court translator translates it into English, thus :—" I have made a Will, you will have to see it." This is the literal translation, and it may be construed by an English Judge to be an admission by the alleged testator that he had *executed* a will. But what the person really meant is " I have prepared a draft of a Will, you will have to settle it."

Suppose again a witness says সে গুলি খেয়ে মরেছিল—and this is translated into " He died of *a* wound from *a* bullet." There is, however, no indifinite article in the Bengali language, and the strict literal rendering should be " He died of bullet-wound." The witness does not mean to say anything about number: there might be one wound and one bullet, or any number of them. And if the latter be the fact, the cross-examining counsel may confound the witness and make him appear to be untrustworthy, to the Court administering justice through the first translation.

The doctrine propounded by the Superior Courts that a Hindu cannot adopt two or more sons successively or simultaneously, appears to be due to some extent to the English indefinite article which is not found in the Sanskrit language, but which is used in the following English translation of Atri's text, —" By a man destitute of a son only, must *a* substitute for the same, always be adopted." From the words "*a* substitute" it is concluded that the power is limited to the adoption of one son only. But the original does not intend to convey any idea as to the number of adopted sons, although the original word for "substitute" is in the singular number, it does not imply any idea or restriction of number, any more than the word "man" in the proposition "Man is mortal."

The translation of the Bengalee word জানি into "I know" creates a great deal of misconception and confusion. A Bengalee would say জানি, when he *knows*, or *knew*, or *believes*, or *has heard of*.

When the originals of title-deeds or of documentary evidence or of recorded oral evidence are ambiguous, a portion of the judge's function is virtually delegated to the translator, who practically decides what meaning is to be put on them, if the ambiguity disappears in the translation.

The best interests of the Brtish Indian Empire require not only that the people of this country should know English, but also that Englishmen, at any rate those that are officially connected with India, should know the language of the people. They cannot be in touch with the people if they be ignorant of their language, and they may unconsciously be unwilling instruments of misgovernment not dreamed of by them, through their ignorance of the sentiments and feelings of the people. It is through sheer ignorance that the rulers and the ruled are likely to misunderstand each other ; and a want of mutual trust and confidence appears to be its natural though deplorable consequence.

There is no reason why the connection between India and Great Britain should not be permanent, and the policy of Government be not shaped in all matters on that footing. Philology has proved that the Indo-Europeans are descendants of common ancestors. Why should not then Englishmen and Hindus recognise each other as distant cousins. It is also due to ignorance to suppose their religion to be different. The religion which Jesus Christ taught appears to be founded on the self-same principle on which the Hindu religion is founded, namely that of Renunciation : the word "Repent" in His teaching seems to be a mistranslation, the proper rendering should be "Renounce." It is also through ignorance that Englishmen think the image-worship of the Hindus to be idolatory, and these images idols. True knowledge is sure to be followed by mutual sympathy which should be the guiding principle of what is said or written by Englishmen or Indians about each other ; and if England, Scotland and Ireland may form one political unity for mutual benefit, India may also be like one of them, to the advantage of all.

To know a people fully and accurately, one must study their language and literature which reflect their character. The Sanskrit literature alone depicts the Hindu people correctly, whose true character cannot be gathered from the modern vernacular literatures which are hybrid productions embodying as they do a mixture of Eastern and Western ideas. An European acquainted with the Sanskrit literature cannot but feel respect and sympathy for the people of this country. With a view to strengthen the bond of union between Englishmen and Hindus, and also to enable Englishmen to learn with ease the Sanskritic languages of the people, Sanskrit ought to be extensively taught in the English Schools and Colleges instead of Greek and Latin. The claim of Sanskrit appears to be far superior to that of the other two, to be included in the curriculum of study for liberal education in Great Britain, having regard to its relation to India. Englishmen are distinguished for their indomitable energy, studious application and constant perseverence ; and it would not be difficult for them when equipped with some knowledge of Sanskrit, to master the vernacular languages here, if they be desirous to do so. Thus there will no longer be any necessity for administration of justice through translations.

ERRATA.

Page 3, line 36, *for* togather *read* together.
„ 10, „ 44, *for* quardrupeds *read* quadrupeds.
„ 45, *for* youngst *read* youngest.
„ 20, „ 39, *for* desease *read* disease.
„ 26, „ 27, *for* quardrupeds *read* quadrupeds.
„ 28, „ 39, *for* refering *read* referring.
„ 31, „ 35, *for* valuabe *read* valuable.
„ 32, „ 29, *for* llke *read* like.
„ 34, „ 9, *for* kindered *read* kindred.
„ 16, *for* brotber *read* brother.
„ 35, „ 20, *for* maintainance *read* maintenance.
„ 36, „ 5, *for* ordaincd *read* ordained.
„ 19, *for* deseose *read* disease.
„ 37, „ 10, *for* here after *read* hereafter.
„ 20, *for* uderstood *read* understood.
„ 38, „ 15, *for* illustrativc *read* illustrative.
„ 40, „ 12, *for* premissing *read* premising.
„ 55, „ 17, *for* twelveth *read* twelfth.
„ 64, „ 42, *for* "the (appointed) daughter's son alone, shall take the entire property of a sonless person" *read* "he alone must give two funeral cakes (one) to his father, one to his mother's father".
„ 65, „ 2, *for* is a repetition of the (rule laid down in) the first half *read* is a superfluous injunction (as it follows from what has been already said).
„ 67, „ 11, *for* deseribed *read* described.
„ 73, „ 33, *for* twelvth *read* twelfth.
„ 74, „ 2, *for* confering *read* conferring.
„ 79, „ 21, *for* extention *read* extension.
„ 83, „ 32, *for* twelvth *read* twelfth.
„ 86, „ 34, *for* refering *read* referring.

शुद्धिपत्रम् ।

Page ३ line १६ *for* कुटुम्बम् भरणम् *read* कुटुम्बभरणम् ।

„ ११ „ १० *for* दंश्रं *read* दंष्ट्रं ।

„ १२ „ २ *for* विवचयाश्च *read* विवचायाश्च ।

„ १२ „ ९ *for* विष्णुवचर्न *read* विष्णुवचनं ।

„ १३ „ २ *for* सवं *read* सर्वं ।

„ १४ „ १५ *for* विहवम् *read* विहतम् ।

„ २० „ २४ *for* सम्भवी *read* सम्भवी ।

„ २१ „ २४ *for* दंश्रमीव *read* दंष्ट्रमीव ।

„ २१ „ २५ *for* एव *read* एवं ।

„ २६ „ ४ *for* प्रजापत्येषु *read* प्राजापत्येषु ।

„ २८ „ २१ *for* दुविभक्ताश्च *read* दुर्विभक्ताश्च ।

„ ३० „ २ *for* वैश्यापुत्रस्त *read* वैश्यापुत्रस्तु ।

„ ३० „ १४ *for* याज्ञवल्कोक्ता *read* याज्ञवल्क्योक्ता ।

„ ३९ „ १० *for* विजानीयत्पुत्रं *read* विजानीयात्पुत्रं ।

„ ४२ „ १६ *for* दौहित्र एव तु हरेदपुत्रस्याखिलं धनं *read* स एव दद्याद्द्वौपिण्डौ पित्रे मातामहाय च ॥

„ ५९ „ ८ *for* मनंशभाजी *read* नंशभाजी ।

„ ६० „ ६ *for* निर्वीजान्यन्यभागिण *read* निर्वीजान्योन्यभागिन ।

„ ६० „ २५ *for* दम्पत्तोः *read* दम्पत्योः ।

„ ६१ „ ४ *for* अन्योन्यनैरपेच्येति *read* अन्योन्यनैरपेच्येणेति ।

CONTENTS.

CHAPTER I.

Partition of Heritage.

CHAPTER II.

Partition during the life-time of the father.

CHAPTER III.

Partition after the father's death.

CHAPTER IV.

Partition among brothers by different mothers.

Page.

CHAPTER IX.

PARTITION OF WOMAN'S PROPERTY.

CHAPTER X.

SUCCESSION TO THE PROPERTY OF A WOMAN DYING WITHOUT ISSUE OF HER BODY, ACCORDING TO THE FORM OF HER MARRIAGE.

CHAPTER XI.

STRIDHANA.

CHAPTER XII.

THE PARTITION OF WHAT WAS CONCEALED.

CHAPTER XIII.

PARTITION AMONG BRETHREN OF DEFFERENT CLASSES.

CHAPTER XIV.

THE PARTICIPATION BY (A SON) BORN AFTER PARTITION.

CHAPTER. XV.

THE PARTICIPATION BY ONE RETURNING (FROM ABROAD) AFTER PARTITION.

CHAPTER XVI.

PARTICIPATION BY OTHER (DESCRIPTIONS OF) SONS.

CHAPTER XVII.

THE AURASA OR REAL LEGITIMATE SON.

Page.

CHAPTER XVIII.

KSHETRAJA OR APPOINTED WIFE'S SON.

CHAPTER XIX.

THE APPOINTED DAUGHTER, AND HER SON.

CHAPTER XX.

THE SON OF THE TWICE-MARRIED WOMAN.

CHAPTER XXI.

THE MAIDEN-BORN SON.

CHAPTER XXII.

THE SECRETLY-BORN SON.

CHAPTER XXIII.

THE SON OF THE PREGNANT BRIDE.

Page.

CHAPTER XXIV.

THE DATTAKA OR GIVEN SON.

CHAPTER XXV.

THE PURCHASED SON.

CHAPTER XXVI.

THE SELF-GIVEN SON.

CHAPTER XXVII.

THE DESERTED SON.

CHAPTER XXVIII.

THE KRITTRIMA SON OR SON MADE.

CHAPTER XXIX.

THE SON BY A SUDRA WOMAN.

CHAPTER XXX.

THE DISCUSSION OF SONSHIP.

Page.

CHAPTER XXXI.

THE EXTENSION OF SONSHIP.

CHAPTER XXXII.

THE ETYMOLOGICAL EXPLANATION AND THE LIKE, OF THE WORD PUTTRA (SON).

CHAPTER XXXIII.

THE REPREHENSIBLE SON.

CHAPTER XXXIV.

THE PARTICIPATION OF, (OR SUCCESSION TO), THE PROPERTY OF A SONLESS PERSON.

Page.

CHAPTER XXXV.

THE PARTITION AND SUCCESSION IN RESPECT OF THE PROPERTY OF THOSE WHO ARE RE-UNITED.

CHAPTER XXXVI.

THE DETERMINATION OF (DISPUTED) PARTITION.

CHAPTER XXXVII.

THE RIGHTS AND DUTIES OF SEPARATED (KINSMEN).

VIVÁDA-RATNAKÁRA

PARTITION OF HERITAGE.

CHAPTER I.

§ 1 & 2—Partition of Heritage, subject of the chapter. 3—Its definition. 4 to 7—Partition of father's property after his death. 8 to 9—Management by eldest brother. 10—Or by any other able brother. 11 to 12—Partition optional. 13—Religious duties common before partition, 14 to 15—Sons dependent on father.

1. Now (the Action called) Partition of Heritage (is explained).

2. Premising this (subject) MANU (says) :—" Thus has been declared to you the law of man and wife based upon affection ; listen now to the law of heritage, and to the mode of having offspring on failure of the (Aurasa or) true son. "

3. NA'RADA (says)—" Where the division of paternal property is instituted by the sons, that topic of litigation is by the wise called Partition of Heritage. "

" Where " means, " in which topic of litigation (or Action) ; " is instituted " means, " is made ".

4. MANU (says) :—" After the death of the father and of the mother, the brothers being assembled, shall divide equally, the paternal estate, for they are not masters while the parents are alive. "

" Equally " means " in equal shares ", that is to say, the specific deduction of the twentieth part &c. (does) not (obtain) here. But (it may be asked) when Manu has ordained the specific deduction of the twentieth part &c. in respect only of partition by those whose father is dead, how (could he here say) equally ? (the answer is) Not so ; that (text of Manu ordaining specific deduction) applies to the eldest and the like who are possessed of merits. Udayakara explained " equally " as being referable to the (residue of the) estate after the specific deductions. But Haláyudha and the Párijáta read *saha* (together) in place of *samam* (equally), and the Párijáta explains *saha* as " with each other ". Haláyudha says, the word *paitrikam* (paternal) is formed by adding an affix after the formation of an uni-residual conjunctive compound (of *mátri* and *pitri*), and hence includes the mother's estate also. Others say, that although the word *paitrikam* (paternal) has been used in the text, the estate of the grandfather and the like, (also,) is intended to be included ; for, partition of such estate also, is shown by the text,—" In the goods acquired by the grandfather &c." It should be understood that both the above are intended, but the succession of sons to the mother's estate, is to take place, under an ancient usage, in default of the daughter and her issue.

5. DEVALA (says)—" When the father is dead, let the sons divide the estate of the father : for sons have not ownership while the father is alive and free from defect."

" Free from defect " means, devoid of defects such as degradation &c.

6. NA'RADA (says)—" When the father is dead, let the sons divide the father's estate. (Let) the daughters (divide) the mother's (estate), and on failure of daughters, their issue ".

The meaning is,—Let the daughters divide the mother's estate ; " on failure of daughters " let " their issue " *i. e.* the daughters' issue divide. " When the father is dead ",—this much alone being sufficient to denote succession, the use of the word " the sons " is for the purpose of including the Kshetraja (appointed wife's son) and other (sons). Hence, when any one of the twelve (kinds of) sons is alive, no other relation can succeed to the estate : the word " father's " (estate) is used for the purpose of showing that in case the gains of science &c. of any of the sons be made separately, there is to be no participation of the same (by other sons). By reason of nearness to the word " daughters " the pronoun *tat* (" their " in *tadanvaya* =" their issue ") has been properly referred to that word (the daughters). LAKSHMÍDHARA's own opinion is also the same. The Prakása and the Párijáta, however, say, " their issue, " means, the daughters' issue such as son, grandson, and the like.

7. SANKHA and LIKHITA (say) :—" Since partition of the estate takes place after his decease, sons cannot divide it while the father lives, even though it was acquired by them independent of him ; they have no power (to make such a partition), since they are not their own masters in respect of wealth or religious duties, when the father is free from defect ".

" Acquired independent of him " *i. e.* acquired by the sons independent of their father, through united efforts in science or the like.

8. Now MANU (says) :—" The eldest alone may take the entire estate of the father, and the rest may live under him as under their father. As soon as the eldest (son) is born, a man becomes possessed of a son, and also discharged of his debt to his own progenitors : the eldest son therefore deserves the whole. That son alone, by whose birth he discharges his debt, and through whom he attains endlessness, is the son begotten from a sense of duty : the rest are considered as begotten from a love of pleasure. The eldest brother shall support the younger brothers as the father (used to do), and these shall be dutiful to the eldest brother as sons. The first-born exalts the family or destroys it : the first-born is in this world the most respectable, and the good never treat him with disdain.

If an eldest brother acts as an eldest brother ought, he is to be revered as a father and as a mother, and if he behaves as an eldest brother ought not, he is still to be regarded as a *bandhu* (an elderly relation)".

9. Likewise (MANU says) :—" The eldest shall not make self-appropriation without giving to the younger brothers."

" The eldest alone may take " means, that the eldest brother who is possessed of all the merits of an eldest brother, shall be independent like the father, in respect of the partible property. " May live under him " means may live in the style approved by him. " Becomes possessed of a son " means, becomes one who has obeyed the Sástras enjoining the procreation of a son. The use of the word " as soon as " signifies, that there is no need of (waiting for) sacraments. " Discharged of debt " signifies, that he satisfies one of the three debts declared by the Sruti—" He becomes born indebted in three debts. " " Discharges " means, satisfies. " Endlessness, " that is, of happiness, the meaning therefore is, endless happiness : " attains " *i. e.* obtains, by being discharged of debts. " Begotten from a love of pleasure " —this is mere eulogium (of the eldest), for it does not denote an exclusion from shares, the younger (sons') shares being (expressly) provided for. " Shall support as the father, " that is to say, shall not defraud them. " Shall be dutiful as the son " that is, shall not envy him. " Exalts the family " *i. e.* the exaltation of the family is (effected) by supporting the younger ones, by all means. " Destroys it ",—this imports mere capability (to destroy). " As an eldest brother ought (to behave)" i. e. the duty of the eldest (brother) is to maintain and protect the younger ones with affection. " As a *bandhu* ", that is to say, he is to be respected as the maternal uncle and the like, by (respectful) rising and salutation, and not to be despised. " Self-appropriation " (Jautaka), is property intended to be separate from theirs : since it is written in the Dhátupatha (lexicon of verbs) that the verb " Yu " means, to disunite. Haláyudha, however, says that *jautaka* (rendered self-appropriation in the text) means, the wife's ornaments and the like.

10. NA'RADA (says) :—" Or let the eldest brother, or an younger brother if able, maintain all the rest if willing, like a father ; for, rank in a family, depends upon ability ".

11. SANKHA and LIKHITA (say)—" (Or) if they choose let them live togather, (because) being united they may develop prosperity ".

" Being united ", that is, aiding one another ; " develop prosperity " means, make prosperity manifest, that is, they become prosperous themselves.

12. MANU (says) :—" Either let them live together ; or if they desire religious merit, let them live apart : religious merit increases by partition, therefore partition is conducive to religious merit ".

Since joint property is not capable of being dealt with, according to the pleasure of a single co-sharer, and since sacrifices and the like which can be performed (only) with property which is the subject of independent ownership, cannot be performed (during joint state), therefore partition which is (otherwise) deducible from reason, has been (not enjoined here, but only) recited, for facilitating (the performance of) such (sacrifices). Hence, the text,—" if they desire religious merit let them live apart ",—

does not imply (either) that there would be religious demerit from the absence of partition, (as it does not embody an *imperative rule* forbidding the joint state,) like the text relating to the eating of the meat of animals killed by poisoned arrows, (or) that there would be religious merit from partition, (as it does neither embody an injunction directing separation,) like the text relating to the performance of the Jyotistoma sacrifice or the like.

13. VRIHASPATI (says) :—" Of those living in commensality, the worship of the *manes* of the ancestors, of gods, and of the twice-born, is common; but of the separated, the same is performed separately in every house. "

" Living in commensality ", means; living unseparated.

14. HA'RI'TA (says) :—" While the father lives, sons are not independent in respect of the receipt, alienation and recovery of wealth ; but if he be prodigal, absent in a remote country, or afflicted with disease, let the eldest son manage the affairs."

" Receipt of wealth " means, taking of joint property, independently of the father ; the Párijáta says, it means the acquisition of wealth ; " alienation " means, gift ; " recovery ", means, taking of such (common) property from the hands of debtors. " Prodigal " means, giving away property at every whim. The author of the Prakása, however, reads the text, as " *kámam díne* " *i. e.*, by the choice (of the father), if he be despondent, instead of " *Káma-dane* " *i. e.* " prodigal ", and says that the term " by the choice " relates to the assent of the father the nearest referrible word, and explains, the word " *díne* " or despondent, as meaning decayed in intellect.

15. SANKHA and LIKHITA (say) :—" If the father be incapable, let the eldest manage the affairs of the family ; or with his consent, a younger conversant with business. But partition of heritage does not take place, if the father be not desirous of it. When he is old, or his mental faculties are impaired, or he is afflicted with a lasting disease, let the eldest, like a father, protect the goods of the rest ; for (the support of) the family is founded on the heritage. They are not independent, while they have their father living, or while the mother is thus existent ".

" Younger " means, a younger brother ; "with his consent" *i. e.* with the permission of the eldest ; " whose mental faculties are impaired ", that is, whose intellect is clouded by nervous debility and the like ; " the family " means, the support of the family ; " founded on the heritage " *i. e.* founded on wealth ; " they are not independent ", that is, they are not competent to make gifts and the like : " while the mother is thus existent," here the construction is, that the sons are not independent while the mother is living and free from defects.

16. Thus in the VIVA'DA-RATNA'KARA ends the chapter on the partition of the heritage.

CHAPTER II.

§ 1—Partition during fathers's life. 2 to 5—Equal rights of father and son in Ancestral property. 6 to 14—Partition of paternal property during his life, 15—Wife's share. 16 to 18—Father's double share. 19 to 21—Specific deductions for eldest and other sons. 22—Where no specific deduction. 23—Distribution by father, of his property not liable to objection.

1. Now, partition during the life-time of the father, (is treated.)

2. On this subject, MANU and VISHṆU (say) :—" But if the father recovers (his) paternal wealth, which could not be recovered, he shall not, if reluctant, share it with his sons, being his self-acquired property."

" Paternal ", means, descended in regular sucession from ancestors ; " could not be recovered ", that is, by his father : he shall not share with his sons, if unwilling, by reason of its being his self-acquired.

3. YA'JNAVALKYA (says) :—" In land acquired by the grandfather, or in corrody (*nibandha*), or in chattels (belonging to him), the ownership of both father and son, is the same."

" Nibandha ", is that which is settled with certainty, such as fixed gain from a mine or the like ; " ownership is the same ", that is, the father has not a larger share in such property, nor can he give it away according to his pleasure.

4. VYA'SA (says) :—" In houses and fields, descended in regular course of succession, the father and son are equal sharers ; but in the property of the father (himself), the sons are not entitled to share, against the will of the father."

5. VRIHASPATI (says) :—" In property immoveable as well as moveable, acquired by the grandfather, the right of the father and the son is declared to the equal. In such property of the grandfather, as was lost and recovered by the father through his own ability, and in what is acquired by science, prowess and the like, the father's ownership is ordained. Of such property, the father may make gifts or distribution according to his pleasure ; and after his death, the sons are pronounced equal sharers ".

" Lost ", that is, taken away by strangers, and not recovered by the paternal grandfather through inability, but recovered by the father through his own ability.

6. On the subject of partition by sons, NA'RADA (says) :—" When the mother is past child-bearing, and sisters are given (in marriage), or when the father is past cohabitation and his desires are extinct."

" Given " means, married ; " past cohabitation ", that is, decayed in the power of cohabitation : " desires are extinct ", that is, desires for worldly enjoyments have ceased. In the Prakása however, two different readings, namely *nirapekshe cha ramane*, and *niraste chápi ramane* are given, but according to the interpretations therein given, the result is substantially the same. Haláyudha however, reads *ramanát* instead of *ramane*, but in that (reading) also, there is no difference in the result.

7. VRIHASPATI (says) :—" On the demise of both parents, partition amongst brothers is allowed, and even while they are both living, it is right, if the mother be past child-bearing."

Here also it is intended to be laid down, " or when the father is past cohabitation."

8. GAUTAMA (says) :—" After the death of the father, sons shall divide the heritage ; or if the father is alive, when he is willing, and the mother past child-bearing."

9. SANKHA and LIKHITA (say) :—" Or partition of heritage, if allowed, is lawful when the father is alive, and it may be made publicly or privately."

" Allowed " means, allowed by the father ; " publicly, " that is, in the presence of arbitrators ; " privately " that is, without the intervention of arbitrators.

10. BAUDHA'YANA (says) :—" By permission of the father, partition of heritage takes place ".

11. HA'RI'TA (says) :—" The father when living may distribute (the whole property amongst the sons) and retire to a forest, or enter the order of old age ; or he may distribute a small portion, and continue to live in his house, reserving the larger portion for himself. Should he lose, he may take back from them, and to such as become indigent he may give a portion."

" Retire to a forest ", that is, adopt a different order of life. The author of the Prakása says that " order of old age " signifies, living in the house as a Vaidic-ascetic after having transferred the property to sons.

HALA'YUDHA AND THE PA'RIJA'TA (say) :—That " order of old age " means, the fourth order of life : in their opinion, by the words "retire to a forest " is intended to mean, adopt the third order of life. In reality however, the particle " or " in the text signifies, indifference : therefore we get a mode of life according to choice, other than the third and the fourth orders of life ; he may adopt the same : in fact, the Vaidic-ascetic desires to continue in the order of the householder, independent (of all concern for worldly affairs). It is to be understood that the passage " or he may distribute a small portion &c., refers to him ; " should he lose ", that is, if he be reduced.

12. On this subject, NA'RADA (says) :—" Or the father when not old, may himself distribute the property amongst his sons, by assigning the best share to the eldest, or in any manner he chooses ".

The word " Or " indicates an alternative ; (hence,) either the father or the sons may make the partition : " when not old " *i. e.* when not disabled by decay, as distinguished from the previous case (of one separating from his sons, when he is past cohabitation): hence it is, that GAUTAMA by the text,—"A son born after partition (gets) the paternal share only"—declares the mode of partition in case of the birth of a son after partition: "best" means, most desirable *i. e.* largest: "in any manner he pleases", that is, the father may divide in equal or unequal shares, according to his pleasure.

13. VISHNU (declares):—"If the father makes the partition amongst the sons, his own will regulates the division of his own acquired wealth."

This refers to property which is acquired without the aid of his father's property.

14. YA'JNAVALKYA (says):—"When the father makes a partition, he may separate the sons according to his pleasure, and either (allot) the best share to the eldest, or all may be equal sharers."

This also refers to self-acquired property, because the equal participation of the father and the son in ancestral property, has been declared.

15. Here again, (he) lays down a special rule with respect to the case of equal distribution,—

"If he makes an equal distribution, the *patnís* or lawfully wedded wives to whom *strídhanam* has not been given either by the husband or by the father-in-law, must be made partakers of equal shares."

If the father makes the sons equal sharers, *patnís* or lawfully wedded wives should be made partakers of equal shares. Thus also it is to be understood, that in the case of unequal distribution amongst sons, the (father's) *patnís* also are unequal sharers; but not the *patnís* of sons and the like, because the father being the person who makes the partition, the word *patní* must be understood as taken relatively to him. If, however, property has not been given to any of the *patnís*, then they also are to be made partakers of the same share of wealth. HALA'YUDHA says, that here son-less *patnís* are also meant. PRAKA'SA says, if *strídhanam* has been given, then half (should be allotted), as laid down in a subsequent passage.

16. NA'RADA (says):—"The father dividing his own (property) may obtain two shares."

"Dividing" i. e. making a division of; "may obtain" *i. e.* may take.

17. VRIHASPATI (says):—"But in a division during (his) life-time, the father may take two shares as his own."

This however appears, from a consideration of SANKHA's text, to refer to a case, in which there is only one son."

18. Accordingly, referring to the father SANKHA and LIKHITA (say):—"If he has only one son, let him set apart for himself two shares, (taking) some thing additional, from amongst bipeds and quadrupeds."

The meaning is, that taking something additional, he shall take two shares.

19. Likewise (they say):—"A bull to the eldest, and a house to the youngest, other than the father's residence."

The meaning of this is: When there are more sons, and the eldest and the youngest are possessed of good qualities, a bull should be given to the eldest, and a house to the youngest, even, against the will of the father, otherwise the rule would be objectionable as being meaningless.

As for what has been said by YA'JNAVALKYA (by the text No. 14) " or all shall be equal sharers ", this means that, when all the sons (are equal) in quality, the equality or inequality of shares, depends upon the will of the father: thus there is no conflict; so says HALA'YUDHA.

The PA'RIJA'TA however says, that *ekaputra* (rendered above into " has only one son " in text No. 18) means, eldest son. The Bháshyakára however, instead of adopting the (above) reading with the word *putra*, reads as follows, " if he is alone, " and says, if he is alone i. e. without a wife, then also he shall take two shares: if he has a wife, he shall satisfy her also with another share. " Something additional ", that is, one from amongst bipeds and quadrupeds, he shall take, in addition to his two shares. The rule about giving something additional to the eldest and the youngest, applies, when they are possessed of good qualities, even against the father's will: otherwise, the rule would be objectionable as meaningless. And the equality of shares ordained by YA'JNAVALKYA applies when all are possessed of good qualities. In the absence of superiority, the equality or inequality of shares depends upon the will of the father: thus there is no conflict. " Other than &c. " means, excepting the house occupied by the father.

20. BAUDHA'YANA (says):—" Heritage shall be divided amongst sons, this is the Sruti (revealed law): the share of all shall be equal, by reason of the absence of any distinction; or the eldest shall take the best of each class of things as his specific deduction, because a text of the Sruti ordains—' Therefore they distinguish the eldest son with property',—or the eldest son shall take as his specific deduction one out of each ten, the rest shall share equally. "

" The eldest shall take the best of each class of things",—the meaning is, that the eldest shall take the best one of the different classes of things. The reason of this is said to be the text of the Sruti,—" Therefore &c. "; " They distinguish ", that is, honour, in preference to other sons, " the eldest son with property " in the shape of specific deduction. (The passage) " or the eldest son shall take as his specific deduction one out of each ten &c. ", marks another alternative, and means, that he shall, even against the will of the father, take as his specific deduction, one out of each ten of the same class of things, such as cows; the alternatives are to be applied, according as the eldest son is possessed of more or less good qualities.

21. A'PASTAMBA (says):—"The father, while living, shall, after having satisfied the eldest with some property, distribute (the rest) equally amongst his sons, excepting the impotent, the insane, and the degraded."

" While living " *i. e.* while living but incapable of begetting children; " with some property " *i. e.* with the best horse (or dress) or the like; by the words " excepting the impotent &c.", all those who are excluded from inheritance, are intended.

The reconciliation (of the different texts relating to specific deduction for the eldest) is, that they are intended to apply (severally), having regard to the extent of property of the eldest, and when there is excess of good qualities.

22. On this subject, MANU (says):—"If there be common exertion amongst joint brothers, then the father shall not, by any means, make an unequal distribution."

"Exertion" means, any effort conducive to the acquisition of wealth.

23. NA'RADA, YA'JNAVALKA and VRIHASPATI ordain:—"Whatever shares, whether equal, lesser or greater, have been allotted by the father to the sons respectively, such shares shall be maintained undisturbed; otherwise (the sons) shall be liable to punishment."

24. NA'RADA (says):—"But those (sons) who have been separated by the father himself with equal, lesser, or larger shares of property, for them that very division shall prevail; for the father is the master of the whole".

The previous text (of Manu) prohibits unequal distribution in the case of common exertion *i. e.* when the property has been jointly acquired by the brothers: but these (texts) lay down unequal distribution of the father's self-acquired property; thus there is no conflict.

25. Thus in the VIVA'DA-RATNA'KARA, ends the subject of partition during the life-time of the father.

CHAPTER III.

§ 1—Partition after father's death. 2—Specific deductions of twentieth and other parts. 3—Specific deduction of other things. 4—Of the same, and Deity &c., for eldest. 5 to 7— Specific deductions for eldest &c.

1. Now partition after the father's death is discussed.

2. On that subject, MANU (says):—"The specific deduction for the eldest is a twentieth part, also what is the most valuable from among all the chattels; for the middlemost, half of that; and a quarter, for the youngest. The eldest and the youngest respectively shall take the just mentioned portions; for sons, other than the eldest and the youngest, the portion shall be the mean. Of all the goods collected, the first-born shall take the best, and shall also get whatever is most excellent, and the best of ten".

This specific deduction refers to the eldest and the like, that are endowed with good qualities. On this subject, the following rules are applicable to different circumstances: when there are many sons born of the same mother, possessed of good qualities, but there is a gradual diminution of the good qualities, then the specific deduction of twentieth part of the common property shall be made for the eldest, "also what is the most valuable property from among all the chattels," shall be given (to him); "for the middlemost, half of that," that is, the fortieth portion and a property of mean value ; "and a quarter, for the youngest." *i. e.* the eightieth portion, and the least valuable property shall be given (to the youngest).

But when the eldest and the youngest alone are possessed of good qualities, then to them the specific deduction just mentioned shall be given ; but the intermediate sons, who are devoid of good qualities, shall get property of mean value. The fortieth portion, which is declared as the specific deduction for the middlemost possessed of good qualities, shall be given by dividing the same equally (when there are more intermediate brothers than one). But when there are many intermediate sons possessed of exceedingly good qualities, then to each of them, should be given a fortieth portion, as his specific deduction.

If the eldest be possessed of exceedingly good qualities, and the others are dovoid of good qualities, then the eldest shall take as his specific deduction, the best of all property, and whatever is excellent in its own kind such as rubies and the like, and the best of each ten of cows, buffaloes and the like.

3. GAUTAMA declares a special rule as applicable to a case, where the eldest is possessed of exceedingly good qualities, and the others are possessed of mediocre qualities :—

"A twentieth part shall belong to the eldest, (besides) a pair, a car with beast having teeth in both jaws, and a cow-bull ; cattle blind of one eye, or aged, or disfigured, or devoid of tail, if there are more than one, shall belong to the middlemost ; a sheep, grain, iron, a house, a car yoked, and one of each sort of quadrupeds, shall belong to the youngest ; all the residue shall be equally (divided)."

"A twentieth part" out of all the paternal wealth "shall belong to the eldest" ; "a pair" of cows ; "beast having teeth in both jaws" such as horses, asses and the like,—with two beasts of any one of these kinds, is the car to be yoked ; "cow-bull" is a bull capable of procreation ; this specific deduction belongs to the eldest, only when possible. In the passage "cattle blind of one eye or aged or disfigured, or devoid of tail, if there are more than one, shall belong to the middlemost",—"aged" means old, "disfigured" means deprived of horns, "devoid of tail" that is, devoid of the tuft of hair at the end of the tail well known as *bende,* this is the specific deduction for the middlemost, if, of these also, there are more than one. In the passage "a sheep, grain, iron, a house, a cart yoked, one of each sort of quadrupeds, shall belong to the youngest",—a sheep means an ewe, grain and iron being spoken of in general terms, something of the kind should be given, "a house" is one house, a car means, a cart, and "yoked" is yoked with bullocks, "of quardrupeds" *i. e.* cows and the like, one of each sort is the specific deduction for the youngst ; "the residue shall be equally divided" the meaning is that what is left, after making the specific deductions, shall be equally divided.

In the same way, when in other texts specific deductions in larger or smaller proportions, are ordained, then a reconciliation is to be made, having regard to the possession or otherwise, of good qualities and the like by the eldest, the middlemost, and the youngest, amongst brothers. In practice, however, the specific deduction for the eldest alone, is taken into account, no notice being taken, of the same, for the middlemost and the youngest, and accordingly the specific deduction of a twentieth for the eldest, is found.

4. HA'RI'TA ordains :—" When a division takes place, a bull from a herd of kine, and a single chattel, or the best (portion), and the Deity, and the house, should be given to the eldest ; the rest shall remove, and build, or if there is only one (homestead land,) then the best should be given to the eldest, and as regards the rest, the order of seniority should be followed."

" A single chattel " means, the best of chattels ; " the Deity " means the image of Vishnu and the like ; " house " means, the paternal house ; " the rest shall build ", *i. e.*, other houses ; when it is impossible to remove from the house, and build other houses, then " the best " *i. e.* the most excellent apartment should be given to the eldest. " The order of seniority should be followed," hence the meaning is—to the middlemost, the mean apartment, and to the youngest, an apartment still inferior, should be given. HARIHARA, however, explains the compound word *devatá-griham* in the above text (translated as " the deity and the house ") to mean the apartment for worshipping the goddess, Durga and the like, and says that the others, after having given the same to the eldest, should build other such apartments (for themselves).

5. A'PASTAMBA ordains :—" In some countries, gold (coin or thing), black cows, the black produce of the earth, belong to the eldest, together with the utensils of the common father."

" Black produce of the earth, " such as (*tila*) sesamum, (माष) pease and the like ; " utensils " mean, vessels for eating, and the like.

6. BAUDHA'YANA declares :—" On the death of the father, the specific deduction for the eldest, is, among the four classes respectively, a cow, a horse, a goat, and a sheep ".

This applies only when the eldest brother is possessed of a small amount of good qualities.

7. DEVALA (says) :—" The mean portion is intended for sons equal in qualities : but a tenth part should be allowed to the eldest whose conduct is in accordance with law."

" Mean portion " means, mean wealth, *i. e.*, a twentieth share : this is intended to apply when the eldest is versed in the Vedas, and the others are devoid of good qualities ; such is the opinion of Haláyudha and the Párijáta. Others, however, say, that when the eldest is versed in the Vedas, and has established the sacred fire, and the others are possessed of good qualities, then a tenth share is for the eldest, and for each of the other sons the mean share, that is, the mean portion, that is, the twentieth part : this is the interpretation of the first half of the Sloka. And the interpretation of the second half is, that when the eldest is versed in the Vedas, and has established the sacred fire, and the others are devoid of good qualities, then the tenth portion is the specific deduction for the eldest; but to the brothers devoid of good qualities, the fortieth part alone should be given by division as stated above.

8. "Thus in the VIVA'DA-RATNA'KARA ends the subject of partition after the death of the father.

CHAPTER IV.

§ 1—Partition among brothers by different mothers. 2 to 5—When eldest born on younger wife, &c. 6 to 7—When equal number of sons by each of several wives. 8 to 9—Equal division. 10 to 11—Status of first-born by birth, and that among twins. 12—Eldest guilty of fraud. 13 to 18—Specific deductions. 19—What eldest entitled to it. 20 to 23—Equal division, and division *per stirpes*. 24 to 26—partition limited to three degrees, when. 27 to 31—Share for brother's widow, and for father's wife and father's mother. 32 to 33—When a member to be honoured. 34—When sharer gives up share.

1. Now, partition among brothers by different mothers (is discussed).

2. On that subject, MANU declares :—" A younger son being born of a first married wife, after an elder son had been born of a wife last married, it may be a doubt in that case, how the division should be made ; (so it is provided),—let the son born of the elder wife, take one most excellent bull as his specific deduction, the inferior bulls other than that, are for those who are inferior to him on account of their mothers."

This doubt relates only to different sons born of mothers of the same tribe with the first-born, because the partition of heritage among sons by mothers of different classes, will be dealt with hereafter. By the term "first-born" is signified the younger son born of the first married wife : this is inferred from what follows in the second line, namely "the inferior bulls are for those who are inferior to him on account of their mothers". The meaning is, that "inferior" *i. e.* less excellent, "bulls other than that" *i.e.* other than the most excellent bull (given to the son by the first married wife) "are for those who are inferior to him" *i. e.* are for those whose mothers were married subsequently to the mother of him *i. e.* the younger son by the first married wife.

3. Having declared seniority by reason of the priority of the mother's marriage, the Sage declares a special rule on that very subject :—" But the first-born born of the first married wife shall take (kine amounting to) sixteen inclusive of an excellent bull, and the rest of the sons shall then take, in rightof their respective mothers : such is the fixed rule."

"(Kine amounting to) sixteen inclusive of an excellent bull" means, fifteen cows and one excellent bull : such a specific deduction is allowed by reason of his superiority of birth. "The rest of the sons," by reason of the juniority of their mothers, shall each take an inferior bull.

The author of the PRAKA'SA (says), that this is mentioned by MANU as the opinion of others and that his (Manu's) own opinion that seniority follows the order of birth, is shewn (by him) in the following text namely,—"Among sons born of wives of the same class, seniority is not in accordance with the priority of their mother's marriage, but seniority is without distinction in accordance with birth."

HALA'YUDHA, however, explains the text as follows :—When the eldest son is born of the last married wife, and the youngest is born of the first married wife, then he who is first born of the last married wife shall take, as his specific deduction one excellent bull, the inferior bulls other than that bull, shall be given, one to each of the sons inferior to him, *i. e.*, younger to the first born, "on account of their mothers", *i. e.* according to inferiority consisting in the order of their mother's marriage : the residue shall be equally divided : when however, the eldest son is born of the first married wife, then a special rule is laid down, in the text,—" But the first born &c. ". Kine amounting to sixteen inclusive of an excellent bull *i. e.* one excellent bull and fifteen cows. The others shall take, in the order of their mothers' marriage, as their specific deduction, each a bull as mentioned before.

4. On this very subject, GAUTAMA (says) :—" An excellent bull is the specific deduction for the eldest : a bull and fifteen cows are the specific deduction for the eldest born of the first married wife, or he shall take equally with a younger son born of the first married wife. "

In conformity with Manu's text the word " eldest " here means, a first-born son by a last married wife, " equally " *i. e.* in the same manner : this is to be understood when all the sons are of the same class.

5. SANKHA and LIKHITA (say) :—" An excellent bull is the specific deduction for the eldest, and a house for the youngest. "

Here also, in conformity with the text of Manu, the word " eldest " is to be understood to be the son of the last married wife.

6. GAUTAMA declares :—" Among groups of brothers by different mothers, there is a special division."

Its meaning is, that when an equal number of many sons is born of each of many wives of the same class, in that case a division among brothers being difficult, the property should be divided into as many shares as there are mothers, and then a special partition with specific deductions of the twentieth part, should be made of each share, among uterine brothers of each group.

7. VRIHASPATI (says) the same thing :—" If sons of the same man by each of his different wives of the same class, be equal in number, they may legally make a partition, by allotting shares to their mothers : but if they be unequal in number though of the same class, then amongst them partition is to be effected by allotting shares to themselves. "

8. VISHNU (says) :—" Sons of equal class shall take equal shares, and shall give the best thing as specific deduction to the eldest."

This applies when the number of sons is unequal.

9. MANU (says) :—" Among brothers equal in respect of the duties of their class, there is no specific deduction such as the best of ten : some trifle only, as a token of respect, should be given to the eldest."

The meaning of this is :—Amongst those who are equal in learning and the like, the specific deduction of the most excellent chattel and the best of ten, should not be made : this again is illustrative ; the prohibition here, is levelled against all specific deductions, by reason of the text " some trifle only ". But something should be given as token of respect, owing to seniority, on account of mere priority of birth. After having written this, the Sage has declared, that when there is a disparity amongst brothers, in respect of qualifications, then it is to be understood, that the text, (No. 2) " for those who are inferior on account of their mothers",—and (No. 3) " but the first born, born of the first married wife ",—would apply. By this is met, what has been stated by some others, namely—that in the texts,—" for those who are inferior on account of their mothers ",—and—" but the first-born, born of the first married wife ",—the adverse argument is stated ; and the conclusion is stated in the text,—" Among sons born of wives of the same class &c." (see § 3), as otherwise there would be inconsistency. Because, all these texts may be taken to lay down different rules, owing to difference of quality and conduct : and this is reasonable, inasmuch as it is not proper to hold, that a text contains an adverse argument, when it may as well be taken to embody a rule ; and as Lakshmídhara holds, that the younger son born of the first married wife, gets a specific deduction on account of being born of the first married wife ; and as the Párijáta also takes the same view.

10. Likewise MANU declares :—" Even in the Swabráhmanya mantras, the invocation is ordained to be made by (the name of) the first born : and of twins in the womb also, the eldest is he, who is first actually born."

The " Swabráhmanya " is a particular mantra recited by the Chhandoga priests in the Jyotistoma sacrifice. The use of the plural number here, is, on account of its repeated use. The invocation is made describing the father by the mention of the name of the first-born son : as " so-and-so's father and so-and-so's grandfather performs the sacrifice ", this has been explained in the Náta-Sútra to refer to the son who is senior by birth, since the text expresses,—" As the eldest among males and females who survive &c..

11. DEVALA (says) :—" In the lower classes, seniority is determined by character, and amongst twins, by priority of birth : of twins (whose priority of birth is unknown) he whose face the father and other ancestors see first after birth, is the first-born, and in that son is vested, the status of seniority.

12. MANU (says) :—" The edlest born, who out of covetousness deprives his younger brother, is not entitled to the status of the eldest, nor entitled to a (special) share, and is liable to be punished by the king." " Deprives ", that is, cheats ; " not entitled to the status of the eldest ", that is, not to be honoured as the eldest.

13. Likewise MANU (declares) :—" After having set apart the deductions in this way, the shares shall be made equal : but if specific deductions are not set apart, the distributions shall be as follows : the eldest son shall receive one share in excess, the next younger shall take half in excess, the other younger sons shall take one share each : this is the settled law. "

" On share in excess, " that is to say, two shares ; the next younger again shall take " half as much in excess, " that is, one share together with another half share ; the other younger sons shall each take one share : this applies, when partition is made without specific deductions. This too is to be understood to apply when the eldest and the next younger are endued with excess of merit and learning, and the others are devoid of merit, by reason of the following text of Vrihaspati relating to the eldest son, and by parity of reason, also to his next younger :—" He, who is senior by birth, learning, and merit, shall obtain two shares of the heritage." The specific deductions of the twentieth and the like, are to be understood to apply, when all are endowed with merit and good conduct and the like, and there is very little disparity amongst them in respect of merit, good conduct, and the like.

14. GAUTAMA ordains :—" Or the first-born shall be a double sharer, and the rest shall take one share each. "

This applies, when the eldest is possessed of excess of merit, and the others are devoid of merit.

15. Likewise,—" Each prior born (brother) shall get one from each class of property, to be chosen by him, and ten cattle. "

The meaning is, that each prior born brother shall get ten from each species of cattle.

16. The same Sage adds—" not of beast which have uncloven hoofs, nor of bipeds."

The meaning is (he) shall not take ten of horse and the like beast having uncloven hoofs, nor of bipeds, that is, female slaves and the like. This again must be understood as meant to apply, when all (the brothers) are equal, and the wealth abundant.

17. VASISHTHA ordains :—"Now partition of heritage among brothers is as follows :—the eldest shall take a double share, and a tithe of cows, and horses ; goats and the like, and a horse shall belong to the youngest ; and what is made of black iron, and household furniture shall belong to the middlemost."

" Double share " means, two shares shall be taken by the eldest : " tithe of cows and horses ", *i. e.* he shall take the best out of each ten of cows and horses. This text of Vasishtha, however, applies when the eldest is possessed of excessive merit, and the other two also are possessed of merit (but not excessive).

18. NA'RADA ordains :—" It is ordained that an additional share shall be given to the eldest and a worse share to the youngest. The rest are to be participators of equal shares, and so also an unmarried sister. Similarly in the case of the appointed wife's sons, lawfully begotten. "

The author of the Prakása reads this text, as *shresthâya tu barah i. e.* the best to the best, instead of *kanisthâya abarah i. e,* worse to the youngest, and has explained the same as meaning " that the first born shall get two shares, and that " the best " means, fit for (managing the affairs of the family, to him should be given something which is " the best. "

" So also the unmarried sister " means, that the maiden sister shall get a share. Distribution in this mode applies to sons legitimate as well as *kshetraja* or begotten on the appointed wife, as will be explained hereafter. The rule laid down in the first portion of the text applies to real legitimate sons, and with respect to the *kshetrajas* the following portion is laid down,—" similarly in the case of the appointed wife's sons lawfully begotten" *i. e.* the partition is to be made in the same manner as has been laid down in the case of the real legitimate sons ; and the sort of *kshetraja* sons meant are those lawfully begotten,—when an impotent person or the like makes over his own wife to a man of the same family or tribe, one born of him at that time is one called lawfully begotten ; to the eldest among them also, an additional share should be given. But if it be asked, how is it possible that the same man should have more than one son, born of his wife by appointment ? The answer is, this refers to twins.

19. On the subject as to what kind of eldest brother, an additional share should be given, VRIHASPATI ordains :—" One who is eldest by birth, learning, and merit, shall get two shares out of the heritage, but the rest shall be participators of equal shares, for he is as a father to them."

20. USANAS (declares) :—" This distribution is ordained among sons born in the direct order of the classes : but partition among sons of the same class, is regulated by equal shares."

The meaning is, that when all the sons are equal by reason of being devoid of good qualities, likewise when all have acquired various kinds of property, although some one may be possessed of good quality, then the partition is to be equal only.

21. YA'JNAVALKYA ordains :—" After the death of the parents, the sons shall equally divide the heritage and debt."

22. Likewise,—" But in case there be improvement of the common stock, the partiton is ordained to be equal ; but among grandsons by different fathers, the allotment of shares is according to the fathers."

This text lays down an exception to the following text of Vasishtha,— ' Amongest them, he who has himself acquired (the property), shall get two shares."

The meaning of the text " But in case there be improvement &c," is, that when an improvement, that is, increase is made by some one, of the common stock, by means of agriculture, trade and the like, then partition of such property is to be equal only, *i. e.*, two shares are not to be allotted to the person making the improvement, the text of Vasistha however is to be reconciled by referring it to cases other than this.

When the property of the grandfather is distributed among sons of different brothers, whose number may be equal or unequal, the share which would have been allotted to their fathers, should alone be allotted to them ;

(jointly *per stirpes*) : but no share shall be allotted to each of them (*per capita*).

23. Upon this very subject, VRIHASPATI (says) :—" But all are equal sharers of that which they have got jointly; their sons, equal or unequal in number, are ordained equal sharers (*per stirpes*)."

That is, sons equal or unequal in number, whose fathers were undivided.

24. KA'TYA'YANA (says) :—" When a son dies undivided, his son shall be made sharer of the heritage, if he has not received maintenance allowance from the grandfather. He shall get his paternal share either from the paternal uncle or from his son, but the very same share should equitably belong to all the brothers; or his son shall be entitled: afterwards, there is a cessation (of right)."

The meaning of this is, when amongst brothers, some one does not exist, then his sons' share does not lapse.

25. DEVALA (says):—" Of the undivided as well as the divided members of the family living together, a second partition of the heritage extends to the fourth (in descent); this is the law."

The meaning is this:—the second partition among those who are either undivided or divided, and living together *i. e.* re-united, extends to the brother, the brother's son, and the brother's son's son. But from his son, who is the fourth, it ceases.

26. Likewise (the same Sage declares):—" To that degree the members of the family are Sapindas, afterwards there is a difference in Pinda, and the equal partition of Pinda and heritage is desired."

This, however, applies, only when the subject of the right is not enjoyed by the claimant for partition (living abroad), but is enjoyed by another residing in that country (where the heritage is situated).

27. VASISHTHA (says) :—" The heritage is to be divided among brothers and childless women till the birth of their sons."

" Women " here means widows of brothers, to whom if with child, shares are to be given: but in case no son is born, the share shall belong to the brothers only: they shall be only maintained. This is the meaning.

28. VISHNU ordains :—" Mothers receive allotments, according to the shares of sons, and so do unmarried daughters."

The term mothers being used in the plural number, every one of them must be a mother, and (accordingly) mothers of many sons are entitled, by reason of there being no authority for considering that one only is meant. If that were not so, then the text is to be taken to refer to the reduction of shares according to the order in the tribe (of the mothers). If there be a single son, he enjoys the whole: GRAHESVARA is also of the same opinion.

29. YA'JNAVALKYA ordains ;—" The mother also, of those making a partition after the death of the father, takes an equal share."

30. After having premised something about the father, VRIHASPATI goes on :—" But in his default, the progenitrix gets a share equally with sons: their mothers are equal sharers, and daughters get a quarter share."

"Progenitrix" here means, mother of son: "mothers" means, father's son-less wives: "quarter share," that is, a fourth part, having regard to that share which is allotted to a brother of the same class, is to be allotted for the purpose of marriage. As for the text of VISHNU,—"Mothers receive allotments according to the shares of sons, and so do unmarried daughters",—that also is to be taken to refer to a fourth share, by reason of this text: the text of VRIHASPATI also intends unmarried daughters.

31. VYA'SA (says);—"But the son-less wives of the father are pronounced equal sharers, and all the grandmothers also are pronounced equal to mothers."

32. VRIHASPATI (says):—"All the sons are entitled to receive the father's heritage according to shares: of them, he who is possessed of learning and has done good deeds, is entitled to get more. By sons whose fame in this world is wide spread in respect of learning, science and prowess, and business and knowledge, and donations and sacrifices, fathers become possessed of (real) male issue."

33. NA'RADA (says):—"He who is engaged in the affairs of the family, and performs its business, is to be honoured by the brothers, with food, dress and conveyance."

34. YA'JNAVALKYA lays down an exception to the two alternatives declared in the text (Ch. II, § 14),—"either allot the best share to the eldest son, or all may be equal sharers",—thus,—"The separation of one who is able to support himself and is not desirous (of participation), may be completed by giving him something."

The author of the PRAKA'SA (says):—Separation *i. e.* partition, is to be made, by giving him something *i. e.* even a trifle, for the purpose of obviating all dispute by his sons. This has been explained by HALA'YUDHA to mean, that when however one does not take a share owing to his ability, the partition should be made by giving something even to him, for the purpose of preventing future dispute by his sons; and he has introduced the following text of MANU saying that it declares the very same thing,—"But amongst the brothers, if any one has a competence from his own occupation, and desires not the property, he may be debarred from his share, by giving him something by way of maintenance."

The author of the PRAKA'SA however taking this to refer to increase of wealth (says),—that when brothers living together and possessed of paternal property, earned additional wealth by means of agriculture and the like, and if one of them does not (exert so to) acquire, he is to be separated with his share, that is to say, the additional wealth produced by the use of his (share of the) wealth, shall not be given to him, but there is no prohibition of the allotment (to him,) of his original share.

In that case (of increase) also, he is not to be entirely excluded, but something should be given him by way of maintenance, that is, deducting the fruits of their labour, the residue should be given to him.

35. Thus in the VIVA'DA-RATNA'KARA, the partition among brothers by different mothers, is finished.

CHAPTER V.

§ 1—Exclusion from inheritance. 2 to 6—The virtuous are entitled to shares, the vicious are not. 7—A person who is outcaste or his issue, or insane, or idiot, or devoid of an organ of sense or action, is excluded from share. 8—Also one afflicted with immedicable disease. 9—Faultless son of excluded, entitled to share, their daughter must be maintained and married. 10—Chaste wife of excluded to be maintained. 11 to 12—An enemy to father and one afflicted with chronic disease, and a dissembler in religion, excluded; but to be maintained except outcaste. 13—Also one born of wife superior in caste, excluded. 14—A text on exclusion. 15—One adopting different order, excluded. 16—Son by superior wife, entitled to maintenance. 17—Issue of irregular marriage. 18 to 20—Initiatory ceremonies of brothers and sisters. 21 to 25—Marriage and fourth share of maiden daughters. 26 to 27—Maiden daughter's right to mother's ornaments. 28—Exclusion of women from inheritance.

1. Now (are mentioned) those that are excluded from shares at a partition.

2. On that subject, A'PASTAMBA (says):—"All co-heirs, who are endued with virtue, are entitled to shares; but he, who dissipates wealth by vice, should be deprived of share, even though he may be the first-born."

"Dissipates" means, spends away. "By vice" means, by gambling and the like: this again is intended to refer to expenses inconsistent with a particular order of life: "deprived of share" means, deprived of so much of his share, as he has dissipated: some, however, say, that it means, deprived of his entire share.

3. GAUTAMA ordains:—"According to some, even a son by a wife of the same class, does not get (a share), if addicted to unlawful acts."

The *áchárya* says, that it follows *a fortiori* from the word 'even,' that sons by wives of different classes do not get. "Does not get" *i. e.* a share.

The author of the PRAKA'SA (says) in this connection,—that this text applies or not, according as the addiction to unlawful acts, is incapable of removal or not.

4. On this subject, MANU (says):—"All those brethren, who are addicted to improper acts, are not entitled to the wealth."

"Addicted to improper acts" means, addicted to gambling and the like: others say, it means, such as cause injury to the family property.

5. On this subject, SANKHA and LIKHITA (say):—"Of one who is excommunicated, the heritage, the oblation of food, and libations of water, cease."

"Excommunicated" means, one with whom his relations have given up the use of the same water-pot, by reason of his guilt, such as disloyalty to the king, and the like.

6. VRIHASPATI declares:—"Though born of a wife of equal class, a son destitute of virtue is unworthy of the paternal wealth. It is declared to belong to kinsmen who are versed in the Vedas, and who offer Pindas to him. A son redeems the father from debt to superior and in-

ferior beings ; consequently, there is no use for one, who acts otherwise. What can be done with a cow, which neither gives milk, nor bears calves. But what purpose is served by that son, who is neither learned, nor virtuous. A son who is devoid of science, courage and good purposes, who is destitute of devotion and knowledge, and who is wanting in conduct, is similar to urine and excrement."

"Distitute of virtue", is explained in the subsequent passages. "Who offer Pindas (or food) to him", means, who give food and raiment to the son who is destitute of virtue.

7. On this subject MANU (says) :—"The impotent and the out-caste are excluded from a share of the heritage, and so are the deaf and the blind by birth ; as well as the madman, the idiot and the dumb, as also those who are destitute of an organ of sense or action. But it is just that the person succeeding, who knows his duty, shall give food and raiment fully to all of them, according to the best of his power. Those who are unwilling to give, become degraded. But if those beginning with the impotent, at any time desire to marry, the issue of such of them as have children, shall be entitled to the heritage."

By the use of the term, "by birth" in the phrase "blind by birth", it is indicated that the blindness must be incurable, not that it shall be congenital. "Idiot" *i. e.*, one destitute of the power of discriminating between what is his own and what is another's. By the use of the term, "destitute of an organ of sense or action", are included those who are not entitled to perform the ceremonies prescribed by the Sruti and the Smriti, such as the lame and the like. "To all of them" *i. e.* the impotent and the like, "fully" *i. e.* so long as they are alive. "Those beginning with the impotent" is, a Bahubríhi compound, in which the import of the term "impotent" is not intended to be included ; (it means the excluded persons beginning with, but exclusive of, the impotent), because the impotent person is incompetent to procreate a child. But the author of the PRAKA'SA says,—that the state of being impotent, is intended to mean, the want of power to procreate a child, in consequence of a defect, which is curable in future : and hence, the Bahubríhi compound is not one in which the import of the word "impotent" is intended to be excluded. "Issue" means, progeny.

8. YA'JNAVALKYA ordains :—"An out-caste and his issue, an impotent person, one lame, a madman, an idiot, a blind man, and a person afflicted with an immedicable desease, and the like, are to be maintained, but are not sharers."

"His issue" means, one born after degradation and the like. "Idiot" is one, whose mind is imperfect : "immedicable disease" means, an incurable disease such as leprosy and the like. "And the like" includes other persons, mentioned by other Sages, as destitute of shares, but entitled to maintenance.

9. The impotent and the like having been declared destitute of shares, their sons also might be inferred to be shareless : the same Sage therefore declares :—

"But their sons, whether (*aurasa*) real legitimate, or the offspring of the wife by a kinsman, are entitled to allotments, if free from (similar) defects: and their daughters shall be maintained until they are given away to husbands."

10. With respect to the wives espoused by the impotent and the like, the same sage declares:—

"Their childless wives conducting themselves aright, shall be maintained: but such as are unchaste, shall be expelled; and so indeed should those who are perverse."

The administering of poison and the like, and not mere quarrelling, is intended to be understood by the state of being "perverse" as here used.

11. NA'RADA ordains:—"An enemy to his father, an outcaste, an impotent person, and one excommunicated, take no shares of the inheritance, even though they are legitimate, much less if they be sons of the wife by an appointed kinsman. Persons afflicted with chronic and painful diseases, an idiot, a madman, a blind man, and one lame, these are to be maintained by the family, but their sons are entitled to shares."

"An enemy to his father", is one who hates his father,—the enmity consisting in beating and the like when the father is alive, and in the omission to offer libations of water and the like in his honour, when he is dead. "One excommunicated", is one the use of whose water-drinking-pot is renounced by (his) relations, because of his guilt, such as the killing of the king, and the like. But the author of the PRAKA'SA reads the word as "*aupapátakí*" (not *apapátrita*), and explains it as meaning one who is guilty of secondary sins. "Chronic diseases", are such as phthisis and the like; and "painful diseases", are such as leprosy and the like. "Family", means the brother and the like.

12. DEVA'LA declares:—"When the father is dead, an impotent man, a leper, a madman, an idiot, a blind man, an outcaste, the offspring of an outcaste, and a person wearing the token (of religious mendicity), are not entitled to a share of the heritage. Food and raiment should be given to them, excepting the outcaste. The sons of such persons, being free from similar defect, shall obtain their father's share of the heritage."

"When dead",—the meaning is, also when he is dead, (that is, whether he is alive or dead). "Wearing the token", *i. e.*, being a great dissembler in religious austerities.

13. On this subject, VISHNU says):—"But an out-caste, the impotent, one afflicted with immedicable disease or deficient (in an organ of sense or action), are not entitled to shares; they are to be maintained by the person taking the heritage; as well as their real legitimate sons; but not those of an out-caste, provided they were born after the commission of the act, (on account of which their parents were out-casted). Neither do those begotten by fathers of an inferior caste on wives of a superior caste, receive a share, even out of the wealth of their paternal grandfather."

"Person taking the heritage" *i. e.* one who takes (their) shares.

14. BAUDHA'YANA ordains :—" Those who are incapable of business, as well as the blind, the idiot, the impotent, those immersed in vice and afflicted with disease, and those incompetent to work, are to be supported with food and raiment, excepting the out-caste and his issue."

" Those incapable of business " means, minors ; " incompetent to work ", are those who are not entitled to perform religious ceremonies and the like. To the same effect it has been laid down,—" Property has been for sacrifice, therefore, it should be entrusted to persons competent to perform religious duties, and not to women, illiterate persons and perverts from religion ". An out-caste and his son are not entitled even to maintenance, as all intercourse with them is forbidden.

15. VA'SISHTHA declares :—" Those who have adopted a different order of life, are also shareless."

" Different order of life " means, an order other than the order of a householder.

16. GAUTAMA (says) :—" But an idiot and an impotent person are to be maintained ; the issue of an idiot, is worthy of a share. One born of a woman of a superior caste, by a father of an inferior caste, is alike to the son of a Sudra woman."

From the word " worthy ", it follows, that when he becomes entitled (by reason of being himself free from defect), then only he gets a share, and not by the (mere) fact of his being the issue of an idiot. " Alike to the son of a Sudra woman ", means, that maintenance such as is allowed to the son of a Sudra woman, should be given, even to those born of women of superior caste, if obedient.

17. KA'TYA'YANA (says) :—" Thus, also the son of a woman married in an irregular order, and one begotten by a man of the same Gotra, as well as an apostate from a religious order, are unworthy of the inheritance. But the son of a woman married in an irregular order, becomes an heir, if he belongs to the same tribe with the father : and so may the son begotten by a man of a different tribe, on a woman espoused in regular order : the son of a woman married in the inverse order, is not entitled to the inheritance : food and raiment without stint, are considered to be due to him by his kinsmen (*bandhu*). But in default of the *bandhu*, he may take the paternal wealth. The kinsmen shall not be compelled to give, when the wealth received by them is not his patrimony."

" The son of a woman married in an irregular order ", means, one born of a woman belonging to a different tribe, married in contravention of the order which is laid down in the Sástras, with respect to the marriage of damsels belonging to different tribes : the provision for the participation of a share made later on, by the passage,—" but the son of a woman married in an irregular order becomes an heir " &c.,—refers to the son of a woman of the same tribe married in contravention of the said order. " One begotten by a man of the same Gotra ", means, one begotten on a married woman of the same Gotra. " Apostate from a religious order ", means, one who having adopted a religious order, falls off from the same. " But the son of a woman married in an irregular order &c. ", means, even if a son of a woman married in an irregular order, be of the same tribe (with the father), then he " becomes an heir ", *i. e.* the participator of a share. In the same manner, " the son begotten by a man of a different tribe ", and born of a woman married in the regular order, becomes the participator of a share. " Son born of a woman married in the inverse order ", *i. e.* on a woman of a superior tribe married by a man of an inferior tribe—is not entitled to the inheritance. " Food and raiment &c. " *i. e.* if he has any kinsmen, they should give food and raiment without stint. But in default of kinsmen, he shall himself take the wealth. When however the wealth received by the kinsmen, is not his paternal property, then they shall not be compelled to give even food and raiment.

18. VRIHASPATI ordains :—" But amongst them, those younger brothers who may remain uninitiated, shall be initiated by the elder ones, from the paternal common property."

According to some, the word *yavíyasas* is the archaic form of the modern *yavíyánsas* ; but others say, that *yavíyasas* (is used in the genitive case and) means, of the younger brother, and governs the word " common property". There is however no difference in substance.

19. VYA'SA ordains :—" But amongst them, those that are uninitiated, shall be initiated by the elder brothers from their paternal wealth ; as also the unmarried daughters, according to law."

The initiation of unmarried daughters, consists in marriage.

20. NA'RADA ordains :—" Of those brethren, however, whose initiatory ceremonies have not, in their order, been performed previously, for them the said ceremonies shall be performed by their brethren from their paternal (i. e. ancestral) wealth alone. If there be no paternal wealth, then the initiatory ceremonies of brothers must be performed by those already initiated, by contributing from their own shares."

Here the initiatory ceremonies are, those beginning with the ceremonies observed on birth, and ending with the ceremony of the investiture with the sacred thread.

21. DEVALA declares :—" To maiden daughters, also should be given property sufficient for marriage, out of their paternal state : and the legitimate daughter of a man without male issue, shall take his wealth like a son".

22. YA'JNAVALKA ordains :—" But the uninitiated should be initiated by brothers who have already been initiated ; sisters also, by giving them a quarter share from their own shares."

23. VISHNU declares :—" And of unmarried daughters marriage shall be celebrated according to wealth."

24. MANU lays down :—" But to maiden daughters, the brothers shall give separately from their respective shares : those who are unwilling to give a fourth part from their shares, shall be degraded."

Here the meaning is not, that a fourth part shall be given deducting from the share of each ; but the intended meaning is, that the fourth part of the share proper for a son of a particular caste, is to be set apart and given to daughters (of that class) for marriage. Hence the meaning is, that out of the four shares of a son by a Bráhmaní wife, and of three shares for a son by a Kshatriya wife, a fourth part of the whole should be given. Here a fourth share only, being mentioned in many texts, that share only should be given; the object, however, is marriage. The provision for the allotment of a fourth share, should be attributed to Vishnu also, in that very manner. The Kalpataru, the Prakása, and the Mitákshará, are also to the same effect. The opinion of Haláyudha and others is, that the allotment of a fourth share, is to be taken to be illustrative, having regard to the text of Vishnu; the purport being, so much should be given as would suffice for the marriage. This is reasonable also, by reason of the propriety of performing the initiatory ceremony of marriage.

25. KA'TYA'YANA (says):—"But a fourth share is ordained, for daughters not given in marriage, and three shares for sons: but when the property is small, her ownership is ordained."

This means, that when the property consisting of the fourth part is small, and more wealth is required for the celebration of marriage, then the "ownership" *i. e.* right, of maiden daughters, extends over so much wealth as would be sufficient for the marriage. Hence so much wealth only, should be given for her marriage, by a brother, deducting from his share. The unmarried daughter shall get the mother's nuptial *strídhana* even when the mother is alive: thus,

26. SANKHA and LIKHITA declare:—"When partition takes place, the unmarried daughter gets the nuptial *strídhana*, consisting of the mother's ornaments of maidenhood."

"Ornaments of maidenhood", such as the *núpura* (bell-anklet), the maiden daughter gets.

27. BAUDHA'YANA (says):—The daughters receive the mother's ornaments and any thing else.

Mother's ornaments, *i. e.*, those worn at the time of (her) marriage, the maiden daughters get, if there is anything other than ornaments, belonging to the mother, and received at the time of marriage, then that also, the maiden daughter gets:

28. BAUDHA'YANA after premising "a woman is entitled", proceeds,—"Not to heritage, for a text of Sruti says,—'Women are considered powerless, and incompetent to inherit'."

The PRAKA'SA (says), "powerless" means, devoid of valour: "incompetent to inherit" means, that they do not get shares. This, however, refers to women other than those for whom inheritance has been provided.

29. Here, in the VIVA'DA-RATNA'KARA or Ocean of Disputes, ends the Wave of Exclusion from Inheritance.

CHAPTER VI.

§ 1—Of things liable to partition. 2 to 3—Residue of joint property after payment of father's gifts and debts, is partible. 4 to 5—What debts payable by all. 6—What, not so. 7 to 8—Ordeal, when concealment of property suspected. 9—Some domestic animals when unequal in number, given to the eldest.

1. Now, what is liable to partition (is dealt with).

2. On that subject, KA'TYA'YANA (says):—"Whatever is inherited from the grandfather, or from the father, or is self-acquired, all that should be divided at a partition among heirs. But having given affectionate gifts out of the heritage, the residue should be divided. And that should be received by their issue, in (their) order down to the fourth."

"Self-acquired," *i. e.* acquired by a member otherwise than in a manner which does not constitute it joint property. Whatever heritage the father promised to give to any one through affection, that is an affectionate gift: having given the same, the remainder is to be divided. The meaning of "down to the fourth", is, that he who benefits another by offering the funeral cake, according to the text,—"To three, must the libations of water be made; for three, is the oblation of food ordained &c.",—shall take his wealth by dividing the same.

HALA'YUDHA, however, says, that the fourth is intended to be counted from him to whom the gift was promised.

3. NA'RADA declares:—"Whatever remains after father's gifts and after paying paternal debts, that should be divided by brothers, so that the father may not remain a debtor."

"Father's gift" here means, property promised by the father to another. The author of the PRAKA'SA, however, prefers the reading "Pitridánevya," but the meaning is the same in this reading also.

4. KA'TYA'YANA (says):—"But all debts incurred for the purpose of the family by a brother, or a paternal uncle, or the mother, must be paid by the co-heirs at the time of partition. That debt shall be paid to the creditor, when after contest, the same is established by evidence: otherwise, they shall not be compelled to pay."

The meaning of the passage "That debt &c.", is, that the debt which has been incurred by the brother or the like, and is doubted after contest *i. e.* disagreement (ending in partition), shall be paid to the creditor, if after litigation the creditor proves it by evidence, and not otherwise.

5. Likewise:—"The paternal debt, the debt connected with a paternal debt, the debt incurred by a relative (for the family), and a debt incurred by a member himself (for the family): such-like debt is payable, jointly by the co-heirs, at the partition."

4

"Paternal debt", is one incurred by the father; "debt connected with a paternal debt", is a debt incurred by a member himself to pay his father's debt; "the debt incurred by a relative", refers to a debt incurred for the family by a relative, other than the brother and the like mentioned in the previous passage; "a debt incurred by a member himself", is one contracted for the family.

6. Likewise:—"Whatever is given for a religious purpose, or through affection, and whatever debt is on account of a member himself, the same shall be divided when perceived: there can be no gift from the patrimony."

It is said in the Kalpataru, that whereas, "whatever" common property "is given for a religious purpose", separately by a member himself, and whatever is given "through affection", and whatever debt is advanced to a stranger by one member himself as creditor: all these being discovered, shall be divided; because from the paternal wealth, it is not proper to make an exclusive alienation. But the authors of the PRAKA'SA and the PA'RIJA'TA say, that a common debt contracted by one member for separate religious purpose, a sum borrowed and given away through affection to some one, and "whatever debt is on account of a member himself" *i. e.* incurred for the purpose of his own enjoyment: all these three, being ascertained to be so, he shall divide i. e. set apart: the meaning is, that it shall be paid by him alone, by whom it was incurred; it shall not be paid by all, from the paternal property. But in fact, all these meanings are intended to be expressed; hence it is proper to construe this text as bearing all these senses.

7. Likewise:—"The visible houses, fields and quardrupeds shall be divided: if concealment of property is suspected, then discovery is prescribed."

"Discovery", means, discovery by ordeal.

8. This is clearly expressed in the following text:—"But household furniture, beasts of burden, milchcattle, ornaments, and workmen, that are visible, shall be divided: and in case of property being concealed, BHRIGU ordains the KOSHA or an ordeal by drinking water in which a deity has been washed.

"Household furniture", means, the mortar and pestle, and the like: "workmen", means, slaves and the like: the rest is well known.

9. MANU ordains;—"Goats and sheep, and one-hoofed animals, when of uneven number, shall not be divided, but the uneven goats and sheep are ordained for the eldest only."

The meaning is, that equal division of an uneven number of goats, sheep and one-hoofed animals, shall not be made by valuation and the like, but they shall be taken by the eldest alone.

Thus in the VIVA'DA-RATNA'KARA ends the chapter on partible things.

CHAPTER VII.

§ 1—Impartible things. 2—Gains of science, present from friend, nuptial gift &c., not partible. 3—Lost hereditary property when recovered by one, not partible. 4—Gains of science & valour, & Strídhana, not partible. 5 to 7—Gains of science. 8 to 9—Affectionate gifts, not partible. 10 to 12—Self-acquired property. 13—Impartible gains of science, described. 14—Impartible gains of valour, described. 15—Impartible nuptial gifts. 16 to 19—Other impartible things. 19—Local and special law of partition. 20—Principles of equitable partition. 21 to 22—Gains of science, when divisible. 23—Acquisition by eldest, shared by younger. 24 to 25—Acquisition by common exertion, divisible. 26 to 27—Acquirer's double share.

1. Now, things not liable to partition (are discussed).

2. On that subject, MANU (says):—"Wealth however acquired by learning, belongs exclusively to him who acquired it, and so does any thing given by a friend, or received on account of marriage, or connected with *madhuparka* *."

"Wealth acquired by learning, and what is received on account of marriage", shall be explained hereafter: "Given by a friend", is received from a friend: "connected with *madhuparka*" *i. e.* received as a mark of respect at the time of giving the *madhuparka*: "belongs exclusively to him" *i. e.* shall not be liable to division.

3. YA'JNAVALKA declares:—"He, who recovers whatever hereditary property had been taken away, shall not give it up to the co-heirs, nor what has been gained by science."

"Whatever hereditary property" *i. e.* property descended from the father and other ancestors, "had been taken away" *i. e.* by others, and not recovered by the ancestors, owing to inability and the like; such property when recovered by one of the co-sharers, shall not be given up to the other co-sharers: here the Mitákshará adds (that this shall be so) when the recovery is made with the consent of the other co-sharers. As for the following text which is quoted as that of HA'RI'TA in the Samhitá,—"If one co-sharer alone recovers by his labour, land which had been formerly lost, the others shall get according to their shares after giving a quarter share"—this is not reasonable, because it is not cited in the Smriti-Mahárnava the Kámadhenu, the Kalpataru, the Párijáta, and others.

4. VYA'SA (says):—"Whatever is gained by science, and wealth acquired by valour, and the *saudáyika* (affectionate gifts from kindred to women) shall not be claimed by the co-sharers."

"Wealth acquired by valour", is what is gained by war and the like. Saudáyika will be explained by a text of Kátyáyana to be cited hereafter (Ch. VIII, § 7).

---

* Madhuparka means guest-offering usually consisting of curds with honey and butter.

5. GAUTAMA (says) :—" A learned co-sharer shall not, if unwilling, give what is acquired by himself to one who is ignorant."

" What is acquired by himself " *i. e.* by means of science.

6. KA'TYA'YANA (says) :—" Never shall a learned man give wealth acquired by science, to those that are devoid of science : but to those who are equal or superior in learning, that wealth shall be given by the learned man."

7. NA'RADA (says) :—" A learned man shall not give, to one who is ignorant, any share from his own property, if the same has not been acquired by him, with the aid of paternal property."

Here this is intended :—When a man, who has acquired science while receiving food and raiment from the common property, acquires wealth by science and without the aid of common property, then he shall not give to the ignorant ; but wealth acquired by science with the aid of common property shall be given even to an ignorant co-sharer. When however at the time of acquisition of science there is no aid from common property, then even if there be aid from the common property at the time of acquisition, the learned shall not give to anybody ; but that property shall belong to the learned alone : because after having mentioned the impartibility of what is acquired without the aid of the father's property, Vyása has separately propounded the impartibility, also of what is acquired by science. Hence the impartibillty of wealth acquired by science, which will be hereafter stated, is to be understood to apply even when there is aid from the common property at the time of the acquisition of wealth, by science acquired without the aid of common property. The commentary of Haláyudha also, is to the same effect. The author of the Prakása, and others however say, that the texts respecting wealth acquired by science and the like, refer to the absence of aid from father's property : this is not acceptable, because reference to both aid, and absence of aid, from common property, in those texts, would be unreasonable.

8. NA'RADA after premising " shall divide ", proceeds—

" Excepting property acquired by valour, and property of the wife, and excepting that which is properly acquired by science : these, they say, are not liable to partition : so also, the affectionate gift by the father. This rule is understood to be applicable, even to him to whom the mother has given her own property through affection, for the mother is as much the owner (of her property), as the father (is of his).

By reason of the use of the expression " her own property ", this text is to be taken as refering to the mother's *strídhana.*

9. VYA'SA (says) :—" Whatever has been given by the paternal grandfather or by the father through affection, or whatever has been given by the mother to one, shall not be taken away from him."

10. YA'JNAVALKYA :—" Whatever else is acquired by the coparcener himself, without detriment to the father's estate, as a present from a friend, or a gift at nuptials, does not appertain to the co-heirs."

" Else ", includes items, other than presents from friends and the like.

11. MANU & VISHNU (say) :—" Whatever is acquired by labour, without detriment to the paternal property, he is not liable to give to his co-sharers, if unwilling, because, that is acquired by himself."

12. VYA'SA declares :—" Whatever property is acquired by one's own exertion, without making use of the father's property, shall not be given to the co-heirs, as also whatever is gained by science."

13. KA'TYA'YANA (says) :—" What has been acquired by learning, after instructions received from a stranger and a maintenance provided by one of a different family, is called wealth gained by learning. What is gained by proving superior learning, after a prize has been offered (by some third person), must be considered as the acquisition of a scholar, and ought not, in general, to be divided among co-heirs. When learning is acquired from a stranger, while receiving a foreign maintenance, the property which is acquired by that learning, is called gains of science. What is gained by the solution (of a difficulty), after a prize has been offered, must be considered as acquired through science, and is not divided at partition. What has been obtained from a pupil, or by officiating as a priest, or for answering a question, or for determining a doubtful point, or through display of knowledge, or by (success in) disputation, or for superior (skill in) reading, the sages have declared to be the gains of science, and not subject to distribution. The same rule likewise applies to the arts, and to increase of price from superior skill in them. A prize which has been offered for the display of superior learning, and a gift received from a votary (for whom a sacrifice was formerly performed), or a present from a pupil (formerly instructed), sages have declared to be the aquisition of science : what is otherwise (acquired), is common (to all co-heirs). Even what is won by surpassing another in learning, after a stake has been deposited, that is pronounced by VRIHASPATI to be gains of science, and impartible. What is obtained by the boast of learning, what is received from a pupil, what is received by officiating as a priest, BHRIGU calls gains of science."

" Increase of price ", means what is received, through the skill of one member, above the (otherwise suitable) price, becomes his : " a prize which was offered for the display of superior learning ", means, what is obtained in this manner, namely—" This is to be gained by one who is free from error in this reading or in this subject of discussion" : this also is not common (property). " What is obtained by the boast of learning," means, what is gained by a boast such as this,—" I alone have studied this science."

14. Now the kind of gains of valour, that is impartible is thus described :—

" When (a soldier) performs a gallant action ; and favour is shown to him by his lord pleased with that action ; whatever property is then received by him, shall be considered as gains of valour. What is taken under a standard, is declared not to be subject to distribution. What is seized (by a soldier) in war, after risking his life for his lord, and routing the forces of the enemy, is named spoil taken under a standard."

15. Now, the kind of nuptial gift which is not common, is declared,—

" Whatever is gained with a damsel of the same caste, at the time of receiving her, that wealth, coming with the damsel, is ordained Sulka causing prosperity; That is known as nuptial gift, which comes with the wife: all this kind of wealth is known as effective of (separate) work."

16. SANKHA & LIKHITA (say) :—" No division of a dwelling takes place, nor of waterpots, ornaments, and whatever has been enjoyed, nor of women, clothes, and channels for draining water: PRAJA'PATI (lord of created beings) has so ordained."

"Waterpots", *i. e.* metallic utensils for water; "ornaments", *i. e.* those only that are actually worn; " enjoyed ", that is, used: it follows from this, that women and clothes that have been enjoyed by any one (of the brothers) are not liable to partition. " Channels for draining water ", are, channels by which water flows (in and out).

17. MANU & VISHNU ordain :—"Clothes, paper (*pattram*), ornaments, prepared food, water, women, family priests or spiritual counsellors, and paths, are declared impartible".

The word "paper" here, means, property recorded in a writing, by reason of Kátyáyana's text,—"Property recorded in a document &c."—and also, of Vrihaspati's text,—" Recorded in writing after giving up debts &c. ". HALA'YUDHA however, says that the word *pattram* here, signifies, vechicles or animals used for draught or riding. " Prepared food ", is, barley or gram meal, the PA'RIJA'TA says, rice and the like. " Women ", means, concubines, as would appear from GAUTAMA's text,—" No partition of women kept &c". The word *yogakshema* in the original, signifying property meant for pious purposes, has been rendered as " the family priests and counsellors " as these latter are the means. "Paths", are, ways for the passage of cattle and the like. The author of the PRAKA'SA says, that the word " *yogakshema* ", means, hereditary livelihood in the kings family. HALA'YUDHA, however, says—YOGA=connection, is a boat or the like means of connection, KHSHEMA=security, is a castle or the like means of security.

18. VYA'SA ordains :—A place of sacrifice, or an object of worship, land, (*pattram*) conveyance, dressed food, water, and women, are not divisible among those of the same *gotra* or family, though distant by a thousand generations".

The author of the PRAKA'SA says, " land " means " land for dwelling house: " *pattram* " means conveyance.

19. KA'TYA'YANA declares :—" But property recorded in a document, what is settled for a religious purpose, water, women, what is a hereditary corrody, worn clothes, ornaments, what is not suitable (for partition),—such things being enjoyed by the co-parceners in a manner suited to the occasion,—the path for cows, the carriage road, clothes that are (actually) worn on the body, (Prayojya) what is requisite for use, or what is intended for arts, should not be divided : so VRIHASPATI declares. Whatever law has been declared applicable to a country, to a caste, or to a class, or to a village, the partition is to be effected in accordance with that alone : so BHRIGU declares."

"Worn clothes", is intended for what is valuable; and "clothes worn on the body", are intended for cheap ones: "what is settled for a religious purpose", is what is set apart for a religious purpose common to all, such as bells and the like for the worship of gods. "Corrody", has been previously explained. "What is not suitable for partition, means, that of which a direct partition is not possible. HALA'YUDHA says, Proyojya, translated as "what is requisite for use",—means, debts advanced. The PA'RIJA'TA says, PRAYOJYA means what is requisite for use such as books: these shall not be partitioned with illiterate parceners. "What is intended for arts" such as painter's brush and the like.

20. Now VRIHASPATI (says):—"Those who say that clothes and the like are not partible, have not considered, that the property of the wealthy, consists of conveyances and ornaments. What is kept common, is unemployed, as it cannnot be given to any one: the same should be divided according to reason, so that it may not be useless: having sold the clothes and ornaments, having recovered the written debts, by giving an equivalent in undressed grain for dressed food, an equitable partition is to be made; water drawn from a single well or tank, shall be taken for use, according to need; a (*setu*) work for irrigation, and a field shall be divided in due proportion; a single female slave shall be made to work by turns in their respective houses; but if there be many, they shall be equally distributed; the same rule applies to male slaves; the benefit derived from family priests or spiritual counsellors, shall be equally shared; and the pasture-ground for cattle, shall be used by the co-heirs, in proportion to their shares."

"What is kept common, is unemployed", *i. e.* being common, is unfit for use. "It cannot be given to any one". *i. e.* it is incapable of being given to any one co-parcener. Here the valuable clothes and the like are pronounced bodily indivisible: hence the texts of MANU and others propounding indivisibility, must be considered as forbidding only the bodily division of apparels of ordinary value, that is to say, as prohibiting partition in any other form, except that which is directed in the case of valuabe apparel: thus there is no conflict. But the author of the PRAKA'SA says that what is of ordinary value and worn on the body shall not be divided, but large wealth consisting of conveyances, ornaments, elephants, and the like, must be divided: and the manner of its division, is declared by the text—" What is kept common, is unemployed &c. ".

21. Now KA'TYA'YANA declares the kind of gains of science and the like, that is liable to division:

" Of brothers, such as have received education in the family or from the father, the property gained by (science or) valour, is divisible: so VRIHASPATI has declared "

The meaning is, that the wealth, which is gained by science or valour of brothers and the like, who have received education in the family *i. e.* from the paternal grandfather, paternal uncle, and the like, or from the father, must be divided.

22. NA'RADA ordains:—" He who protects the family of a brother studying science, shall take, be he ever so ignorant, a share of the wealth, gained by that science".

"Ignorant" *i. e.* devoid of science.

23. MANU ordains:—" After the death of the father, whatever wealth the eldest son acquires, a share of that belongs to the younger brothers, provided they have duly cultivated science."

The meaning is, after the death of the father whatever wealth is acquired by the eldest, by means of science or the like acquired without the expenditure of joint funds; in the wealth so acquired, two shares belong to the eldest, and one share to each of the younger brothers, provided they are given to the study of science.

24. " But when all are ignorant, and property is acquired by their exertion, it is to be understood that such property though not descended from the father, should be equally divided".

When all the brethren being devoid of science acquire wealth by agriculture and the like, then of such property, though not descended from the father, the distribution must be equal. But no deduction and the like should be made, upon the ground that any one has consumed a larger share.

25 Having premised self-acquired property, GAUTAMA (says):—

" Those devoid of science shall divide equally".

" Those devoid of science ", means, devoid of science which would have caused the property to become the exclusive property of any one.

26. VASISHTHA (says):—" But he amongst them, who by himself produces, shall take two shares ".

When one amongst many acquires, by means of agriculture and the llke, with the aid of common property, then he is entitled to two shares, and the rest to one share each.

27. VYA'SA declares:—" When property is acquired by valour and the like, with the aid of any common property such as a conveyance or a weapon, therein the brothers are sharers, to him (*i. e.* the acquirer) two shares are to be given, the rest are equal sharers".

This is to be understood to intend property acquired by means of science, valour aud the like, other than gains of science, valour and the like technically so called.

28. Thus in the VIVA'DA-RATNA'KARA, the chapter on impartibles is finished.

CHAPTER VIII.

§ 1.—Duties in respect of Strídhana. 2.—Abstraction of property, forbidden to women. 3 to 4.—Ornaments, and gifts by relations. 5.—Husband's gifts. 6.—Limit of gift to woman. 7.—Gift by affectionate kindred, and woman's right over same including immovables. 8.—Husband's gift and heritage. 9.—Relations appropriating woman's property, punishable. 10.—Subsistence, Sulka, &c., Strídhana cannot be taken by husband except at distress. 11.—Relations have no control over woman's property, must be compelled to refund with interest, Strídhana if taken forcibly. 12.—When husband not liable to refund wife's property taken. 13 to 14.—When husband lives with another wife, he must refund ; unchaste woman not entitled ; woman must reside in husband's family.

1. Now, the duties in respect of Strídhana (are discussed).

2. On that subject MANU says :—" Women shall not make abstraction from family (property) common to many, nor even from her husband's own property, without permission."

Here by the word " family, " is intended family-property by reason of contextual association : hence, out of joint property " abstraction " *i. e.*, secret appropriation of property, should not be made by women without the permission of the owners. Likewise, "from even husband's own property" *i. e.*, from husband's property held not in common with other members of the family, secret appropriation should not be made, without the permission of the owner of the property. This is the meaning.

3. MANU and VISHNU ordain :—" Whatever ornaments may be worn by the females during the lifetime of their husbands, the same shall not be divided by the heirs : they become degraded, if they divide these."

MEDHA'TITHI as quoted by the PRAKA'SA says that, such ornaments also as were worn for the purpose of beauty by the permission of the husband, although not (actually) given by him, shall not be taken by the heirs.

4. On the same subject, A'PASTAMBA (says) :—" Ornaments belong to the wife, so also property given by relations, according to some."

" Property given by relations", means, such property called Jautaka as is received at marriage : the meaning is, that that also belongs to the wife alone.

5. NA'RADA ordains :—" Whatever is given by the affectionate husband to the wife, she shall, even when he is dead, enjoy or give away the same according to her pleasure, excepting immoveable property. "

6. Of property given by the husband, the amount which can be the subject of independent use, is thus shown by VYA'SA :—"But of the property, a gift of two thousand *panas* may be given to the wife : whatever property is given by the husband, she may enjoy according to her pleasure. "

It is said (by the wise), that, the words—" a gift of two thousand *panas* " *i. e.* a gift amounting to two thousand *panas*,—indicate, that if the property be small, the gift also is to be small ; and that as it has been laid down that—" Self-acquired property may be given away according to one's pleasure",—this text is intended to refer to joint property. But the PRAKA'SA says, that when, females whose husbands are excluded from inheritance and who are declared to be entitled to maintenance, are separated; to them, no more than two thousand *panas* should be given.

7. KA'TYA'YANA (says) :—"That which is received by a married woman, or a maiden in the house of her husband or of her father, from her brother * or from her parents, is termed the gift of affectionate kindered. The independence of women who have received such gifts, is recognised (in regard to that property;) for it was given by them (their kindred) for the sake of their mildness and for their maintenance. The independence of women in regard to the gifts of their affectionate kindred is ever celebrated, both in respect of donation and of sale, according to their pleasure, even in respect of immoveables."

The passage "from the brotoer (husband) or parents" is illustrative. Hence whatever is received by a married or unmarried woman, in the house of her husband or in the house of her father, from her mother, or from her father, or from their relations, is the gift of affectionate kindred. "Mildness", that is, want of violence: hence the meaning we get, is,—"for it is given by them" *i. e.*, by their father and the like, "for their maintenance" so that, they may not be violent for want of property.

Thus the result is, that women are independent in respect of property given by affectionate kindred, including immoveables; but as regards property gifted by the husband, they are so in property other than immoveable.

8. Likewise, (KA'TYA'YANA says) :—"The husband's *dáya* (heritage or gift), the wife may use according to her pleasure, when the husband is dead: but when he is living, she shall preserve it, or otherwise commit it to his family. A childless (wife), preserving unsullied the bed of her husband, and abiding by her venerable protector, shall enjoy (the husband's property) until her death, with moderation, afterwards the *heirs* shall take."

Here husband's *dáya* is property which is the subject of the wife's ownership through her relationship to the husband: that again is twofold, (1) what is subject of the wife's ownership, after the death of the husband, in default of any other heir, (2) or what is subject of the wife's ownership, even during the life time of the husband, through relationship to him. As regards the first of these, "the wife may use" *i. e.* deal with, "according to her pleasure", anything other than inmoveables, (and) living with her venerable protector, and keeping unsullied the bed of her husband, shall pass her days. In respect of inmoveables, it is said she "shall enjoy until her death"; after her, the heirs shall take. As regards the second, it is said "but when he is living, shall preserve it" *i. e.*, shall protect his property, following the husband's directions, with respect to expenditure. This is in accordance with the PRAKA'SA. HALA'YUDHA and the PA'RIJA'TA however say, that "husband's *dáya*" is Strídhana given by the husband. Of these, the opinion of the Prakása is preferable; for, with respect to also the property devolving from a

* Another reading is husband.

sonless man, and becoming the subject of the wife's ownership, there exists the Expectancy (or the reader's desire to know the incidents thereof); as regards, however, the meaning suggested by the context, it is even rejected, as in the case of the prohibition of abstraction (§ 2); because predominance must be given to the Expectancy.

9. MANU ordains :—" The same care should be taken of chaste women, whether they are sterile or sonless, or destitute of kindred or widowed or diseased. If their kinsmen misappropriate that (Strídhana) whilst they are living, the virtuous King shall inflict on them the punishment of a thief."

" Sterile ", means, barren : " sonless ", means, those whose sons are dead : " destitute of kindred ", means, those whose paternal and maternal kindred are dead.

10. DEVALA ordains :—" Her subsistence, her ornaments, her *sulka*, her gains, are her Strídhana ; she herself shall enjoy it exclusively : her husband has no right to use it, except in distress. In cases of unnecessary donation or enjoyment, he shall refund to the wife with interest ; but he has right to use the wife's property, also for relieving the son's distress. "

" Subsistence ", is property given for maintainance : " gains ", are what is received from kindred : " Sulka ", is property given to a bride with a view to marriage : "unnecessary donation &c.," that is, when (the husband) taking her property for necessary purposes, uses it in unnecessary donations or enjoyment, then, he shall refund it with interest. But he may take Strídhana for relieving the son's distress, even without the consent of the wife.

11. KA'TYA'YANA (says) :—" Neither the husband, nor the son, nor the father, nor the brothers, are competent to take or give away Strídhana property. If any one of these persons takes the woman's property by force, he shall be compelled to refund it with interest, and shall also incur punishment. If such person having obtained her consent consumes the property amicably he is liable to pay the principal only, when he becomes possessed of property. If seeing any of them diseased, or distressed, or oppressed by creditors, she gives property, through affection, then he may repay if he wishes."

The meaning of the last verse is :—Seeing the husband or the like overtaken by disease and the like, whatever property is given by the woman to the husband or the like, that shall be repaid by the husband or the like if he wishes.

12. YA'JNAVALKYA ordains :—" The husband is not liable to refund the property of the wife taken by him, in a famine, or for the performance of a religious duty, or during illness, or while under restraint "

" Religious duty ", that is, such as must be performed. " During illness ", means, during such illness as that in which he is disabled from working ; the wife's property taken for the removal of such (illness), is not to be refunded to the wife.

13. KA'TYA'YANA declares :—" But if the husband have a second wife, and do not live with her, he shall be compelled to restore her the

property, though given to him through affection. If food, raiment and residence be withheld from the woman, she may exact her own, and may likewise take a share of his heritage. This is the rule of law, ordained by LIKHITA: when she has got, she shall live in the husband's family. But if she be afflicted with desease, and in danger of her life, she may remove from there to the family of her relatives. But a wife who does act injurious to the husband, is shameless, wastes her husband's wealth, and is addicted to adultery, is not worthy of the Strídhana. Property has come into existence for sacrifice, therefore it should be entrusted to virtuous persons, and not to women, to the ignorant, and to the vicious. The Strídhana promised by the husband (to a wife), should be given, by the son as a debt of his, if she live with the family of her husband, and not, if she lives in the family of her father."

When the property has been given by a wife through affection, but the husband does not approach her, even after the catamenial period, and likewise her food, raiment and residence are withheld, then she shall recover by force, her property, even when given, on seeing the husbaud overtaken by deseose and the like: that also (food &c) she ought to receive without labour, and even then (*i. e.*, when the husband is ill &c.) the same is to be exacted from the husband and the like. This is the rule of law laid down by the Sástras. "Having got" such property, she shall reside only in the family of her husband. In case of serious illness, she may go to the family of her relatives. This is the meaning of the verses ending with "family of her relatives."

14. Here in the VIVA'DA-RATNA'KARA, ends the topic relating to the duties in respect of Strídhana.

CHAPTER IX.

§ 1—Partition of woman's property. 2 to 6—Mother's property goes to sons and unmarried and unprovided daughters. 7 to 12—Paraphernalia, Yautaka, and father's gifts, go to daughters, in their default to their sons; then to sons, then to husband: but parents' gifts go to brothers.

1. Now, partition of woman's property is determined.

2. On that subject MANU (says):—When the mother is dead, all the uterine brothers and the uterine sisters shall equally divide their maternal heritage"

"Equally" *i. e.*, without deduction for the eldest and the like: "sisters" here, intend unmarried and unprovided, according to the text of VRIHASPATI, to be cited below.

3. Likewise:—"If they (sisters) have daughters, to them also, should be given out of affection, something from their maternal grandmother's property, according to shares"

"They" *i. e.*, the sisters: "according to shares", *i. e.*, according to largeness or smallness of property.

4. Likewise:—"Gifts subsequent, as also what is given by the affectionate husband: that becomes the property of the issue, if she dies during the lifetime of the husband."

The definition of "gifts subsequent", will be given here after. HALA'YUDHA says, that this text is laid down for the purpose of prohibiting the husband's connection with these two kinds of property, when she dies even when the husband is alive.

5. VRIHASPATI declares:—"Woman's property belongs to children: the daughter also is a sharer of the same, but if there be an ungiven one, the married daughter gets only something as a token of respect."

"Children", means, sons; "sharer of the same", means, entitled to get a share equal to that of him: "ungiven" means unmarried. Hence by force of this text, the participation of equal share with the brothers, is to be uderstood, of unmarried daughters only, in the text of Manu also. But to the married, something should be given according to their rank.

6. GAUTAMA declares:—"Woman's property belongs to daughters, ungiven and unprovided."

This is not intended to exclude the son's share, but to establish the participation by daughters: "unprovided", means, married but childless, wife of a poor husband, and disliked by the husband.

7. MANU ordains:—"But whatever Yautaka property belongs to the mother, that is to be allotted to the maiden daughter alone"

Here *yautaka* means, what is given to a woman, by the father and the like, at the time of marriage.

HALA'YUDHA however says, Yautaka is what is given to a woman for purchasing articles of her food, and increased by her own skill, and that therein the brothers and the married sisters have no shares; but married daughters, who are childless, or disliked by their husbands, have equal shares (with the maiden daughters).

8. VASISHTHA ordains:—"The mother's paraphernalia, the daughters shall divide."

"Paraphernalia", means, dress, mirror, combs and the like.

9. Having premised, "shall divide after (death)", YA'JNAVALKYA declares:—"Of the mother, the daughters, the residue, after payment of debts, in their default the issue.

The "residue" *i. e.*, what is left "after payment of debts" *i. e.*, the mother's debts. Hence what is left of the Yautaka and paraphernalia property, after payment of the mothers debts, the unmarried and the unprovided daughters shall divide: this is the meaning of a part of the text. "In their default" *i. e.*, in default of the daughters, "their issue" *i. e.*, daughter's son and the like: this refers to marriage in the Bráhma and the like (approved) forms.

10. Likewise VISHNU declares after having premised "in marriages", "of all descriptions, that property of mothers, goes to daughters."

11. MANU ordains:—"But whatever property is given to a woman, by her father at any time, the Bráhmaní daughter shall take, or the same shall belong to her issue."

When the husband, or issue of her body, does not exist, and there are co-widows of different castes, and they have daughters, then, the Bráhmaní daughter is entitled to the property of her mother's co-widow, which was given by the father (of the co-widow): in her default, her son: this is the meaning. The author of the PRAKA'SA says, property given by the father, is illustrative of any Strídhana: this is the opinion of Asaháya and Medhátithi.

12. KA'TYA'YANA ordains:—"In default of daughters, that heritage belongs to sons: but what is given by Bandhus (parents) belongs to Bandhus; in their default, it goes to the husband. Sisters having husband shall share with *bandhabas i. e.*, brothers. This is the settled lawful partition of woman's property."

Paraphernalia, Yautaka, and father's gifts, go to sons, in default of daughters. As regards Strídhana other than these, those mentioned before (are entitled.) In default of those mentioned before, the property goes to the husband alone.

13. Thus in the VIVA'DA-RATNA'KARA, the subject of partition of woman's property is finished.

CHAPTER X.

§ 1—Succession to property of woman destitute of issue. 2 to 4—In approved forms of marriage, property received at the time of marriage, goes to husband, mother, brother and father in their order; in other forms, to mother, brother, father and husband in their order. 5 and 6—Parents' gifts, Sulka, and gifts subsequent, go to mother and brother, in disapproved forms. 7 and 8—Appointed daughter's property goes to sister, and then to husband. 9 and 10—On death of betrothed damsel, mutual presents, refunded; Sulka goes to bridegroom. 11—Maiden's property goes to brother, mother, and father. 12—Sister's son and other heirs.

1. Now is discussed, succession to the property of a woman dying without issue of her body, according to the form of marriage.

2. On that subject NA'RADA (says):—"Woman's property belongs to issue, in default of issue, it goes to the husband, in the four forms of marriage commencing from the Bráhma; in the other forms, it goes to the father: so the wise have declared."

The term "four forms", is not intended for excluding the fifth: hence, in the Bráhma, Daiva, A'rsha, Gándharva, and Prájápatya forms, the property of a woman destitute of issue, goes to her husband on her death; in the other forms *i. e.*, Rákshasha, A'sura and Paisácha, it goes to the father: this refers to woman's property received at the time of marriage.

3. Likewise MANU ordains:—"The property in the Bráhma, Daiva, A'rsha, Gándharva and Prájápatya forms, is intended for the husband alone: but whatever property is given to her in the A'sura and like marriages, is intended for the mother and the father, if she dies without leaving issue."

4. DEVALA (says):—"The property of a woman, on her death, is common among her sons and daughters; in default of issue, the husband, the mother, the brother, or the father, shall take."

The husband shall take in the Bráhma or the like forms of marriage, the mother in A'sura and the like. Thus it is to be understood, the intention of MANU and NA'RADA is to be gathered by taking the order mentioned by Devala.

5. On this subject GAUTAMA (says):—"The sister's Sulka belongs to the uterine brothers, after the mother, some say even before her."

The wealth received by the sister from her husband's house, in the A'sura and the like forms of marriage, belongs to the uterine brothers, after the mother, *i. e.*, if the mother be dead. Some say, that such property of sisters belongs to the uterine brothers, even before the mother's death. Haláyudha says, this is the opinion of others.

6. YA'JNAVALKYA ordains:—"What is given by the parents, the brides price (sulka), and gifts subsequent, the brothers get, on the death of a woman without bearing issue"

By "Sulka", is here intended, that on taking which the daughter is given away in marriage: "gifts subsequent", will be defined hereafter: "brothers", *i. e.*, uterine brothers. This also refers to A'sura or the like marriage.

7. MANU ordains:—"If the appointed daughter dies at any time without bearing a son, the husband of that appointed daughter shall take the property without hesitating."

This is to be understood to refer to a case in which the sonless woman has no maiden daughter or sister.

8. To this effect PAITHINASI' (says):—"If an appointed daughter dies without bearing a son, her husband is not entitled to her effects: it is to be taken by a maiden daughter, or by a sister."

Here the property is to be taken by the sister, in default of the maiden daughter.

9. YA'JNAVALKYA (says):—"A man withholding a damsel after giving her, is liable to punishment, and shall pay the expenditure with interest: if she dies, then every thing is to be taken back, after paying the expenditure on both sides."

A person who after giving a damsel, *i. e.*, by word in betrothal, withholds her without any fault, is to be punished by the king, and is to be compelled to pay to the bridegroom, his expenditure with interest: but there is no offence in withholding for a good cause, as is declared in the following text,—" Even after (verbal), gift a damsel may be withheld, if a better bridegroom turns up. " If however the betrothed damsel dies by chance, then, whatever was given by the father for the honour of the first bridegroom's relations, and whatever rings and the like were given by such relatives: " paying " *i. e.*, taking into account, both of the same, the rest shall be taken back.

10. SANKHA (says) :—After premissing " is entitled "

" To the Sulka, the bridegroom himself."

11. BAUDHA'YANA (says) :—" The heritage of a deceased damsel, her uterine brothers themselves shall take ; in their default, it belongs to the mother ; in her default, it belongs to the father "

Here by " damsel ", is intended, a maiden.

12. VRIHASPATI declares :—" The mother's sister, the maternal uncle's wife, the paternal uncle's wife, the father's sister, the mother-in-law, and the wife of an elder brother, are pronounced similar to the mother, when these have no *aurasa* son, no daughter's son, or their son, their property is received by the sister's son and the like."

The meaning is, in default of Aurasa and the like, the sister's son and the like, shall get the property of the mother's sister and the like.

13. Thus in the VIVA'DA-RATNA'KARA ends the succession to the property of a woman dying without issue, according to marriage.

CHAPTER XI.

§ 1—Definition of Strídhana. 2—Six kinds of woman's property, this enumeration not exhaustive. 3—For, another kind called A'dhivedanika is enumerated. 4—It is described. 5—Vishnu enumerates another kind called Anvádheya or gift subsequent. 6 and 7—Texts enumerating Strídhana 8—Husband's control over what is earned by mechanical arts and what is received from stranger. 9 and 10—Different kinds of Strídhana, defined.

1. Now STRI'DHANA is defined

2. On that, MANU and KA'TYA'YANA (say) :—" What is given before the nuptial fire, what is given in the bridal procession, and what is given to a woman through affection, and what is received from the mother, the brother, or the father, are ordained the sixfold property of woman. "

"What is given before the nuptial fire" *i. e.*, what is given by any one at the time of the marriage: "what is given in the bridal procession", means, what is sent with a damsel, when she is taken to the house of her husband. MEDHA'TITHI says,—"what is given in the bridal procession", means, what is given by the father-in-law and the like, when she is taken back from her husband's house to her father's house: that also is to be included, for parity of reasoning: "what is given through affection", means, what is given by the father and the like, by reason of being pleased by her good conduct, piety, skill, and the like. The adjective "sixfold", is intended for the denial of a lesser number, but not for the denial of a higher number, because YA'JNAVALKYA has declared "gifts for alleviation of the grief", as an additional kind of woman's property.

3. Thus, YA'JNAVALKYA (says):—"What is given by the father, the mother, the husband, and the brother, and what is received at the nuptial fire, and also the gift for alleviation of the grief, are denominated woman's property."

4. And the same sage has given the following definition,—

"An equal amount should be given, as a gift for alleviation of the grief, to the wife superseded, by the husband marrying another wife, if *strídhana* has not been given to her (by the husband): but if it has been given, half is ordained."

A wife, after whom another wife is married, is said to be "superseded."

5. (Strídhana is not sixfold) also because VISHNU ordains "gifts subsequent" as an additional kind of woman's property. Thus he says:—

"What is given by the father, the mother, the son, and the brother, what is received before the nuptial fire, the gift for alleviation of the grief, the Sulka (bride's price), and the gift subsequent, are defined woman's property."

6. NA'RADA (says):—"What is given before the nuptial fire, what is given in the bridal procession, and likewise what is given by the husband, what is given by the brother, and by the parents, are ordained the sixfold property of woman."

Here also, the intention is not the denial of a larger number.

7. DEVALA (says):—"The subsistence, the ornaments, the Sulka, and the gains, are woman's property."

8. KA'TYA'YANA (says):—"Whatever wealth is gained by the practice of mechanical arts, and what is received through affection from a stranger, therein the ownership of the husband always exists: but the rest is woman's property."

Whatever wealth, other than the (two) kinds mentioned, is acquired by a woman, therein the wife alone has ownership; this is the meaning.

9. Likewise (KA'TYA'YANA says):—"Whatever is given to a woman at the time of marriage, before the nuptial fire, is pronounced by the wise to be woman's property, named, 'gift before the nuptial fire'.

Whatever a woman receives when taken away from her father's house, is denominated woman's property, under the name of 'gift in bridal procession': this is 'gift in bridal procession', according to Kátyáyana."

10. Likewise (KA'TYA'YANA says):—"Whatever is given through affection by the mother-in-law or by the father-in-law, on the occasion of her salutation by touching the feet, is called 'gains of amiability': whatever is received by a woman, after marriage, from the husband's family, or from her own family, is called 'gift subsequent'. Whatever is received by a woman after marriage through affection, from the husband or the parents, is 'gift subsequent' according to Bhrigu. Whatever is received as price of workmen on houses, on furniture, on carriages, on milking utensils, and on ornaments, is called Sulka."

The meaning is, whatever property is given to women in the shape of bribe, to send their husbands who are workmen on houses &c., for the purpose of performing such work, is Sulka. 'Gift from affectionate kindred', has already (Ch. VIII, § 7) been described in some other connection, and is therefore not explained in this chapter.

11. Thus, in the VIVA'DA-RATNA'KARA, ends the subject of definition of woman's property.

CHAPTER XII.

§ 1—Partition of concealed property. 2 to 4—Equal distribution of property concealed at partition, and subsequently discovered; member concealing property is not guilty of theft. 4—What has been improperly divided, or subsequently realized, and what had been stolen or lost and subsequently recovered or found respectively, shall be equally divided; concealed property shall not be recovered from the member, by force; member not liable to pay compensation for enjoying larger portion. 5—Force shall not be used towards member concealing joint property, recovery of which should be effected by gentle means and artful contrivance.

1. Now is discussed, the partition of what was concealed.

2. On that subject, MANU (says):—"If after all the debts and property have been duly divided, anything is subsequently discovered, all that should be taken equally."

3. YA'JNAVALKYA (says):—"When separated kinsmen discover effects concealed by any member, they shall divide the same in equal shares: this is the law."

Here although partition follows from the general rule, still by force of this separate text, it is made known, that there is no offence of theft, in the concealment of common property: so says Haláyudha.

4. KA'TYA'YANA declares:—"Whatever is concealed by any one, the sons should, after the death of the father, assemble and divide with their brethren, in equal shares: BHRIGU says, what is concealed by different members, and what has been improperly divided, and what

has been received subsequently, shall be divided in equal shares. Whatever is acquired by a separated co-parcener, shall belong to him alone: but whatever was stolen, or lost, of the aforesaid property, shall be divided afresh. Whatever effect has been stolen by a kinsman, shall not be recovered by force: undivided kinsmen shall not be compelled to pay (compensation) for enjoyment."

"Stolen", means, what has been stolen by a stranger: "lost", means not found: "aforesaid property" means property coming from the paternal grandfather. By the words—"shall not be recovered by force", it is intended, that the same should be recovered by some artful contrivance. "Shall not be compelled to pay for enjoyment" means, that at the time of partition shall not be compelled to pay compensation for enjoyment, on the ground, that he has enjoyed a larger portion.

5. VRIHASPATI ordains:—"In case of concealment of a debt or deposit belonging to the joint family, the payment of the same shall not be enforced by force but by having recourse to an artful contrivance causing indirect loss. When men who hold property, are dishonest, wicked and avaricious, they shall be dealt with by gentle means through some deception or deprivation of interest."

The meaning of "In case of &c.", is, that if any one makes concealment of a debt or deposit belonging to the joint family, the person who conceals shall not be compelled by force, to give the thing concealed, but by having recourse to an artful contrivance causing indirect loss, *i. e.* causing loss of property belonging to the concealer.

6. Thus ends in the VIVA'DA-RATNA'KARA, the chapter on the division of concealed property.

CHAPTER XIII.

§ 1—Partition among brethren of different castes. 2—Specific deduction for Bráhmana son, and then shares for sons of four castes in the regular order, are 3, 2, 1½, and 1 share. 3 and 4—In partition without specific deduction, the shares for sons of four castes, are 4, 3, 2, and 1, in regular order. 5—A passage showing shares for sons of a Kshatriya to be 4, 3 and 1, and of a Vaisya to be 4 and 1. 6 to 11—Shares are, 4, 3, 2, and 1 for Bráhmana's sons, 3, 2 and 1, for Kshatriya's sons, and 2 and 1 for Vaisya's sons; different shares; distribution explained. 12—Sons of one class, equal sharers. 13—Súdras have wives of one class, their sons equal sharers. 14 to 18—Son of the next inferior case, if endowed with virtues, equally shares with son of next superior caste. 19 to 21—Land of Bráhmana, got by acceptance of gift, taken by Bráhmana son alone; ancestral land shared by twice-born sons only. 22—Bráhmana's son by Sudrá wife, gets a third. 23—Sudra son, of the twice-born, gets half. 24 to 27—Son of twice-born by a not married Sudrá woman, gets maintenance, &c.. 28—Son of inferior man by superior wife, is alike to son by Súdrá wife. 29 to 31—Sudra's son by Súdrá woman not married by him, may get a share; when, gets half; gets whole, in default of heirs down to daughter's son.

1. Now, partition among brethren of different classes, is discussed.

2. On that subject, MANU (says):—"This provision of partition is to be understood to refer to those of the same womb. Listen now to the mode of partition among those born of one person on many and various wives: when a Bráhmana has four wives in the regular order

of castes, the following partition is pronounced to apply to sons born of them ; an agricultural labourer, a bull for impregnating cows, a conveyance, an ornament, and an apartment, shall be given to the son of a Bráhmaní wife, as his specific deduction, and a share (marked) by superiority : the son of a Bráhmaní wife, shall take three shares ; the son of a Kshatriyá wife, shall take two shares ; and the son of a Vaisyá wife, shall take a share and a half ; and the son of a Súdrá wife, shall take one share."

"Those of the same womb", means, those belonging to the same caste ; "born of one person", means, begotten by one person : the grammatical connection is, "those begotten by one person on many and various wives", *i. e.* wives born in different castes : "an agricultural labourer", is a ploughman, "a conveyance", *i. e.* a horse or the like ; hence a ploughman, a bull for impregnating cows, a conveyance, an ornament, and an apartment, shall be given to the son of a Bráhmaní wife : of his three shares, one should be marked by superiority *i. e.* shall be so constituted as to be distinguished by excellence ; the gift of a bull for impregnating cows, and so forth, is to be made, if possible.

3. Accepting partition without specific deduction, it is declared :— "Or all the properties should be divided into ten shares : and one versed in law shall make a lawful partition in the following manner,—the son of the Bráhmaní wife shall take four shares ; the son of the Kshatriyá wife, three shares ; the son of the Vaisyá wife, two shares ; and the son of the Súdrá wife, shall take one share."

The singular number in the term "son of the Bráhmaní wife", is not intended (to have any importance) : so, this very rule applies, when there are many sons of the Bráhmaní wife.

4. NA'RADA (says) :—"Among those born of women married, but inferior in caste, there is the diminution of a share in regular order."

"Inferior in caste", such as the son of a Kshatriya wife, and the like, are to the son of a Bráhmaní wife ; "married", *i. e.* lawfully wedded : "diminution of a share" such as three shares of a son born of a Kshatriya wife and the like, (as compared with the four shares of a son by a Bráhmaní wife, The reading in some copies is, "belonging to different castes", instead of "inferior, caste" : there also, the meaning is the same.

5. BHI'SHMA, in the *Mahábhárata* (says):—"O son of Kuru ! two wives are ordained for the Kshatriyas also : there may be a third *i. e.* a Súdra woman, but it is not ordained in the holy writ. O Yudhisthira ! the property of a Kshatriya should be divided into eight shares : the son by the Kshatriya wife, shall take four shares from the father's property, and shall also take whatever implement of war belonged to the father ; the son by the Vaisya wife, shall take three shares ; and the son by the Súdra wife, the eighth share. He again takes what is given by the father, and is not entitled to take, if not given. O son of Kuru ! a Vaisya has one wife, or he may have a Súdra woman for a second wife : but it is not ordained in the holy writ. O excellent descendant of Bharata ! the property of a Vaisya should be divided into five shares : O Lord of men ! I shall state the distribution amongst their sons : four shares shall be taken by the son of the Vaisya wife from the father's

property: O descendant of Bharata! the fifth share shall belong to the son by the Súdra wife: he also shall take the paternal property, if given, and is not entitled to take, if not given."

"Holy writ", here means the Veda: hence, though not ordained by the Vedas, if a Súdra woman is married by a Kshatriya impelled by inclination, as his third wife, then her son also, is entitled to a share: this is the meaning: and similarly in the subsequent passages. "Implements of war", *i. e,* means of war, such as a broad sword and the like.

6. YA'JNAVALKYA declares:—"The sons of a Bráhmana, are according to their caste, entitled to four, three, two and one share: those born of a Kshatriya, to three, two and one, and of a Vaisya are entitled to two shares and one."

This text applies, when a Bráhmana has four wives, and a Kshatriya three. Here again, when the sons by the Kshatriya and the Vaisya wives, are endowed with superior virtues, then the rule of distribution mentioned in the Mahábhárata applies, but when they are of inferior quality, then the rule propounded by Yájnavalkya shall apply; thus, there is no conflict.

7. VISHNU declares:—"If a Bráhmana has sons in the four castes, they shall divide the paternal heritage into ten parts: then the son of the Bráhmaní wife shall take four shares; the son of the Kshatriyá wife, three shares; the son by the Vaisya wife, two shares; and the son by the Súdra wife, one. If, however, a Bráhmana has three sons, excepting a son by a Súdra wife, then the property should be divided into nine parts, and they shall, in the order of the castes, take shares, composed of four, three, and two parts. If there be no son by the Vaisya wife, then having divided into eight parts, they shall take four, three and one, if there be no son by the Kshatriya wife, then dividing into seven parts, they shall take four, two, and one. Should there be no son by the Bráhmaní wife, then dividing into six parts, they shall take three, two, and one. Amongst the sons of Kshatriyas, Vaisyas, and Súdras, the partition should be made in the same way. If a Bráhmana has sons by Bráhmaní and Kshatriyá wives, then, out of the property divided into seven parts, the Bráhmana shall take four shares, and the Kshatriya, three. If a Bráhmana has Bráhmana and Vaisya sons, then out of his property, divided into six, the Bráhmana shall take four shares, and the Vaisya shall take two. Again if a Bráhmana has a Bráhmana and Súdra son, then his property shall be divided into five parts, and the Bráhmana shall take four parts, and the Súdra one: again, if a Bráhmana or a Kshatriya has Kshatriya and Vaisya sons, then his property should be divided into five parts, the Kshatriya shall take three shares, and the Vaisya, two shares. Again, if a Bráhmana or a Kshatriya has Kshatriya and Súdra sons, then his property should be divided into four parts, the Kshatriya shall take three parts, and the Súdra, one. Again, if a Bráhmana, or a Kshatriya, or a Vaisya, has a Vaisya and a Súdra son, then his property shall be divided into three shares, the Vaisya shall take two shares, and the Súdra, one."

8. SANKHA and LIKHITA (say):—"Among those, born of wives belonging to other castes, there is a diminution of heritage by halves, in the order of castes."

9. VISHNU declares:—"If there be two sons by a Bráhmaní wife, and one by a Súdrá wife, then the two sons of the Bráhmaní wife, shall take eight shares, and the son of the Súdrá wife, one. Again, if there be two sons by the Súdra wife, and one by the Bráhmaní wife, then by dividing into six shares, the Bráhmana shall take four shares, and the two sons by the Súdra wife, two shares. In this manner, distribution shall be made, in other cases also."

10. VISHNU further declares:—"A single son of a Bráhmana, whether by a Bráhmaní, Kshatriyá or Vaisyá wife, takes the whole property: so a Kshatriya or a Vaisya son of a Kshatriya; a Vaisya son of a Vaisya, and a Súdra son of a Súdra."

When a Bráhmana has only one son, born of any one of his wives belonging to the three castes commencing with the Bráhmana, then he alone will take the property, whether he be a Bráhmana, a Kshatriya or a Vaisya. Similarly also, if a Kshatriya has a Kshatriya or a Vaisya son born of any of his two wives (belonging to the two castes), then he alone takes the whole. Similarly also, an only son of a Vaisya takes his entire property, and an only son of a Súdra takes his whole property; a third and a second wife of a Kshatriya and a Vaisya respectively, is not expressly mentioned here, by reason of not being supported by the Vedas: this rule will apply if a Kshatriya and a Vaisya marry a wife of the third and the second caste respectively (counting from their own caste), although the same be unlawful.

11. VASISHTHA ordains:—"If a Bráhmana has Bráhmana, Kshatriya and Vaisya sons, then the son of the Bráhmaní wife shall take three shares, the son of the Kshatriya wife, two shares, and the rest shall take one."

"The rest" *i. e.* sons by a Vaisya wife. Here Vishnu and Vasishtha declaring different modes of distribution, (the apparent conflict) should be reconciled by reference to the superiority or inferiority in the good quality of the sharers.

12. MANU ordains:—"All sons of the twice-born, begotten on wives of equal caste, or (of a different caste) shall equally divide, after having given specific deductions to the eldest."

When the twice-born have many sons on different wives belonging to the same caste, and likewise many sons by different wives of even a different caste, as is implied by the particle "or", then they shall divide equally, after having given something, as a specific deduction, to the eldest.

13. Likewise:—"But for a Súdra, a wife of the same class, and not one of a different class, is ordained: those born of her, are equal sharers, though there be hundred sons."

14. BAUDHA'YANA ordains:—"If between a son born of a wife of the same caste, and one born of a wife of the next (inferior) caste, the one born of the wife of the next inferior caste, is endowed with good qualities,

then he shall take the share of the eldest; since, one possessed of good qualities, becomes the protector of many."

15. VRIHASPATI (says):—"A son begotten by a Bráhmana, on a Kshatriyá wife, becomes equal sharer with a Bráhmana son, if senior by birth, and endowed with good qualities: likewise, a son born of a Vaisyá wife."

16. GAUTAMA (says):—"The son of a Bráhmana by a Kshatriyá wife, is entitled to a share, equal with the first born, *i. e.* all excepting the (deducted) portion of the eldest son."

"All" *i. e.* the bull and the like. "Excepting the (deducted) portion of the eldest son", means, that the specific deduction for the eldest son, shall not be made.

17. Likewise:—"When sons by a Kshatriyá and a Vaisyá wife, co-exist, then as he (the son by a Kshatriyá wife is equal sharer) with the son by a Bráhmaní wife."

The meaning is, as the son of a Bráhmana by a Kshatriya wife, is equal sharer with a son by a Bráhmaní wife, similarly, when there is no son by the Bráhmaní wife, but there are sons by the Kshatriyá and the Vaisyá wife, the son by the Vaisyá wife, being endowed with good qualities, is equal sharer with the younger son by a Kshatriyá wife, who is destitute of good qualities: the son by the Kshatriyá wife, is, like the son of a Bráhmaní wife, deprived of the portion of the eldest.

18. "If born of a Kshatriya father."

If similarly, two sons are born of a Kshatriya father, one by a Kshatriyá wife, and the other by a Vaisyá wife, then the very same is the mode of distribution (between them.) Likewise, the same rule would apply to two sons of also a Vaisya, one by a Vaisyá wife, and the other by a Súdrá wife. Similarly, the declaration, by Baudháyana, of the allotment of the portion of the eldest, in such a case, applies, when the son by a wife of the same caste is younger, and devoid of good qualities; but if the younger be endowed with good qualities, then the share shall be equal: thus, there is no conflict.

19. VRIHASPATI declares:—"Land received by acceptance, shall not be given to a son by a Kshatriyá or the like, wife: even if his father gives, on his death, the son by the Bráhmaní wife shall take it back."

20. The senior MANU (says):—"That son, who is born of the Bráhmaní wife, shall get the land come through sacred knowledge. All the twice-born sons shall take the ancestral house and the field."

"Come through the sacred knowledge", means, acquired by acceptance of gift, by officiating as a priest, and the like means: "the twice-born", means, belonging to the three superior castes. The Párijáta says—"come through sacred knowledge", means, acquired by the acceptance of a gift.

21. VRIHASPATI ordains:—"A son begotten by the twice-born on a wife of the Súdra caste, is not entitled to the land. One, born on a woman of the same class, shall get the whole; this is the settled law."

22. DEVALA (says) :—" When a Súdra is the only son of a Bráhmana, he gets a third : the remaining two shares shall be taken by the Sakulya, or the Sapinda, or him who is the giver of the funeral oblation : in default of the Sakulya, the giver of the Pinda, or the preceptor, or a pupil. In the utmost difficulty (to find an heir), let those shares be allotted, to any person sprung from the same original stock."

The two shares shall belong to the Sapindas, and in their default to the Sakulyas, and in default of the Sakulyas, the preceptor, or the pupil, shall get. " In the utmost difficulty " *i. e.* in default of the Sapindas, Sakulyas and the like, the share shall be given to a person " sprung from the same original stock " *i. e.* the original stock of the father of that Súdra son. The Párijáta says, that this refers to a Súdra son endowed with good qualities.

23. VISHNU (says) :—" If a Súdra be the only son of the twice-born, he takes half ; the other half is to be disposed of, in the same way, as property left by a person dying without male issue."

" The twice-born ", means, other than Bráhmanas *i. e.* Kshatriyas and Vaisyas, because Devala has declared a third share for the son of a Bráhmana by a Sudra wife, the rest is to be allotted to some Bráhmana.

24. MANU (says) :—" Whether there be any other son or no other son, more than a tenth share cannot lawfully be given to the son of a Súdra wife. The son of a Bráhmana or a Kshatriya or a Vaisya by a Súdrá wife is not entitled to the heritage : whatever his father gives, that becomes his property."

" Any other son ", means any son by a twice-born wife : " no other son " *i. e.* no such son. On this subject Laksmídhara says, that when the father being pleased, gives property to a son by a Súdrá wife, then let him give only a tenth share ; hence in his opinion, the passage— " son by a Sudra wife is not entitled to the heritage ", suggests that he is not entitled to heritage, if not given by the father.

But HALA'YUDHA and the PA'RIJA'TA have explained the text as prohibitory of the allotment of a share, by saying that the first rule is referable to the son by a married Súdrá woman, who is utterly destitute of good qualities, and that the second rule is referable to a son by an unmarried Súdrá woman, who is destitute of good qualities.

25. VRIHASPATI (says) :—" The son by a Súdrá woman of a person destitute of male issue, being obedient and virtuous, gets maintenance, the Sapindas shall get the rest."

This must be referred, to a son by a woman not married, as the context relates to women not married.

26. On this snbject, GAUTAMA declares :—" Even a son by a Súdrá woman, of a person destitute of male issue, shall get property for maintenance, if obedient like a disciple."

The meaning is, that even a son by a not-married Súdrá woman, of a person belonging to the three superior castes, who has no twice-born son, shall get " property for maintenance " *i. e.* something yielding maintenance, such as agricultural lands and the like, if he be obedient like a disciple *i. e.* rendering service.

27. As for the declaration by SANKHA and LIKHITA, that what has not been given by the father to him, should be given,—in the following text :—

"A son by a Súdrá woman, is not entitled to a share of the property: whatever his father, gives him, that alone is his share ; to him should also be given a bull and a cow, black iron, and black grain excepting *tila* (sesamum) ;"

that refers to the son of a not-married Súdrá woman.

28. GAUTAMA (says) :—"A son born of a father of an inferior caste and a mother of a superior caste, is like the son of a Súdrá woman."

The meaning is, that these, though born of other castes, are, like the son of a Súdrá woman, entitled, only to a source of maintenance, like a disciple.

29. MANU (says) :—"The son of a Súdra begotten on a female slave, or on a female slave of a male slave, being permitted, shall get a share : this is the settled law."

"A son begotten by a Súdra on a female slave" *i. e.*, on a woman falling within one or other of the descriptions of slaves, given in the text,—"There are slaves of seven sorts, namely one made captive under a standard, one becoming a slave, in consideration of maintenance &c."—"or on the female slave of a male slave", *i. e.* on a not-married female slave of a male slave falling within the said descriptions, is so entitled, if permitted (by the father): this is the settled law. The Kalpataru says that the "female slave of a male slave", means, the female slave of a man-servant.

30. YA'JNAVALKYA (says) :—"A son though begotten by a Súdra on a female slave, is entitled to a share by (the father's) choice ; but after the father's death, (the legitimate) brothers shall make him partaker of a half share."

The meaning is,—"gets a share by choice" *i. e.*, by the father's choice : if after the death of the father, there are sons born of married wives, then they shall make the son of the female slave, partaker of a half share, in comparison to their own share.

31. What should be done in default of a son by a married wife, is declared (by YA'JNAVALKYA) :—"If there be no legitimate brother, he shall take the entire property, in the absence of the daughter's son."

In default of a son by a married wife, and also in default of a married wife, a daughter and a daughter's son, the son by a female slave alone shall take the whole property, after the death of the father.

32. Thus, in the VIVA'DA-RATNA'KARA, the subject of partition amongst sons by wives of different castes (is finished).

CHAPTER XIV.

§ 1—Share of son born after partition. 2 & 3—Such son takes father's share ; or takes share out of reunited property, when any other son became reunited with father. 4.—He alone takes father's acquisition made after separation from other sons. 5 & 6—A son in womb at time of partition, takes share by re-opening the partition.

1. Now, the participation by (a son) born after partition (is discussed).

2. MANU (ordains) :—" But let a son born after partition, take only the paternal wealth, or let him divide with those that are re-united with him."

A son born after the (other) sons have become separated from the father, shall take the entire share of the father, when the father is dead : when the father is living, he shall get only a share out of the father's wealth (should he separate from the father) ; by the particle " only ", it is indicated that (he is to take) not also out of the share of a separated brother.

3. VRIHASPATI (declares) :—" When the half brothers, or whole brothers, have become separated from the father ; and they have brothers subsequently born, these however shall take the father's share : one born before (partition) is not entitled to the paternal share, nor is one born after partition, to the brother's share."

" One born before, " is one born before partition *i. e.*, one who has become separated : he is not entitled to the father's share ; " one born after partition " *i. e.*, one born of the separated father, is not entitled to the brother's share :—this is the meaning.

4. Likewise, (VRIHASPATI ordains) :—" What is acquired by the father himself after having become separated from the sons, all that belongs to (the son) born after partition ; those born before are ordained, not entitled. As in wealth, so also in debts, and in gifts, pledges and sales, they are independent of each other, excepting mourning, libations and exequial rites."

5. YA'JNAVALKYA (declares) :—" After the sons have been separated, one who is born of a woman equal in class, shares in the distribution : his allotment shall be made out of the visible estate, corrected from income and expenditure."

6. VISHNU (ordains) :—" Those separated from the father, shall give an allotment, to one born subsequently."

Both of these texts refer to one who was in the womb at the time of the partition, and has been born, subsequently to the partition. By these it is declared, that those that have become separated shall, out of their own shares, make out the allotment of one, who was in the womb at the time of the partition, and has been born after partition.

The opinion of Manu and others, that a son who is born after partition, is entitled to the wealth of the separated father,—refers to a son other than the one just mentioned. The distinction is based on the imperceptibility of (the fœtal existence of) one begotten at the time of partition. But if the pregnancy is perceptible, then partition itself cannot take place.

This is the view of the author of the PRAKA'SA.

But HALA'YUDHA cites the text of YA'JNAVALKYA, after having cited the text of VISHNU, and says :—"The meaning of this is that, if the son born after partition, of a woman equal in class, is endowed with virtues, then he gets a share from all visible and invisible property, that was previously divided ; but if he is possessed of bad qualities, then he gets a share from the residue left after paying off the debts contracted by the brothers,—of only the visible *i. e.*, only the perceptible land and the like, and paddy and the like produce of landed property."

7. Thus, in the VIVA'DA-RATNA'KARA, is finished the subject of participation by a son born after partition.

CHAPTER XV.

§ 1—Share of one absent at time of partition. 2—Absent co-heir entitled to share, when appears. 3—Even seventh descendant of co-heir absent at distant place, entitled to share, after return. 4—If such co-heirship is known by tradition to old men of the village.

1. Now, the participation by one returning (from abroad) after partition, (is discussed).

2. On this (subject) VRIHASPATI (declares) :—"Whether partition has or has not been made ; whenever a co-heir appears, he is entitled to a share, if he shows common property."

"Shows" *i. e.*, proves—"I also have a share in it."

3. Likewise, (the same sage declares) :—"Be it debt, or a writing, or a house, or a field, which descended from his paternal ancestor, he shall take his due share of it, when he comes, even though he have been long absent. If a man leave the common family, and reside in another country, his share must, no doubt, be given to his descendants, when they return,—be the descendant third, or fifth, or even seventh, in degree, he shall receive his hereditary allotment, on proof of his birth and name."

As for the restriction declared by DEVALA, namely, that amongst the undivided or the divided (co-heirs), participation extends to the fourth in descent, that refers to a case in which the co-parcener resides in the same locality, and the like ; but this relates to a case in which the co-parcener resides in a place which is distant or difficult to reach, and the like :—thus there is no inconsistency.

4. Likewise, (the same sage ordains) :—" To the lineal descendants, when they appear, of that man whom the neighbours and old inhabitants know by tradition to be the proprietor, the land must be given by the agnates."

5. Thus, in the VIVA'DA-RATNA'KARA, is finished, the participation by a co-heir returning from abroad, after partition.

CHAPTER XVI.

§ 1—Participation by sons other than Aurasa. 2 & 3—Putriká and Aurasa, equal sharers. 4—Aurasa son's superiority. 5 to 7—Kshetraja and his procreator uncle, equal sharers. 8 and 9—Sons of same woman by different men, without appointment. 10 and 11—Aurasa and Kshetraja sons. 12—Aurasa and Dattaka sons. 13—Aurasa and other sons of equal and unequal castes. 14 to 18—Different shares for different sons. 20 to 30—Texts enumerating twelve kinds of sons, laying down rank among sons, dividing them into two sets of six each, and declaring their shares or right to maintenance &c. 31—Son of any description, entitled to inherit father's property, in preference to all other heirs. 32—Order among sons. 33—Enumeration of sons of middle and inferior rank. 34—Text condemning some sons.

1. Participation by other (descriptions of) sons, is now (discussed).

2. On that subject, MANU declares :—" If after a daughter has been made a *putriká* or appointed to raise male issue for her father, a son is subsequently born, then the distribution must be equal, since the female has not seniority (or specific deduction for the eldest)".

" A son " *i. e.*, a real legitimate son ; " subsequently " to the appointment of daughter : " the female " *i. e.*, one made *putriká* or appointed daughter. *putriká* or daughter converted into son, is described by Manu, in the text,—" A sonless man shall, in this manner, make a daughter *putriká* &c."—which will be cited in the chapter on the description of the son (called *putriká* : see Ch. XIX, § 11.)

3. VRIHASPATI declares :—" The *aurasa* or real legitimate son alone is proclaimed owner of the paternal wealth, the *putriká* is pronounced equal to him ; the other sons, however, shall be maintained."

4. MANU (says) :—" The *aurasa* son alone is master of the paternal property : to the rest, however, livelihood shall be given, for want of cruelty."

"To the rest" *i. e.*, to those to whom allotment of a share is prohibited ; " livelihood " *i. e.* maintenance ; " for want of cruelty " *i. e.* out of kindness.

5. Likewise (MANU declares) :—" Should a younger brother beget a son on the wife of an elder brother, then the distribution shall be equal : this is settled law."

The meaning is,—A son begotten by a younger brother, appointed to raise issue, on the wife of a sonless undivided elder brother, shall get an equal share while separating from the progenitor uncle, after the death of the father, but not specific deduction and the like, by reason of the seniority of his (legal) father.

6. On this very subject, is the following text, indicating the reason (of the above rule):—"That the secondary should be equal to the principal, is not reasonable under the law: the father is principal in procreation, hence the son is entitled by law to take that (*i. e.*, equal) share."

The author of the PRAKA'SA explains this text, thus:—The secondary, *i. e.* the subsidiary *i. e.* the appointed wife's son: that he should be equal to the principal *aurasa* son, is not reasonable under the law, since here the father *i. e.*, the progenitor uncle alone, is the principal.

But LAKSHMI'DHARA (says);—Here the word "secondary" means, secondary character: (thus, the first line of the text would be—"The secondary character of the principal is not reasonable under the law:) there is, however, no difference in the result. "By law", *i. e.*, by law laid down in the Sástra.

7. Likewise (MANU says)—"He who protects the estate and also the wife of a deceased brother, shall, having begotten a son for his brother, give that estate to him alone."

The meaning is,—he who protects the wealth and the wife of a separated sonless deceased brother, shall, having procreated a son on her, according to the law relating to the procreation of a KSHETRAJA or appointed wife's son, give that wealth to that son alone; but must not himself appropriate the brother's estate through covetousness.

8. Likewise (MANU says):—"If an *aurasa* or real legitimate son and a *kshetraja* or wife's son claim the same estate, then each shall take exclusive of the other, whatever is his own father's estate."

Here "wife's son", is one procreated by a person not appointed; "father's estate", is what is given to the mother, by the father for making a provision for the son.

Others, however, put on it the plain meaning, namely, that each takes the estate left by his own father.

9. "But among sons by different fathers, the allotment of shares is according to the fathers: each shall take, exclusive of the other, whatever is his paternal estate."

"Among sons by different fathers", (means), among those begotten on the same woman by several (men).

10. When by the continuous treatment of the disease, or through the discovery of a remedy of the disease (of the husband), the disease is cured by the use of medicine and the like, after a *kshetraja* son has been begotten (on the wife), by appointment in the prescribed mode, and an *aurasa* or real legitimate son is afterwards born, then the question arises, whether the *kshetraja* son is entitled, to a mere provision for main-

tenance, or to a share? and in case he be entitled to a share, then what is his share?

On this, MANU declares:—"But a fifth or a sixth share shall be given to the *kshetraja* son, out of the paternal wealth, by the *aurasa* son, while he is dividing the paternal heritage."

This alternative of a fifth or a sixth share, is to be settled, having regard to endowment of the Khetraja son, with good qualities, or the contrary.

11. Likewise (MANU declares):—"The *aurasa* and the *kshetraja* sons are entitled to the father's heritage: but the ten others, are, in succession, entitled to become members of the *gotra*, and to get a share of the heritage."

Here the first half (of the text) recites the rule laid down in the preceding text. "The ten", *i. e.*, the Dattaka or given son, and others; "in succession" *i. e.*, the next in order on failure of the first; "entitled to become member of the *gotra*" *i. e.*, entitled to perform the duties of a kinsman,—this is said by ASAHA'YA A'CHA'RYA; "entitled to get a share of the heritage" *i. e.*, of the father;—this however (is the case) in default of the *aurasa*, the *putriká* and the *kshetraja* sons.

12. Having premised the subject of sonship, VASISHTHA says:—"If, after he has been adopted, an *aurasa* son is born, he (the adopted son) is entitled to a fourth share, should (the wealth) be not applied to rites for prosperity."

"He" *i. e.*, the son other than the *aurasa* son; "he" *i. e.*, the adopted son: 'if the property be large'—is understood (as the condition for the fourth share); the meaning of the words—"should be not applied to rites for prosperity", is, should the wealth be not applied *i. e.* appropriated to rites for prosperity, such as sacrifices.

13. KA'TYA'YANA declares:—"But if an *aurasa* son is born, (other sons) that are of equal class, are ordained to be entitled to a third share: but those that are unequal in class, are entitled to food and raiment."

The meaning is, that if an *aurasa* son is born, then the Dattaka and the rest are entitled to a third share, when they are of the same class.

Now, a fourth share is declared (by VASISHTHA), in the case of a son previously adopted, but by this (is declared) the participation of a third share: these are to be reconciled by reference to possession of good qualities or otherwise.

It also appears from this text, that the provision of mere maintenance in the text of Manu (§ 3), namely,—"to the rest, however, livelihood shall be given for want of cruelty,"—is intended for only sons that are unequal in class.

14. On this subject, VRIHASPATI ordains:—"And the other sons beginning with the *kshetraja* son, are entitled to fifth, sixth and seventh share."

"Beginning with the *kshetraja* son" *i. e.*, the *kshetraja*, the *kánína* or maiden-born son, and *paunarbhava* or son of a twice-married woman, are respectively entitled to fifth, sixth and seventh share: this is the meaning.

15. HA'RI'TA ordains :—" One making distribution, shall allot a twenty-first share to the maiden-born son, a twentieth to the son of a twice-married woman, a nineteenth to the wife's secretly begotten son, an eighteenth to the appointed wife's son, a seventeenth to the appointed daughter's son, and the rest to the real legitimate son."

" The rest " *i. e.*, sixteen shares.

16. In the BRAHMA-PURA'NA (it is laid down):—" Although the *aurasa* son is the youngest, he enjoys the whole property ; the *kshetraja* son enjoys the third share ; the appointed daughter's son, a fourth ; the Kritrima or son made, a fifth share ; a son secretly born, a sixth share ; the deserted son, a seventh share ; the maiden-born son, an eighth share ; the son of the pregnant bride, a nineth share ; the purchased son gets a tenth ; the son of the twice-married woman, the next (*i. e.*, eleventh) ; the self given son, a twelveth ; and the son by a Sudra woman enjoys a thirteenth as his share, out of the father's wealth."

17. The declaration by Vrihaspati, of a sixth share for the maiden-born son, and the declaration by Háríta, of a twentieth share for the very same son, and the declaration in the Brahma-purána of an eighth share for the very same son—are to be reconciled by reference to possession of the very best qualities, to want of good qualities, and to possession of mediocre qualities, respectively.

The declaration by Vrihaspati, of a seventh share, for the son of the twice-married woman, the declaration in the Brahma-purána, of an eleventh share for him, and the declaration by Háríta, of a twentieth share for that very son, are to be reconciled by reference to possession of the very best qualities, to possession of good qualities, and to the want of good qualities.

Likewise, in the case of the *kshetraja* son. It has already been said that secretly born sons are not entitled (in competition with the Aurasa son).

Here, the passage of the Brahma-purána answers the question, namely, what share does any one of the thirteen sons, get out of the father's property ?

The text of Háríta, namely—" One making distribution &c.,"—and the text of Sankha and Likhita, (§ 20) namely,—" The adjustment of shares among the six co-heirs, &c."—show the distribution after the father's death, among the six heirs equal in class : of them, the first applies, when the five sons are inferior to the Aurasa son in qualities ; and the second applies, when they are equal to the Aurasa in qualities.

18. Again SANKHA and LIKHITA ordain :—" A donkey belongs to the seniormost son, over and above (his share) ; in his default, to the appointed wife's son and the appointed daughter's son : on failure of both of them, to the other three sons ; in their default, those sons that are not heirs, if equal in class, take the entire heritage."

It is to be understood here, even those that are not heirs (in competition with other sons) take the heritage, the next in order on failure of the first.

19. Likewise,—" The deserted son, the son of the pregnant bride, the given son, the purchased son, the son of a Súdrá woman, and the self-given son,—these six sons are not heirs ; according to their quality, is here the declaration by the great sages, of their participation of different shares, in conflict with one another, which is to be reconciled by reference to absence of good qualities, or to possession of good qualities, or to possession of still superior excellent qualities."

20. SANKHA and LIKHITA (say):—" The adjustment of shares among the six co-heirs,—the real legitimate son, the appointed wife's son, the appointed daughter's son, the twice-married woman's son, the maiden-born son, and the wife's secretly begotten son—these six sons are *bandhus* or kinsmen and *dáyádas* or co-heirs : they are of the same *gotra* with the father and the paternal grand-sires ; the heritage, the funeral oblation, and the Sapinda relationship, belong to them : the wealth is to be divided into ten shares ; two shares belong to the father ; two, to the real legitimate son ; three, to the appointed wife's son and the appointed daughter's son (jointly) ; and one, to each of the others : to the other sons, livelihood (shall be allowed)."

" Bandhu-Dáyáda " i. *e.*, entitled to the *gotra* or membership of the family, to Pinda or funeral oblations, and to libations of water,—and entitled to the heritage ; this very matter is explained in the next passage, namely,—" they are of the same *gotra* &c.".

By this it is declared, that the joint property being divided into ten shares, two shares belong to the father ; two, to the real legitimate son ; one share and a half, to the appointed wife's son and the appointed daughter's son, each ; and one share shall be given to the twice-married woman's son, the maiden-born son, and the wife's secretly begotten son, each : to the other sons, livelihood shall be given ; but this takes place when there are the six sons entitled to be co-heirs.

21. GAUTAMA ordains:—" The real legitimate son, the appointed wife's son, the given son, the deserted son, the son made, and the wife's secretly begotten son, are entitled to the heritage ; the maiden-born son, the son of the pregnant bride, the twice-married woman's son, the appointed daughter's son, the self-given son, and the son bought, are entitled to the *gotra* or membership of the family, and to a fourth share in default of the legitimate son and the rest."

They are said to be entitled to the *gotra* or membership of the family, as in that character they perform the son's duty by offering the funeral oblation of food and libation of water, and by performing the funeral ceremony and the like.

But this declaration, that the maiden-born son and the others are only entitled to the *gotra* or membership of the family,—is made for the purpose of prohibiting their participation of a share, when there is even any one of the real legitimate son and the like.

They are entitled to a fourth share in default of the real legitimate son and the like, when the father is living ; but if the father is dead, and there is a failure of the real legitimate son and the like, then they are, in their order, entitled to take the entire heritage.

This participation of a fourth share takes place, when they are endowed with good qualities ; while the Brahma-puráńa applies, when they are possessed of bad qualities : thus there is no conflict.

The declaration in the text of SANKHA and LIKHITA, of participation of shares, by the son of a twice-married woman, and by the maiden's son, and the prohibition of the same in the text of GAUTAMA, are to be reconciled by reference to equality or unequality in class : for it appears from KA'TYA'YANAS text, that those unequal in class, are entitled to food and raiment, (but not to any share).

In this manner, should be explained, the text of SANKHA and LIKHITA, declaring that the deserted son and the given son are not entitled to heritage, and the text of GAUTAMA, declaring them to be entitled to heritage, by reconciling them as being applicable to different cases.

22. Having described the son of the pregnant bride, the given son, the son bought, the self-given son, the deserted son and the son by a Súdrá woman, and referring to the real legitimate son and the like, VASISHTHA declares again,—

" Of him, however, who has not a single heir of the first group, these take the share."

23. HA'RI'TA ordains :—" Six are Bandhu-Dáyáda,—the son begotten by a man himself on the chaste wife, the appointed wife's son, the son of a twice-married woman, the maiden's son, the appointed daughter's son, and the secretly begotten son of the wife—are Bandhu-Dáyádas ; the given son, the purchased son, the deserted son, the pregnant bride's son, the self-given son, and the son suddenly seen (the son made), are not Bandhu-Dáyáda."

By reason of being a member of the Gotra, arises the status of Bandhu or relation, as well as the status of Dáyáda or heir. LAKSHMI'DHARA, however, says that Bandhu-Dáyádas are those who take the heritage of Bandhus (or relations of the father.)

The purport, however, is the same, as showing the superiority and inferiority, respectively, of the first six, and the second six, sons.

24. MANU ordains :—" Of the twelve descriptions of sons of men, mentioned by MANU sprung from the self-existent, six are kinsmen and heirs, and six are not heirs but kinsmen : the real legitimate son, the appointed wife's son, the son given, the son made, the secretly begotten son of the wife, and the deserted son, are the six heirs and kinsmen ; the maiden-born son, the pregnant bride's son, the purchased son, the twice-married woman's son, the self-given son, and the son by a Súdrá woman, are the six who are not heirs but kinsmen."

25. BAUDHA'YANA declares :—" The real legitimate son, the appointed daughter's son, the appointed wife's son, the given son, the son made, the secretly begotten son of the wife, and the deserted son, are pronounced

entitled to the heritage; the maiden's son, the pregnant bride's son, the purchased son, the twice-married woman's son, the self-given son, and the son by a Súdrá woman, are pronounced entitled to the Gotra or membership of the family."

26. Having described the real legitimate son, the appointed daughter's son, the appointed wife's son, the maiden-born son, the secretly begotten son of the wife, the deserted son, the son of the pregnant bride, the twice-married woman's son, the given son, the self-given son, the son made, and the purchased son, DEVALA ordains,—

"These twelve sons have been propounded for the purpose of offspring: (they are either) begotten by the father himself, or procreated by another man (on his wife), or received (in adoption), or self-given. Among these, the first six are heirs of kinsmen, the other six inherit only from the father: the rank among sons is distinguished in the order of enumeration. All these sons are pronounced heirs of a man who has no real legitimate son: but should a real legitimate son be afterwards born, they (*i. e.*, subsidiary sons) have no right of primogeniture. Of them such sons, as are equal in class, are entitled to a third share; but those of a lower tribe, must live dependent on him, being supplied with food and raiment."

27. Having described the real legitimate son, the appointed wife's son, the appointed daughter's son, the twice-married woman's son, the maiden-born son, the secretly begotten son of the wife, the pregnant bride's son, the given son, the son bought, the self-given son, the deserted son, and the son begotten on any woman,—VISHNU ordains:—

"Of these, the first in order is superior, he alone takes the heritage, and he must maintain the others."

28. NA'RADA declares:—"The real legitimate son, the appointed wife's son, the appointed daughter's son, the maiden daughter's son, the pregnant bride's son, the secretly begotten son of the wife, the twice-married woman's son, the deserted son, the given son, the purchased son, the son made, and the self-given son,—these are pronounced the twelve kinds of sons: of these, six are kinsmen and heirs, and six are not heirs but kinsmen; each prior in order is superior, and each next in order is inferior; when the father is dead, they are entitled to his wealth, in their order; on failure of each superior, the next inferior gets the wealth."

29. Having described the real legitimate son, the appointed daughter's son, the appointed wife's son, the secretly born son of the wife, the maiden daughter's son, the twice-married woman's son, the given son, the purchased son, the son made, the self-given son, the pregnant bride's son, and the deserted son,—YA'JNAVALKYA ordains:—"In default of the first among these, the next in order, is to offer the funeral oblation and to take the heritage."

30. Here some description of son is stated by some sage to be heir of kinsmen, and by some sage to be not so; this conflict is to be avoided by reference to his being endowed with good qualities, or to his being devoid of good qualities.

In the enumeration of the twelve sons, for the purpose of showing the superiority of the prior in order, the same description of son is placed in a superior position by some sage, and in an inferior position by some other; this is to be understood to imply the possession of good qualities by the former, and want of good qualities in the latter.

Similarly in other cases also, the conflict is to be avoided, in this very manner.

31. MANU ordains:—"Neither brothers, nor fathers, but sons are ordained entitled to heritage."

Likewise,—"In default of each superior, the inferior is entitled to the heritage; but if there be many equal, all become entitled to the heritage."

"Equal", *i. e.*, as regards possession of good qualities, or as regards description.

32. SANKHA and LIKHITA declare:—"In default of each superior, the inferior is entitled to the heritage."

The purport is,—"in default of each superior" *i. e.*, the real legitimate son and the like, "the inferior" *i. e.*, the appointed wife's son and the like.

33. VRIHASPATI declares:—"The given son, the deserted son, the purchased son, the son made, and the son by a Súdrá woman,—these, if pure by birth, and pure in conduct, are ordained sons of the middle class; the appointed wife's son is reprehended by the virtuous, and so are twice-married woman's son, the maiden-born son, the pregnant bride's son, and the wife's secretly begotten son."

34. HA'RI'TA declares:—"Sons by Súdrá women, self-given sons, as well as purchased sons,—all these are, no doubt, sons like Súdras and deserters of family: he who turns back to his own family, and goes to a different family, is, no doubt, a deserter of family, by reason of that misconduct. One that goes away in distress, and one who appears of his own accord, and the son of a Vaishnaví,—all these three sons are pronounced by MANU, deserters of family."

"Vaishnaví," is here a Súdrá woman.

35. Thus, in the VIVA'DA-RATNA'KARA, is finished the participation by other descriptions of sons.

CHAPTER XVII.

§ 1—Aurasa son. 2 and 3—Aurasa, first among twelve kinds of sons. 3 to 8—Aurasa is son begotten by a man himself on his lawfully wedded wife of equal caste, who was not married to any other man. 8—A son begotten by a twice-born on a twice-born wife, though not equal in class, is Aurasa 9—Aurasa begotten on wife of equal class, superior.

1. Now, the *aurasa* or real legitimate son is defined.

2. On this VASISHTHA (says):—" Twelve descriptions of sons are recognized by the ancient sages : the first is the *aurasa* or real legitimate, who is begotten by a man himself on his own lawfully wedded wife."

3. VISHNU (says):—" Now there are twelve sons : the first is procreated by a man himself on his own wife."

4. MANU (declares):—" He who is procreated by a man himself on his lawfully wedded wife is known as *aurasa*, or sprung from the breast, and primary son."

5. DEVALA (declares):—" He who is begotten by a man himself on a lawfully wedded wife, and is named the *aurasa* son, is the principal propagator of the father's lineage."

6. YA'JNAVALKYA ordains:—" The *aurasa* is born of the lawfully wedded wife."

7. A'PASTAMBA (says):—" Sons of one approaching in due season, a woman of equal class, who had no previous (husband) and who is ordained by the Sástras (are *aurasa*) ; they have connection with rites, and have non-exclusion from the heritage."

" *Apúrvám* " *i. e.*, who had no previous husband ; the meaning according to the author of the Prakása is, one who was not even betrothed to another man : " who is ordained by the Sástras " *i. e.*, who is ceremoniously wedded according to the rites of marriage sacrament ; " with rites ", such as the establishment of the holy fire, and the like : " non-exclusion from the heritage"—the meaning is,—in their case only, the non-exclusion from the entire heritage should be made.

8. BAUDHA'YANA ordains:—" One begotten by a man himself on a lawfully wedded wife of equal class is known *aurasa*. Thus it is propounded in the scripture—" You are sprung from every limb, you are descended from the heart, you are one's own self, called by the name *puttra*, may you live for hundred autumns."

The PA'RIJA'TA (says):—" Wife of equal class," means, a twice-born wife for the twice-born, and a Súdra wife for a Súdra, not a Bráhmaní wife for a Bráhmana, nor a Kshatriyá wife for a Kshatriya ; otherwise, a son of a Kshatriyá woman married by a Bráhmana, could not be included under any of the twelve kinds of sons.

9. SANKHA and LIKHITA (say) :—" But a Bráhmana shall espouse a woman of the same class ; in her, the bodies of the ancestors are born again : let him address his own self in the person of his son ; thus it is said by ancient sages—" You are sprung from every limb &c," and—" Ancestors seize the infant fœtus, like a garland of lotus ; (and say) as a man's own self is here, so art thou reproduced : for the benefit conferred on the father and the mother, a man's own self (reproduced) is called *puttra* ; since thou deliverest from what is called *put*, hence thou art named *puttra*."

10. Thus in the VIVA'DA-RATNA'KARA, is finished the subject of the description of Aurasa son.

CHAPTER XVIII.

§ 1—Kshetraja or appointed wife's son. 2—He is second, or inferior to Aurasa. 2 to 5—Kshetraja, is a son begotten by a Sapinda, or a Sagotra, or a man of a superior caste, on the wife of a man who is dead, or impotent, or afflicted with incurable disease, by the appointment of the husband or elders. 6 to 11—When, he is son of two fathers.. 11 to 13—How, *pindas* offered by son of two fathers.

1. Now KSHETRAJA or appointed wife's son is described.

2. On this (subject) VASISHTHA (declares) after (describing) the *aurasa* son,—

" On failure of him, the Kshetraja son begotten on a woman appointed, is the second."

" Appointed ' *i. e.* either by the husband or by the elders in the family ; " the second " *i. e.* a little inferior to the Aurasa son.

3. VISHNU says,—" The Kshetraja son is the second, begotten on an appointed woman, by a Sapinda, or by a man of a superior class."

4. MANU ordains :—" He, who is begotten on the lawfully appointed bed of a man who is dead or impotent or afflicted with disease, is known as the Kshetraja son."

" Bed ", means, wife : " afflicted with disease ",—here disease is intended to be incurable ; " lawfully " *i. e.* in the mode of being sprinkled with clarified butter, &c..

5. YA'JNAVALKYA—" The Kshetraja son is one begotten on the wife, by a *sagotra* (*i. e.* member of the same *gotra*), or by any other."

" By a *sagotra* " *i. e.*, by a man born in one's own *kula* or family ; " by any other ", *i. e.*, by a man belonging to a superior tribe.

6. BAUDHA'YANA :—" He, who is begotten by another on the authorized wife of a man deceased or impotent or afflicted with disease : he alone is son of two fathers, belongs to two *gotras*, and becomes entitled to the obsequies and the heritage of both fathers."

"By another," *i. e.* by the brother-in-law or the like, who is destitute of (any other) male issue. In the compound word *dvi-pita*, the regular affix (*ka* as in Dvi-pitrika) is omitted, as the rule requiring it after compound words, is optional ; "belongs to two *gotras*" *i, e.*, becomes a member of the *gotras* of both fathers ; "obsequies" *i. e.*, rites in honour of paternal ancestors.

7. YA'JNAVALKYA—"When a son is begotten by a sonless man, on another's wife by appointment, he is pronounced the heir of both of them, and offers oblations to them."

When, however, the brother-in-law or the like, is himself the father of male issue, and is appointed to raise male issue for the owner of the soil (*i. e.*, the husband of the woman), then the son belongs to the owner of the soil, and not to the owner of the seed (or the progenitor).

Where, however, even one having a son, enters into a special contract in the shape of the following agreement, namely,—"A son begotten on this, woman shall belong to us both," there the son belongs to both even.

8. MANU (says,)—"The owners of the seed and of the soil, are found in this world, to be joint owners, of the produce, of what is given for the seed, with a special contract".

9. NA'RADA and KA'TYA'YANA (say),—"When one man's seed is sown in the soil of another, with his assent, the child is ordained to belong to those very owners of the seed and of the soil."

10. SANKHA and LIKHITA (say),—"ANGIRA's maintains, that the child belongs to him who performs the initiatory rite with sacred texts : USANA'S says, that the crop is divided into two, when the seed is sown with the assent of the owners of the seed and of the soil."

11. HA'RI'TA (says),—"When the husband is alive, the son is called *kshetraja*, by reason of want of independence ; when dead, the son is called Dvyámushyáyaṇa or son of two fathers, by reason of the seed being subsequently sown ; the soil does not bear fruit without seed, nor does the seed grow without soil, so both being seen (to be necessary for production,) the child belongs to both (the owners) : this is the opinion of some. The first *pinda* or funeral oblation, is for their progenitor ; in the ancestor-worship, two *pindas* should be offered, or in a single *pinda* the names of both (ancestors) should be pronounced : his son (shall pronounce two names) in the second *pinda* (offered to the paternal grandfather) ; his grandson (shall pronounce two names) in the third *pinda* (offered to the paternal great-grandfather) ; and while mentioning the three partakers of *lepa* (or remnant of oblations *i. e.* the three remoter ancestors, shall pronounce two names) up to the seventh degree : this is the opinion of others."

When the husband is alive, then a son born of the wife, though begotten by another person, belongs to the husband alone : the reason why, is,—"by reason of the want of independence" *i. e.* of the wife. When the husband is dead, then although the wife's want of independence remains unchanged, because it is laid down in the text—"A sonless widow preserving unsullied the bed of her husband &c." (Ch VIII. para 6),—yet a child born of the widow, is styled the Dvyámushyáyana son of both: the reason why, is,—"by reason of the seed being subsequently sown *i. e.*, in the field. Even in the case of a living husband, indeed, he is not the sower of the seed. The union of the effects of the two parties, is the cause of their offspring: this is stated by the words,—"the soil does not bear fruit without seed": "both," means, the owners of the seed and the soil. "In a single pinda the names of both," should be pronounced *i. e.*, in each oblation, two names should be pronounced, according to A'pastamba, who declares—"If a person be the son of two fathers, he must offer each *pinda* to two ancestors." "His son, in the second &c.", means, his son (shall pronounce two names) commencing from the second *pinda*. While pronouncing the names of the three partakers of *lepa* (remnant of oblations), shall mention two names (of two ancestors in each degree).

12. NA'RADA lays down:—"The sons of two fathers, shall separately offer, oblations of food and libations of water, to two (sets of ancestors), and shall likewise, get half from the heritage of the owner of the seed and the owner of the soil."

This text refers to a case, where the owner of the seed has a begotten son, and the owner of the soil, also has somehow an Aurasa son, subsequently born. But if both be destitute of other sons, he shall take the entire property of both.

13. BAUDHA'YANA (says):—"It is declared in the Scriptures: when a son of two fathers offers *pindas* (oblations of food) there shall be two names in each *pinda*, the three *pindas* shall belong to the six (ancestors). One doing so, is not mistaken."

"Is not mistaken," *i. e.*, guilty of any defect.

14. Here, in the VIVA'DA-RATNA'KARA, ends the chapter on the appointed wife's son.

CHAPTER XIX.

§ 1—Puttriká or appointed daughter, and her son. 2—Puttriká, third, comes back to her father, if there be no brother. 3 to 1—Described, she or her son is her father's son ; Puttriká may be made by express contract, or without the same, may be made mentally, or by force of her father being sonless ; this son succeeds to the legal father's property. 10—Puttriká inherits mother's Stridhana, and brother's estate. 11 to 15—Mode of making Puttriká, expressly. 16—Modes of making Puttriká. 17—How, Pindas offered.

1. Now, the appointed daughter, and her son, are described.

2. On that subject, VASISHTHA (says) :—"The appointed daughter is known as the third (description of son) : a brotherless daughter of a man, comes back to her fathers : having returned, (she) obtains the status of a son."

The meaning is :—the third description of son is the *Puttriká*, equal to the begotten son, by reason of her performing, his duties : "having returned, obtains the status of a son" *i. e.*, with respect to the father's line of ancestors.

3, SANKHA and LIKHITA (say) :—"The appointed daughter is similar to the son : this is the opinion of PRACHETAS. Her issue, the appointed daughter's son, is giver of funeral oblations to both the maternal grandfather and the paternal grandfather : there is no difference in this world between a son and a daughter's son, as regards benefit ; hence, by reason of doubt, a brotherless damsel shall not be espoused."

"Benefit", is, by deliverance from the infernal region called *put* : "by reason of doubt", in the shape, whether she has been constituted a son or not.

4. After describing the *aurasa* or begotten son, YA'JNAVALKYA (says) : "Equal to him, is the appointed daughter's son."

5. DEVALA (says) :—"Equal to him, is the appointed daughter's son, he becomes the heir of the sonless father and also maternal grandfather, like a son."

6. BAUDHA'YANA declares :—after premising "Another (description of son")—"is the daughter's son, born of the daughter after contract, and called the appointed daughter's son."

"A son born of a daughter after contract", means, after an agreement in the form that "the son that will be born of her, will be my son" : (he) is known (as) a son called the appointed daughter's son. The word "another" is to be taken in relation to the *aurasa* son. In the Kalpataru, the reading for 'अन्य' *i. e.*, "another" is 'अस्या', and the meaning of it is clear.

7. MANU ordains :—"The daughter's son takes the entire inheritance of the sonless father : the (appointed) daughter's son alone, shall take the entire property of a sonless person."

"Sonless", means, destitute of the *aurasa* (begotten) son. The PRAKA'SA says, the second half is a repetition of the (rule laid down in) the first half. Udayakara, in his commentary on Manu says, that this is a declaration of a rule with the reason for the same.

8. Having premised the *aurasa* or begotten son, DEVALA declares:— "Similar to him, is the appointed daughter's son; he becomes the heir; he alone shall give a *pinda* (funeral oblation) to the father and maternal grandfather. In this world, there is no distinction in law, between a son's son and a daughter's son; for their mother and father are sprung from his body. When a daughter, whether not made or made (appointed daughter expressly), gets a son from a husband of equal class, by him the maternal grandfather becomes the father of a son; he shall offer funeral oblation, and obtain the property."

Here the word daughter's son, means, the son of an appointed daughter, whether (expressly) made or not made.

9. With respect to the right of a daughter made (appointed daughter), VRIHASPATI declares:—"Just as her right arises to her father's property, even when *bandhus* (*sagotra* relatives) exist; similarly, her son also becomes owner of the mother's and maternal grandfather's property."

10. SANKHA and LIKHITA (say):—"The unmarried daughter gets the property of a woman: her son's property also, is received by the unmarried daughter alone."

Here, the word "her", refers to the mother of the unmarried daughter; the property of her son, who is born after the time (of appointing the daughter), and dies without bearing male issue, is received by the unmarried daughter alone, *i. e.* is received by the appointed daughter alone, by reason of her being equal to a uterine brother: this is the purport.

11. MANU declares:—"A sonless person shall make his daughter a Puttriká (appointed daughter) in the following manner: the son that may be born of her shall become performer of my *sráddha.*"

"Performer of my *sráddha*", means, performer of funeral obsequies and the like.

12. VASISHTHA ordains:—"To thee, I shall give this brotherless damsel, bedecked with ornaments; the son that may be born of her, shall be my son."

13. GAUTAMA ordains:—"A sonless father, after having worshipped Agni (fire) and Prajápati (lord of creatures), and having made an agreement,—that the son (born of her) shall be mine, shall give away (in marriage) an appionted daughter. Some are of opinion, that a daughter may be made *puttriká* by mere intention."

Having worshipped Agni aud Prajápati *i. e.*, having performed the A'gneyi and Prájápatya sacrifices. This fire-sacrifice prescribed in the Smriti, may refer even to a single description of sacred fire, and be performed in the domestic fire; and in default of the same, the worship only (of fire) may be made: this is said by HARIHARA. "By mere intention",—this recites what has previously been laid down.

14. VRIHASPATI declares,—" (An appointed daughter) is made, after having worshipped Agni, (the God of fire) and PRAJA'PATI (the lord of created beings): so GAUTAMA has ordained. Others, however, say that one thought of, becomes the appointed daughter of a sonless person."

" One thought of" *i. e.*, one intended in mind, in this manner,—that this daughter must be (my) appointed daughter.

15. VISHNU (says) :—" She becomes *putriká* or appointed daughter, who is given (away in marriage), by the father with this condition,— 'The son that may be born of her shall be my son.' A daughter becomes *putriká* or appointed daughter, when she is destitute of brother, even if she is not given in marriage in the mode prescribed for a *putriká*."

16. In the BRAHMA-PURA'NA (it is laid down),—" That damsel is known as an appointed daughter, who is made alike to a son by her sonless father, either in his mind, or in the presence of the king, fire, and relations, or any where else, before conception, or who is given to the bridegroom without taking the bride's price : such a daughter receives an equal share from the paternal share."

17. MANU ordains :—" The appointed daughter's son shall offer the first *pindá* or funeral oblation to the mother ; the second to her father ; and third, to the father of the father."

That is, (to the father of the father) of her.

18. Thus, in the VIVA'DA-RATNA'KARA, the subject of the appointed daughter and her son is finished.

CHAPTER XX.

§ 1—Twice-married woman's son. 2 to 5—Twice-married woman, and her son, described.

1. Now (is described), the son of the twice-married woman.

2. On that, VISHNU (says) :—" The fourth (description of son) is the twice-married woman's son."

3. MANU declares,—" He, that is produced by a woman abandoned by the husband or widowed, who remarries according to her own pleasure, is called, the son of a twice-married woman."

" Is produced " *i. e.*, from a man of an equal caste ; " remarries ", means, causes herself to be married by another man.

4. YA'JNAVALKYA ordains,—"A son born of a (twice-married) woman, whether there was consummation or not, of her marriage with the first husband, is the twice-married woman's son."

5. KA'TYA'YANA declares,—"When a woman espouses another husband, after having forsaken an impotent or degraded husband ; the son born of her, is the twice-married woman's son ; it is clear that the son belongs to the progenitor."

6. Thus, in the VIVA'DA-RATNA'KARA, is finished the subject of the twice-married woman's son.

CHAPTER XXI.

§ 1—Maiden's son. 2—He is described, he becomes his maternal grandfather's son. 3—He is described. 4 and 5—When, he becomes his mother's husband's son.

1. Now (is deseribed), the maiden-born son.

2. On that subject, VASISHTHA (says) :—" The maiden-born son is the fifth : the ancient sages ordain :—He, whom a damsel, herself unmarried, produces from sexual appetite in her father's house, becomes his maternal grandfather's son, under the name of Kánína or maiden-born,—and they quote on this subject (this text),—When an unmarried daughter produces a son, by a man of equal class, by that son the maternal grandfather becomes the father of male issue ; he shall offer funeral oblation and get the property."

3. BAUDHA'YANA declares :—" If a man approaches a damsel who is not initiated, or who is not fully parted with ; a son born of her is maiden-born."

" Who is not initiated ", *i. e.*, on whom the sacrament of marriage has not been performed ; " who is not fully parted with " *i. e.*, who is not given away (un-betrothed.)

4. In the BRAHMA-PURA'NA (it is said) :—" But a son begotten by a man of equal class, on a damsel not given away, in her father's house, is maiden-born son : that son belongs to him, to whom she is given (in marriage.)"

5. NA'RADA declares,—" A maiden-born son, a son born of a pregnant bride, and one who is born of a married woman secretly : the husband of the mother is known, their father : they again are ordained to be entitled to shares."

" A son born of a pregnant bride ", is one, who was in the womb of a bride, at the time of marriage, and is born afterwards."

The PA'RIJA'TA (says) :—If, however, the maternal grandfather is sonless, then the maiden-born son and the pregnant bride's son become his son ; but if he is father of a son, then they belong to their mother's husband, and to both, if both be destitute of male issue.

6. Thus, in the VIVA'DA'-RATNA'KARA, is finished, the subject of the maiden born son.

CHAPTER XXII.

§ 1—Secretly born son of the wife. 2 and 3—He is described, his status when the procreator doubted to belong to inferior caste.

1. Now, the secretly-born son, (is described).

2. On that, VISHNU (says) :—" The secretly-born son is the sixth this son belongs to him, of whose bed he is born."

3. MANU ordains :—" When a son is born in the house, but it is not known, by whom he is begotten, he is called secretly born in the house, and belongs to him, of whose bed he is born."

" Born of bed ", means, born of wife : when the owner of the seed is not known, he belongs to the mother's caste ; this is so, in the absence of any doubt, with respect to the coition being with a man of an inferior caste ; in case of such doubt, the son is, as if born (of a superior woman and inferior man married) in the inverse order of castes, and unfit for performing funeral obsequies.

4. Thus, in the VIVA'DA-RATNA'KARA, (is finished), the subject of the secretly-born son.

CHAPTER XXIII.

§ 1—Pregnant bride's son. 2 and 3—He is described, he belongs to his mother's husband, sacred rite of marriage inapplicable to his mother's marriage.

1. Now, the son of the pregnant bride, is described.

2. On that subject, VISHNU declares :—" The son of the pregnant bride is the seventh ; he is the son of a woman who is initiated (*i. e.*, married) when pregnant ; the son belongs to the husband."

The author of the Prakása condemns the (performance of the) initiatory sacrament (of marriage) for a pregnant woman, putting her forward as a virgin, as it is declared (by MANU),—" The sacred texts relating to marriage rite, are applied to virgins alone ;"—and then states, by way of conclusion, that others are of opinion, that the performance of the initiatory sacrament of re-marriage in the form prescribed in the ATHARVA-VEDA, is found in the scripture.

But, in reality, the term " is initiated", intends the sacrament consisting of HOMA and the like rite, other than the sacrament caused by the sacred texts relating to marriage.

3. MANU ordains,—"When a bride with child, is espoused, whether known or unknown to be so, that child belongs to the husband, and is called the son of the pregnant bride."

4. Thus, in the VIVA'DA-RATNA'KARA, is finished, the subject of the pregnant bride's son.

CHAPTER XXIV.

§ 1 – Dattaka or given son. 2 to 4—He is described ; parents may give ; connection with natural father's Gotra and estate, ceases ; why, parents may give ; gift of only son ; gift and acceptance by woman ; mode of adoption ; when doubt about caste of the boy.

1. Now, the Dattaka or given son, is described.

2. On that subject VISHNU (says) :—"The Dattaka or given son is the eighth ; he (belongs to him) to whom he is given, by the mother or the father."

"Belongs to him", is understood.

3. MANU ordains :—"That son who is equal (in caste), and affectionate, and whom the mother or the father give with water, in distress, is known as the Dattrima or given son. Whose *given* son is endowed with all good qualities, his estate shall be taken by that son though received from a different *gotra* or family. The given son shall not get the *gotra* or family, and estate of his progenitor ; the *pinda* or funeral oblation follows the family and the estate, (therefore) the giver's *swadhá* or funeral oblation (which would have been offered by that son, if not given away in adoption), ceases."

"In distress" *i. e.*, in default of son of the adopter ; "equal" *i. e.* equal in caste ; Medhátithi, however, says, that "equal", is not equal in caste, but in virtues suitable for the family ; "affectionate" *i. e.*, devoid of fear and the like ; "good qualities" *i. e.*, caste, learning, and conduct ; although right to the estate follows from the very status of son, still the declaration (of it) in the passage "whose given son, is endowed &c.", is intended for the receipt of a share by the given son who is endowed with good qualities, when an *aurasa* or begotten son is subsequently born, and for the receipt of maintenance only by one, devoid of good qualities ; *gotra*, such as Kásyapa, descended from a *rishi* or patriarch, is well known. The offering of funeral oblation also ceases, since by the general rule, it follows the family and the estate ; the word *swadhá*, means, Sráddha and the like.

4. VASISTHA ordains,—"A son springing from the virile seed and uterine blood, is an effect, whereof the mother and the father are the causes ; the mother and the father (therefore,) are competent to give,

or sell, or abandon him. But an only son shall not be given or taken, for he is designed for the lineage of ancestors. But a woman shall not give or accept without the permission of the husband. A person about to adopt a son, shall invite the relations, shall inform the king, shall perform the burnt sacrifice (accompanied) with Vyáhritis within the house, and then accept one, whose relations are near, or even one, whose relations are not near : if a doubt arises, one whose relations are at a distant place, should be placed as a Sudra ; since it is well-known, that many are saved by one."

Like gift, sale and abandonment also shall not be made. Sale takes place, at a time of distress, and abandonment, in case of inability to maintain. The Prakása says, that in case of extinction of lineage, there is great defect, as funeral oblation, libation of water, and performance of obsequial rites, cease. Both the father and the mother have severally the right to give. There is, however, this distinction, that when the father is alive, the mother may give with his permission, and even without it, when he is not alive ; "shall invite his relations", *i. e.*, shall call together his kinsmen for the allotment of share to the (Dattaka) or given son. "Shall accept one whose relations are near", *i. e.*, whose maternal uncle and the like relations are near : this is for receiving information, about name and caste and the like : in the absence of his relations, "even one whose relations are not near', (may be accepted), after having been satisfied in respect of name and Gotra, from other strong evidence : "if a doubt arises" *i. e.*, about his being a Bráhmana and the like, in the mind of one who has somehow adopted a boy whose relations are distant ; then he "shall be placed as a Súdra" *i. e.*, as a son by a Súdrá woman, by making him entitled to maintenance only. "Many are saved by one", because many ancestors are saved by only a single son, therefore such a boy alone should be taken, about whose caste and the like there is no doubt.

Thus ends in the VIVA'DA-RATNA'KARA, the Chapter on the given son.

CHAPTER XXV.

§ 1—Purchased son. 2 to 4—He is described ; his caste.

1. Now, the purchased son, is described.

2. On that, VISHNU (says) :—"The purchased is the nineth."

3. BAUDHA'YANA declares :—" He, who is taken for sonship, from the hands of the mother and the father or either of them, is the purchased son."

4. MANU ordains :—" He who is purchased from the mother and the father, for sonship, is the purchased son, whether his equal or unequal."

The PA'RIJA'TA (says) :—" Equal", means, of the same class : in his default, " unequal " *i. e.*, one not of the same class. But the author of the Prakása says, that although there is the word " unequal " in the text, still a man of the inferior caste, shall not take one of a superior caste for sonship, nor shall a man of a superior caste, take one of an inferior caste for sonship, as regards the words " equal " and " unequal " Medhátithi says, they have reference to quality amongst those of the same caste.

5. Here ends in the VIVA'DA-RATNA'KARA, the subject of the purchased son.

CHAPTER XXVI.

§ 1—Self-given son. 2 & 3—He is described ; he must be destitute of father and mother, or abandoned by them.

1. Now, is described, the self-given son.

2. On that, VISHNU (says) :—" The tenth description of son is one, who comes of his own accord : he belongs (to him), to whom he comes."

" To him ", is to be added to complete the sense.

3. MANU ordains :—" He who is destitute of the mother and the father, or who is abandoned without any cause, and who delivers himself (in adoption), is ordained the self-given son."

" Without any cause " *i. e.*, without any guilt : " delivers himself " *i. e.*, gives himself in adoption, by declaring that " I become your son."

4. Thus ends in the VIVA'DA-RATNA'KARA, the Chapter on the son who comes of his own accord.

CHAPTER XXVII.

§ 1—Deserted son. 2 to 5—He is described ; he must be deserted by the parents, or by either of them—by reason of poverty or guilt.

1. Now, is described, the deserted son.

2. On that, VISHNU (says):—" The deserted son is the eleventh, he is one deserted by the mother or the father, and is accepted by a person, (whose son he becomes.")

" Whose son he becomes ", should be added to the text for completing the sense.

3. MANU ordains :—" He who is deserted by the mother and the father, or by either of them, and is accepted as a son, is ordained the deserted son."

" Deserted" *i. e.*, abandoned. Abandonment is made, by reason of inability to maintain on account of extreme poverty, or by reason of some fault. The acceptance again must be made as a son, and not merely with the desire of saving life.

4. VASISHTHA declares :—" The deserted son is the fifth : who is deserted by the mother and the father, and is accepted for sonship."

The declaration of his being the fifth, is made, by counting him as the fifth in the second set of six.

5. Thus, in the VIVA'DA-RATNA'KARA, ends, the Chapter on the deserted son.

CHAPTER XXVIII.

§ 1—Kritrima or son made. 2 to 4—He is described. 5—Sons belonging to the same caste, preferable ; caste of some sons, how determined.

1. Now, is described, the Krittrima son or son made.

2. On that, MANU ordains :—" When one who is equal, who is able to discriminate between merit and fault, and who is endowed with the qualities of a son, is made a son ; he is known as the Krittrima son or the son made."

MEDHA'TITHI (says):—Here also, " equal ", means, equal in quality : " who is able to discriminate between merit and fault " ; *i. e.*, discriminate that there is merit in the performance of the funeral ceremony of the mother and the father, and fault in non-performance ; " endowed with the qualities of a son", *i. e.*, with a desire to serve, and the like.

3. BAUDHA'YANA ordains :—" One, who being equal and desirous, is made a son, is the Kritrima son, or son made."

" Desirous," means, having the desire, *i. e.*, thinking in his mind that— " I shall become this person's son, if he will accept me for sonship" : " equal," *i. e.*, one of the same class.

4. On this subject, YA'JNAVALKYA (says) :—" Kritrima is one who is himself made a son."

5. Likewise, he says :—" This rule declared by me, relates to sons of the same class, (if there be a son of the same class. ")

" If there be a son of the 'same class", is to be added to the text, for completing the sense. The maiden's son, the secret-born son, the son of the pregnant bride, and the son by a twice-married woman, are deemed to be of equal class, through their procreators, but not in their own character, by reason of their not being within the definition of the status of belonging to a Varna or one of the four primitive classes, or belonging to a Játi or a mixed class : this is said in the Prakása.

6. Thus, in the VIVA'DA-RATNA'KARA, is finished, the subject of the son made.

CHAPTER XXIX.

§ 1—Son by a Sudra woman. 2 & 3—He is one begotten on a Sudra woman married or not. 4 & 5—Pársava. 6—Principal sons, and substitutes of son. 7—Aurasa and Putriká are principal sons, the rest substitutes. 8—12—Brahma-purána on sons of persons of different castes.

1. Now, is described, the son by a Sudra woman.

2. On that subject, VISHNU (says) :—" The twelvth description of son, is one begotten on any woman."

" On any woman," means, on a Sudra woman, whether married or not married (by the father).

3. VASISHTHA declares :—" They say, that the son by a Sudra woman, is the sixth."

Here also, his being the sixth, has reference to the second set of six : he is certainly the twelvth, in relation to the *aurasa* or begotten son. " They say," here, indicates dispute, and that has reference to the right to take the heritage : for, Manu has declared this, including the son by the Sudra woman. Hence, the applicability of both rules is, according to the possession or want of good qualities.

4. MANU (says) :—The son, whom a Bráhmana begets on a Sudra woman, through passion, is ordained Párasava, because, he is a corpse though fulfilling his duty."

"Fulfilling his duty," *i. e.*, confering trifling benefit on the person considered as his father; he is even as a corpse, because the benefit is inconsiderable.

5. BAUDHA'YANA declares:—"The son, begotten on a Sudra woman by a Bráhmana, is a *Párasava*".

6. On this subject, MANU (says):—"The eleven descriptions of sons beginning with the Kshetraja or the appointed wife's son as described above, are, by the wise, called substitutes for the son, for (fear of) non-compliance with the rite. All these sons begotten from the manhood of others, who have been described while dealing with the subject of sons, belong to him from whose manhood they are sprung, and not to any other."

"Substitutes for the son,"—means, substitutes for the *aurasa* and the appointed daughter's sons: since, in their default, they are declared, to be performers of their duty, according to Vrihaspati's text to be cited hereafter. The reason of this is: "for non-compliance, *i. e*,. for fear of non-compliance with the rite, that is, with the ordinance,—"son must be produced." This ordinance is imperative, and it must somehow be given effect to: hence, in the second text, it is shewn by the prohibition of their being the principal sons, by the portion—"belong to him from whose manhood they are sprung,"—that they are only substitutes: "not to any other," indicates, that the status of being a principal son cannot be extended (to the secondary sons.)

7. VRIHASPATI ordains:—"Of the thirteen descriptions of sons that have been described by Manu in succession, the *aurasa* or begotten son and the Puttriká or the appointed daughter are the causes of lineage; as oil is substituted, by the wise, for clarified butter, so are the eleven descriptions of sons, in default of the *aurasa* and the Puttriká."

8. It is declared in the BRAHMA-PURA'NA:—"The given son, the self-given son, the son made, the purchased son, and the deserted son shall always be maintained: they belong to a different *gotra* (primitive stock), their funeral oblation is separate, they perpetuate a different lineage, they are liable to pollution for three days, on occasions of birth and death, among the relations of the adoptive father who gives food and raiment, as well as of the natural father who is the owner of the soil and the seed."

By this, their liability to pollution for three days, has been declared, as a matter arising in connection,

9. Likewise, (it is declared in the BRAHMA-PURA'NA):—"Bráhmanas have rarely a *párasava* son of the servile Sudra class: but persons of the royal class, who are labouring under a curse, and are gradually dying out, and are always engaged in warfare, have sometimes these descriptions of sons."

By this is removed the doubt as to the inadmissibility of these descriptions of sons, (among twice born classes.)

10. Likewise, it is declared in the BRAHMA-PURA'NA:—"If there be either the *aurasa* or begotten son, or the appointed 'daughter-son, then

their, (other) eleven descriptions of sons, beginning with the Kshetraja or wife's son, being of a different *gotra*, are known to be mere perpetuators of the lineage; all of them perform, like slaves, their Sráddhas on specified occasions.'

The term appointed daughter-son, means, the appointed daughter herself as son. The eleven descriptions of sons, beginning with the Kshetraja, are the sons other than the *aurasa* or begotten son and the *puttriká* or appointed daughter. The construction is, that if there be an Aurasa or Puttriká, then the wife's son, and the like, are perpetuators of the lineage only. "Like slaves," that is, in the same manner in which slaves have to perform.

11. Likewise (it is declared in the BRAHMA-PURA'NA):—The secret-born son, the maiden-born son, the pregnant bride's son, the appointed wife's son, and the twice-married woman's son, these five are prohibited to the Vaisyas, for fear of punishment from the king: the wealthy Vaisyas may have all the rest."

By this also, has been declared, the admissibility of the secondary sons of a Vaisya. Thus, the admissibility of the secondary sons has been declared for the Bráhmana, the Kshatriya, and the Vaisya.

12. It is next declared that, in the case of a Sudra owned by his master, the procreation of a son by himself, is rare:—

"Of the Sudras, whose occupation is slavery, who depend for livelihood on others, and whose person is under the control of others, there can be no son anywhere."

Then, in answer to the question, cannot a son be born from a slave? it is declared;—

"Therefore, from a male slave and a female slave, a slave only is born."

"A slave only," that is, a son owned by the master, "is born"; but in no mode of affiliation can the son be independent of the master: this is the meaning.

13. Thus, in the VIVA'DA-RATNA'KARA, is finished, the subject of the son by a Sudrá woman.

CHAPTER XXX.

§ 1—Discussion of sonship. 2—Question is, whether son belongs to the owner of the seed, or to the owner of the soil. 3—Son belongs to the owner of seed, for spiritual purpose. 4 to 7—Son belongs to owner of soil. 8—Such is thec ase, in the absence of agreement to the contrary. 9 to 11—Same rule applies to crops and lower animals. 12—Such son, not heir. 13—Of sons begotten by appointment. 14 to 16—Sons belong to both, by agreement. 17—Adoption by such son, of family usages, and offer of *pinda* by him.

1. Now, is set forth, the discussion of sonship.

2. On that subject, VASISHTHA (says):—"They dispute, whether the son belongs to the owner of the soil, or the son belongs to the progenitor."

3. A'PASTAMBA declares:—"Without being careless, preserve this lineage; (so that) another's seed may not scatter in the soil: the son belongs to the progenitor. For spiritual purpose, the cultivator makes this lineage useless."

"Without being careless," *i. e.* without being guilty of carelessness: "lineage," means, the series beginning with the son and the grandson: and "another's seed may not scatter" *i. e.*, be sown, "in the soil." The son belongs to the progenitor, *i. e.*, becomes benefactor of the owner of the seed. "For spiritual purpose" *i. e.*, for the purposes of the next world: "useless," *i. e.*, infructuous.

4. "Those versed in ancient law, recite a text on this subject ordained by Váyu:—No man should sow his seed in the wife of another: just as the arrow of one, hitting a game in the wound (made by another's arrow), becomes useless, so the seed scattered in the wife of another, is lost."

"The arrow of a person hitting a game in the wound, made by another's arrow, becomes useless", *i. e.*, the game is declared to belong to the first hitter alone.

5. "The wise pronounce, that a man is this much only, namely,—that he is, his wife and his progeny and himself; and likewise this, that a woman is ordained wife and husband."

Just as the wife, the self and the progeny, these three are called the man; similarly, the husband and the wife, these two, are called the woman.

6. One man's wife, even if purchased, cannot be the wife of another man also, hence it is declared, to remove the doubt that, a woman, if sold or abandoned by her husband, may become the wife of another man:—

"A wife cannot be severed from the husband by redemption or abandonment."

"Redemption", is here sale, and "abandonment" is desertion.

7. Likewise, (MANU says):—"As in the case of a cow, a she-camel, a female slave, a she-goat, an ewe and a she-buffalo, so in the case of wives of others, the progenitor does not become entitled to the progeny. The owners of the seed sowing in another's soil, do no-where get the

benefit of the crop produced, but the owners of the soil get the same. If a bull procreates a hundred calves on another's cows, the calves belong to the owner of the cows alone, the seed of the bull becomes useless. In the same manner, the seed of one who is not the owner of the soil, but who sows in another's soil, causes the fruit to belong to the owner of the soil; the owner of the seed, does not get the fruit."

8. This very matter is specially laid down thus:—" Where the owners of the soil and the owners of the seed, have not come to any agreement in respect of the fruit, then visibly the fruit belongs to the owner of the soil, because the soil is superior to the seed."

The meaning is, that where there are not the owner of the soil and the owner of the seed, the crop belongs to the owner of the soil, and not to the owner of the seed.

9. The very same thing is clearly stated :—" When a seed carried away by flood or wind, sprouts up in another man's soil, that should be known to belong to the owner of the soil alone : the owner of the seed does not get the fruit."

The meaning is, that in the same manner, with respect to also the subject in question, the superiority belongs to the wife. "Flood", is, flowing water: "carried", is, brought.

10. The subject is concluded (by the same sage),—" This rule should be known to apply to the progeny of cows, mares, female slaves, she-camels, she-goats, ewes, birds, and she-buffaloes."

" This rule ",—namely, that the owner of the seed is not entitled to the fruit.

11. SANKHA & LIKHITA declare:—" That seed which is scattered, without the knowledge of the owner of the soil, belongs only to the owner of the soil."

12. GAUTAMA declares :—" The son begotten by one person, in the wife of another man, is not entitled to participate."

13. With respect to the law of appointment (for raising issue on another man's wife), GAUTAMA (says) :—" Not exceeding two ; the child belongs to the progenitor : without agreement : belongs to the living husband, (being born) in the soil : (if maintenance received) from the stranger, then his : by reason of maintenance, belongs to the husband alone : or belongs to both."

" Not exceeding two ", means, that in appointment, the man appointed shall not procreate any more sons, after the second. " The child belongs to the progenitor ", means, that if he does procreate, the child belongs to him : " without agreement ", means, that if there be agreement, the child may belong to either or both ; without agreement, the child belongs to the soil. " Belongs to the living husband (if born) in the soil ", means, the son that is born in the soil, that is, in the wife of a living husband, who is incapable of procreation, belongs, even if third, to the owner of the soil, even without agreement : (" if maintenance received) from the stranger, then his ", means, that if however the stranger *i*, e., the owner of the seed, maintains the woman, then the first child belongs only to him : "by reason of the maintenance, belongs to the husband", means,—if however the husband himself maintains (the woman), then the child belongs to him alone. "Or belongs to both", means, that where both are desirous of having a child, then the said child belongs to both.

14. NA'RADA declares :—"There cannot be a crop without soil, nor can it be without seed, hence the child is found to lawfully belong to both the father and the mother."

15. SANKHA and LIKHITA (say) :—"It is the maxim of the Scripture, that the child does certainly belong to the soil : some saints say, the child belongs to the mother ; the son of two fathers, pronounces."

"The son of two fathers, pronounces", that is, he pronounces the names of two fathers in a single *pinda* (funeral oblation).

16. An instance is mentioned :—"Of VASISHTHA and KA'SHYAPA standing in water, one comes out of the water, and procreates a child unknown to the people."

"One", *i. e.*, either begets in the soil of the other. What follows from it ? is thus declared :—

"Thus the child belongs to them equally."

17. Another special rule is declared :—"Because, sons begotten in the soil of another, offer *pinda* (funeral oblation) and water, also (to the procreator) after offering to one : and take the heritage, and adopt the family religious usages."

"Adopt" *i. e.*, accept, that is, perform the family religious usages. "Sons begotten even in the soil of another", shall offer *pinda* and water also to the procreator, after offering to the one, *i. e.*, to the husband of the mother.

18. Thus, in the VIVA'DA-RATNA'KARA, ends, the Chapter on the discussion of sonship.

CHAPTER XXXI.

§ 1—Extension of sonship. 2 & 3—Sonship of fraternal nephew, and f co-wife's son. 4—Some are of opinion that when these exist, other substitutes of son should not be made.

1. Now, is described, the extension of sonship.

2. On that subject, MANU (says):—"Of brothers born of the same (parents), if one has a son, then all of them become by that son, fathers of male issue: this was declared by MANU. If among all the wives of the same man, one brings forth a son, then all of them become by that son, mother of male issue: so MANU has ordained."

3. VRIHASPATI declares:—"If there are many uterine brothers begotten by the same father, then a son being born to any one of them, all of them are ordained fathers of sons. The very same rule applies to many wives of the same person, if one is mother of a son, he is the giver of *pinda* to all of them."

4. With respect to the passage,—"all of them become by that son &c.", ASAHA'YA says, that, when men have a brother's son, and women a co-wife's son, then the appointed wife's son and the like substitutes of son should not be made. The PA'RIJA'TA also says the same thing and so UDAYAKARA in his commentary on Manu.

5. Thus, in the VIVA'DA-RATNA'KARA, ends, the Chapter on the extension of sonship.

CHAPTER XXXII.

§ 1—Etymology of the word Puttra—son. 2 to 4—Puttra is derived from *put* an infernal region, and from *tra* to protect, meaning 'saviour from *put*'. 5 and 6—On birth of son, father is exonerated from debt of ancestors. 7—Virtuous son saves ancestors. 8.—Superiority of first-born son, for spiritual purposes. 9 and 20—Son, grandson, and greatgrandson, means of heaven. 11 and 12—Son, means for heaven, there is no heavenly region for sonless man. 13—Many sons are desirable for spiritual purpose.

1. Now, are stated, the etymological explanation and the like of the word Puttra (son).

2. On that subject, MANU and VISHNU (say):—"Because a son saves the father from the infernal region called *put*, therefore he is called *puttra*, by the self-existent himself."

3. HA'RI'TA declares:—"An infernal region, of the name of *put*, is declared; and one whose lineage is extinct, is liable to go to the infernal region; and because he saves from it, therefore he is ordained Puttra."

4. VRIHASPATI ordains:—"Because, the father is saved by the son, from the infernal region called *put*, by even seeing the face; therefore he should try for the birth of a son. Son's son, and an appointed daughter's son, are both means of attainment of heaven, and are proclaimed equal, with respect to the heritage, and to the presentation of Pindas."

5. MANU and VASISHTHA (say):—"If a father sees the face of a son born living, he transfers his debt to him and attains immortality."

6. SANKHA, LIKHITA and PAITHI'NASI (say):—"A father is delighted by a son, on whatever woman begotten; by that giver of *pindas* to ancestry, he becomes exonerated from his own debts."

7. HA'RI'TA (says):—"A son who is pure, competent, religious in youth, and the controller of his own faults, saves the ancestors."

8. SANKHA and LIKHITA (say):—"The sacrificial fire, the three Vedas, sacrifices in which hundred gold coins are paid to the officiating priest as his fees, are not equal to a sixteenth part of the birth of the eldest son. A man who has many sons, and whose sons and grandsons are worthy, and who is not wanting in the performance of the sacrifices prescribed in the Veda, has the heaven in his hands, even when living."

9, SANKHA, LIKHITA, VISHNU, VASISHTHA and HA'RI'TA (say):—"By a son, a man conquers the worlds; by a son's son, he attains immortality; and by a son's son's son, he attains the region of the sun."

10. YA'JNAVALKYA (says):—"Because, continuation of lineage in this world, and attainment of heaven, are, through son, grandson and great-grandson; therefore, women should be enjoyed, and made well-guarded."

11. VASISHTHA declares:—"It is ordained in the Scripture, that infinite are the heavenly regions, for a man having son; but there is no heavenly region, for a sonless man: let the eaters be childless,"

"Let the eaters", *i. e.*, those that are given to eating *i. e.*, the demons, "be childless" *i. e.*, sonless. The purport is, that it is a great injury, which suggests the idea of demons. The extinction of the lineage of the enemy, is his greatest destruction, hence the same is desired.

12. Another text (says):—"May I hereafter attain to, immortality, by means of progeny"

The intention is, that I may attain to immortality by means of progeny *i. e.*, sons. The author of the Prakása says, that the former curse refers to the enemy, and the latter in the form of blessing, refers to one's ownself.

13. Likewise,—"The son's son and the appointed daughter's son, are both means for the attainment of bliss; they are equal in respect of *pinda*—oblation of food, and libation of water. By a sonless person, should a son be made, by any means, for the purpose of oblation of food, libation of water, and funeral rite, as well as for the perpetuation of name. The ancestors fearing fall into the infernal regions, are anxious for many sons; any one of them, who will go to Gaya, shall save us: they shall perform the *sráddh* accompanied by the gift of a bull, perform the *sráddh* at Gaya, shall perform sacrifices and charities, shall maintain

us in the old age, and shall offer Sráddha every day. Just as a man crossing water with a bad raft, is drowned ; similarly by a bad son, a father falls into the dark regions of hell."

14. Thus, in the VIVA'DA-RATNA'KARA, ends, the chapter on the etymological explanation of the word Puttra (son).

CHAPTER XXXIII.

§ 1—Reprehensible sons. 2—Son begotten on woman not appointed, and one begotten by husband's brother on woman having son, are censured. 3—Son unlawfully begotten even on woman appointed. 4—Son begotten by any other when there is husband's brother. 5 to 7—Sons unlawfully begotten on another's wife. 8—Two sons begotten on a woman by two men, get their respective father's property.

1. Now, are discussed, the reprehensible sons.

2. On that subject, MANU (says):—" A son of a woman not appointed, a son begotten by the husband's brother on a woman having son, both these begotten by a paramour, and begotten through passion, (respectively), are not entitled to any share."

" Son of a woman not appointed," is one, who is begotten after the death of the husband on a woman, without the permission of her venerable protector : " share," *i. e.*, a share of the heritage of the owner of the soil : this also includes the presentation of funeral oblation &c. This refers to a son begotten on a woman obtained on payment of price, according to NA'RADA's text hereinafter cited.

3. Likewise :—" A son unlawfully begotten on a woman, who was even appointed, is not entitled to the paternal heritage, since he is to be deemed to be begotten by an outcaste."

" Unlawfully, " *i. e.*, contrary to the rule prescribed for appointment.

4. GAUTAMA (says):—" A son begotten by any other, when there is the husband's younger brother, is not entitled to a share."

If the husband's younger brother is living, then a son begotten by any other man, is not entitled to a share.

5. NA'RADA (says) :—" Those that are begotten on an un-appointed woman by one or many, are not entitled to the heritage (of the owner of the soil) : all of them become sons, only of the owners of the seed. They shall give oblations to the owner of the seed, if their mother had been received on payment of Sulka, but if she was approached, without payment of Sulka, then they become giver of *pinda* to her husband only."

" Un-appointed woman, " is an incontinent woman : "are not entitled to the heritage," *i. e.* they do not get the heritage of the owner of the soil. The author of the Prakása, however, says that, they do not get the heritage of the mother, the mother's husband, and the maternal grandfather.

6. Is he to offer *pinda* without any distinction ? It is said in answer :—"They are to offer *pinda* to the owner of the seed, if their mother was obtained by the payment of Sulka."

If the mother was obtained, by the owner of the seed, on payment of price to the owner of the soil. Hence, the passage—"but if she was approached without payment of Sulka &c.,"—(§ 5) is reasonable.

7. NA'RADA again says, while dealing with twice-married and incontinent women :—"Sons begotten on a woman, who has been obtained on payment of Sulka, belongs to the progenitor, but if she is approached without the payment of Sulka, the fruit belongs, only to the owner of the soil."

8. MANU (says):—"When two sons of a woman, begotten by two persons, dispute with respect to property, of them, each should take, what belonged to his father, and not the other."

The PA'RIJA'TA (says):—The term woman here, means, one other than, a prostitute, a twice-married woman, and an incontinent woman.

9. Here ends, in the VIVA'DA-RATNA'KARA, the chapter on the reprehensible sons.

CHAPTER XXXIV.

§ 1—Participation of, or Succession to, estate of a sonless man. 2—Son born of widow by appointment. 3 & 4—Widow's succession. 5 to 7—Daughter's succession. 8 & 9—Succession of mother, and father's mother. 10—Brother's succession. 11—Order of succession according to Manu. 12 & 13—Same according to Paithínasi and Devala. 14—Same according to Yájnavalkya. 15—Vishnu. 16—Vrihaspati. 17—A'pastamba. 18—Baudháyana. 18—Nárada. 20 to 23—Bráhmana's property does not go to King. 24 to 27—King shall protect infant's property. 28—Or relatives protect the same. 29 to 32—Heir shall perform Sráddhas for deceased proprietor : Son must offer Pinda, even when he gets no property. 33 & 34—Heirs of persons belonging to religious orders.

1. Now is discussed, the participation of, (or succession to), the property of a sonless person.

2. On that subject, MANU (says):—"(The widow) of a deceased sonless person, shall procure a son from a man, belonging to the same Gotra, and to him shall hand over all the estate that there may be."

The widow of a deceased sonless person, shall cause a son to be begotten (on herself), by a person belonging to the same Gotra *i. e.*, either by the husband's brother or by a Sapinda, and shall give to him all the estate, which was the subject of the ownership of her deceased husband, and not take the same herself. This is said in the Párijáta, but the author of the Prakása says, that the king himself shall procure a son, through a person belonging to the same Gotra, and give (the estate) to him. But here, there is no distinction as to the result.

3. The senior MANU ordains:—"The sonless widow herself, keeping unsullied the bed of her husband, and practising austerities, shall offer *pinda* to him, and shall take the whole property."

"Sonless," means, destitute of the twelve descriptions of sons: "practising austerities" *i, e.*, ascetic observances prescribed for a widow.

4. VRIHASPATI (says):—"In the Scripture, and in the codes of law, as well as in popular practice, a wife is declared by the wise, to be half the body of her husband, equally sharing the fruit of pure and impure acts. Of him, whose wife is not deceased, half the body survives: how then should another take his property, while half his body is alive. Let the wife of a deceased sonless man, take his share, notwithstanding kinsmen, the father, the mother, or a uterine brother. be present: dying before her husband, a wife devoted to the husband, partakes of his consecrated fire: or if her husband be dead (before her, she partakes of) his wealth. This is the ever-existing law. Having taken his moveable and immoveable property, his gold and silver, grains, carriage and clothes, she shall duly cause (herself) to offer his monthly, half-yearly and other funeral repasts. With presents to his *manes*, and by pious liberality, she shall honour the paternal uncle of her husband, his *guru*, (*i. e.*, elderly relation), his daughter's sons, sister's sons, and maternal uncles, and also old and helpless persons, guests and females."

Some say, that the widow can perform even the Párvana-Sráddha, in order to prohibit the same, the Sráddhas (which may be performed by her) are enumerated by the term monthly, six-monthly and other funeral repasts. Here by the term "monthly," is expressed, the twelve monthly Sráddhas. By the term "six monthly," is meant, the two Sráddhas performed on the days previous to the performance of the sixth monthly and the twelvth monthly Sráddhas. By the term "other" is included the Sráddha to be performed on the eleventh day, and the Sapindí-karana-Sráddha, and the Sráddha to be performed every year on the anniversary of the day of death. Hence, (she) shall not perform any other Sráddha, otherwise this text would be meaningless, as these Sráddhas have been prescribed by other texts. "Devoted to the husband," means, chaste. Likewise, the causal form, in the term "cause to offer," is used in a reflexive sense *i. e.*, to indicate that she shall cause herself to offer; just as in the sentence,—Ráma caused (himself) to reign. Udayakara however, in his commentary on Manu's Code, says, that the word "devoted to the husband," has been used, with the intention of expressing its primary sense, hence as devotion to the husband must end with concremation (with the deceased husband's body), therefore "cause to offer," must mean, cause *another* to offer. In this way however, widows who may be endowed with good qualities, other than devotion to the husband in the above sense, would not be entitled to inherit, but this is not approved by many. Thus, when there is the chaste wife living, she is entitled to the estate of a sonless person.

5. NA'RADA declares that in her default, the daughter if alive, is entitled :—

"On failure of male issue, the daughter inherits, for she is equally a cause of perpetuating the race, since both the son and the daughter are the means of prolonging the father's line."

6. MANU declares :—"The son of a man is even as himself, and the daughter is equal to the son, how then can any other inherit his property, notwithstanding the survival of her, who is as it were himself."

7. On this subject, VRIHASPATI (says):—"Of men, the daughter like the son, springs from every limb, how can another man take her father's property ? A daughter of equal class married to a person of equal class, who is chaste and devoted to obedience, gets the sonless father's property, whether appointed or not."

8. VRIHASPATI further (says):—"The mother, or by her permission the brother, is known to take the estate of her son, who is dead, without leaving a widow or a son."

"By her permission," means, by the mother's permission.

9. On that subject, MANU (says):—"The mother shall take the heritage of her sonless son, and when the mother too is dead, the father's mother shall take the estate."

Here the term "sonless," is intended to express, the absense of son, widow, and the like : the succession of the father's mother, is to be understood to take place, in default of the father, the brother and the like. Because, in default of the mother, the succession of the father and the like, is settled. "Heritage," means, property receivable by an heir.

10. GAUTAMA (says):—"The share of a deceased person, not re-united, belongs to the eldest brother."

The meaning is, that if amongst brothers who are separated, but not re-united, one dies, without issue, his share belongs to the eldest brother only : this also is to be understood to apply, in default of the widow, the mother and the father.

11. MANU declares:—"The father or the brother, of a sonless person shall take the heritage : libations of water should be made for three, and for three are ordained the funeral oblations of food : the fourth is the giver of them : the fifth has no concern with them. To the nearest Sapinda the inheritance next belongs : after them, the Sákulya or a person belonging to the same family, or the preceptor, or the pupil, becomes the heir."

"Sonless," means, destitute of primary and secondary sons ; "nearest," means, the most proximate. "Inheritance" *i. e.*, the inheritance of the sonless person. The word "Sakulya," here means the Samánodaka.

12. PAITHI'NASI declares :—"The property of a sonless person goes to the brother, in his default the mother and the father get : or the inferior wife, or a Sagotra, a pupil, or a fellow student."

"Inferior," means, one who performs in a small degree, the austerities enjoined to a widow, other than devotion to the husband ; and not one, who performs them in their entirety ; for she is preferable to the brother, as regards succession to the husband's estate ; nor one who is unchaste, for she is liable to be banished. As for mere maintenance declared by Sankha in the text,—"Maintenance shall be allowed to his wives until death ; provided they preserve unsullied the bed of their husbands : but it shall be resumed, if they act otherwise,"—that refers only to unchaste women, who are devoid of the austerities prescribed for widows. As for the succession of the parents when there are brothers, declared by Yájnavalkya in the text—" the parents and brothers likewise, "—that refers to property acquired by the father, the paternal grandfather and the like. But what is acquired, without detriment to paternal property, belongs to brothers alone, when parents exist.

13. DEVALA declares,—" Then the uterine brothers shall divide the heritage of a sonless person, or the equal daughters, or the surviving father ; brothers of the same caste, the mother and the widow, according to the order ; in their default, those belonging to the same *kula* or family living together, shall take."

" Equal," means, equal in class ; " the surviving father " *i. e.*, if he be desirous (of enjoying property :) apprehending a conflict (of authorities) here, Haláyudha avoids it by saying that " according to the order " means, according to the order propounded by Yájnavalkya and the like ; and premising that this is the principle of the Sástras here, he has also written that the succession of persons beginning with the widow and ending in the learned Bráhmana, applies to the estate of a sonless Bráhmana, and that ending in the King applies to the estate of a sonless person other than the Bráhmana ; and having regard to this, words in the text of Sankha and Likhita, also, must be construed together, though separated by other words. That the order of succession given in the texts of Yájnavalkya and Vishnu, is to apply to the text of Devala, which does not give the order, appears to be intended by the author of the Kalpataru, who has cited the text of Yájnavalkya and Vishnu after quoting the text of Devala.

But in reality the part of Paithínasi's text which lays down, that " the property of a sonless deceased person goes to the brother," refers to property other than what is acquired by the father, the paternal grandfather and the like ; and so also the part, " in his default the parents take :" as regards the remaining portion (of that text,) certainly no order is found ; so there is no conflict.

14. YA'JNAVALKYA ordains :—" The widow (Patni) and daughters also, the parents, brothers likewise, their son, an agnate, a cognate, a pupil, a fellow student : in default of the first among these, the next in order is entitled to the estate of a sonless person departing for heaven : this rule applies to all classes."

The meaning is that, among the widow, the daughter, the mother, the father, the brother, his son, an agnate, a cognate, a pupil and a fellow student, in default of each preceding one, the next in order becomes heir.

The word Patní or the widow here, intends a wife endowed with excellent virtue.

Here, by sonlessness is intended the absence of son's son and son's son's son also ; this explanation is given by the author of the Prakása ; and this is also reasonable, being supported by usage.

Although the joint succession (of the parents) appears, at the first sight, by reason of the joint mention in the term "parents" (in Yájnavalkya's text,) yet as the text (§ 8) "The mother is known to be the heir of her deceased son, destitute of widow and son,"—shows the succession of the mother in default of widow and son ; therefore, the father's succession in default of the mother, is shown by this text.

15. VISHNU ordains :—"The property of a sonless man goes to the widow ; in her default, it goes to the daughter ; on failure of her, it goes to the mother ; in her default, it goes to the father ; in his default, it goes to the brother ; on failure of him, it goes to the brother's son ; in his absence, it goes to a *bandhu* (*i. e.*, Sapinda) ; on his default, it goes to a Sakulya, on failure of him, it goes to a fellow student ; in his default, it goes to the king ; excepting the property of a Bráhmana."

Here, the term *Bandhu*, means Sapinda ; and the *Sakulya*, a Sagotra : this is said by Misra.

16. VRIHASPATI declares (the heirs) after the daughter and the daughter's son :—"In his default, the uterine brothers, the brothers son, the Sákulyas, the Bándhavas, the pupils, and the learned Bráhmanas are entitled to the property. If the deceased be devoid of issue and wife, and devoid of brother, father and mother, then the Sapindas that are equal (in degree) shall divide according to due share, his estate consisting of the half of his collected wealth ; half of it shall be carefully set apart for the monthly, the six-monthly and the annual Sráddha. When there are many *gnatis* (Sápindas,) Sakulyas and Bándhavas, he who is the nearest among them, shall take the estate of a sonless person."

The locative case in the words monthly &c., has been used to indicate the object.

17. Refering to a sonless person, A'PASTAMBA (says) :—"In default of the son, the nearest Sapinda ; on failure of him, the preceptor ; in his default the pupil, or his daughter being appointed, shall employ (his property) for his good."

18. BAUDHA'YANA (says) :—"The paternal greatgrandfather, the paternal grandfather, the father, the man himself, the uterine brothers, and a son, a son's son and a son's son's son born of a woman of the same class : these partaking of undivided heritage are called Sapindas ; those partaking of divided heritage are called Sákulyas : if there are not issue of the body, the property goes to them (Sapindas and Sákulyas) in default of the Sapinda, the Sakulya ; on failure of him also, the preceptor or the priest takes ; in his default the King."

This definition refers to inheritance ; but it does not refer to pollution on deaths and births of relations, and the like : as regards these (*i. e.*, pollution &c.), those that are of the same *pinda* (or body), are Sapindas ;

and take the share of one that is born, and of one that is dead, respectively."

But the property of a deceased re-united person, a re-united relation takes, but not the (ordinary) heir: but a uterine brother shall take the property of a uterine brother: "but of a uterine brother, a uterine brother," means, that when a uterine brother and a half brother are (both) re-united, then the uterine brother alone shall take.

10. Now is stated what takes place on the death of a re-united person, when there are a uterine brother not re-united, and a re-united half brother.

"But the half brother who is re-united, shall take the property, but not a half brother (even if not re-united) : but the united (through the same mother) though not reunited shall take, not a half brother (though re-united)."

The construction of the text is, that a half brother who is not re-united shall not take the property. By this, the re-union of the half brother is declared to be the cause of inheritance, because inheritance and non-inheritance depends upon its existence or non-existence respectively: but the word "re-united" should not be construed also with what follows; hence, even one not re-united, takes the property; then, in answer to the question who is he ? it is declared, the united *i. e.*, sprung from the same virile seed and uterine blood, *i. e.*, the uterine brother; hence, being a uterine brother though not re-united, is declared by this to be the cause of inheritance; hence, as both (that is, being re-united, and being uterine brother) are the causes of inheritance, therefore even both of them are declared to be takers of the property. If the reading be, as in the Kalpataru, namely,—"shall not take the property of a half brother," the meaning would be the same. The meaning is, the property of a re-united half brother, shall not be taken by a re-united half brother (alone). Others however approve of the plain meaning, namely,—but a re-united half brother shall not take the property of a half brother.

11. KA'TYA'YANA (says) :—" Of the re-united however, the re-united, and of the separated the separated, are known to become heirs in default (of the widow and the like) : each takes the share of the other, if sonless."

The re-united are heirs, of the deceased re-united coparceners : those who are separated, are known to become heirs of deceased separated coparceners, "in default" means, in default of the widowed wife and the like.

12. VRIHASPATI declares :—" He, who being separated, lives together, through affection, with the father, or a brother, or a paternal uncle, is called the re-united."

The term "or" indicates that there is no force in the enumeration, hence a person who lives together after separetion even with any other co-heir, such as a paternal uncle's son, becomes re-united and is recognised as such in all places. In the Prakása, however, it is said, that here, there is a restriction by force of the enumeration.

13. Thus, in the VIVA'DA-RATNA'KARA, is finished, the chapter on partition and succession in respect of the property of a re-united co-heir.

CHAPTER XXXVI.

§ 1.—Determination of disputed partition. 2 to 5—Partition is proved by writing, by agnate and cognate relations or other witnesses, as wel' as by various facts and circumstances raising presumption of separation.

1. Now, is discussed the determination, of (disputed) partition.

2. NA'RADA (says) on this subject :—"If there be a doubt with respect to the status of partition among co-heirs, the determination (is to be made) by means of agnates, by a deed of partition, and from engagement in separate transactions. Amongst undivided brethren religious ceremonies are common : in case of separation their religious ceremonies are different ; of the separated co-parceners, the gift, the acceptance, the cattle, the food, the house, the fields, and acquisitions, and cooking, and religious ceremonies and income and expenditure, are known to be different. Separated brethren, and not brothers who are undivided, can become witness, or surety for each other, or make gifts to, and acceptance from, each other. Those, amongst whom these transactions are separately made, are presumed to be separate even without writing."

"If there be a doubt with respect to the status of partition" *i. e.*, in the shape whether a partition has been made or no, "amongst the co-heirs:" "the determination" is to be made by means of agnates: "deed of partition," means, a deed shewing partition: "engagement in separate transaction," *i. e.*, by means of engagement in separate transactions such as income, expenditure, and the like: "religious ceremonies," *i. e.*, the group of ceremonies beginning with that in honour of the Vishwadevas: "income," *i. e.*, receipt of wealth, "expenditure," parting with wealth. The purport is, that this sloka will apply, if (the fact of partition is) not otherwise made out.

3. YA'JNAVALKYA (says) :—"In case of denial of partition, partition is known to be made out by agnates, cognates, witnesses, and writing, and by separate houses and fields."

4. Likewise :—"It is ordained, that among brethren, between husband and wife, between father and son, there cannot be surety-ship, the relation of debtor and creditor, and the giving of evidence, when they are joint."

The word "mutually" is to be added to the text. Although A'pastamba says that there is no partition between husband and wife, still, because in some case, partition between husband and wife is shewn by Yájnavalkya in the passage—"if the shares are made equal, the wives should be made equal sharers,"—this text of Yájnavalkya is to be understood to intend such partition : thus there is no conflict.

5. VRIHASPATI (aays) :—"Those, who have separate income, expenditure and wealth, who carry on money-lending and trade severally, are separate from each other."

"Severally" *i. e.*, without association *i. e.*, independently of each other. The word "separate" in the expression "separate income, expenditure and wealth" is to be construed with all.

6. Thus, in the VIVA'DA-RATNA'KARA, is finished the chapter on determination of (disputed) partition.

CHAPTER XXXVII.

§ 1—Rights and duties of separated co-heirs. 2 and 3.—They may deal with their shares independently of each other, subject to certain restrictions set forth in the chapter on Non-delivery of Gifts. 4.—After enjoyment of a share allotted on partition, no dispute can be raised about it.

1. Now, are discussed the rights and duties of separated (kinsmen).

2. On that subject, NA'RADA declares :—"If many born of the same person, whose religious ceremonies are different, whose transactions are different, and whose occupations and qualities are different, be not unanimous as to what is to be done."

By the expression "if many born of the same person," are intended those born of a common male ancestor : "whose religious ceremonies are different," *i. e.*, who perform the (five) great sacrifices and the like, separately from each other : "whose transactions are different," *i. e.*, whose professions such as money-lending and the like are separate : "whose occupations and qualities are different," *i. e.*, who are separately occupied (Kshatriyas) in the protection of subjects, (Vaisyas) in agriculture, (Sudras) in service and the like : "be not unanimous as to what is to be done," means, can not act together.

3. The consequence of what has been premised in the above Sloka, is (thus) declared :—"They may give away or sell their shares, they may do all that, according to their pleasure, for they are the masters of their own wealth."

Here the term "all" should be limited, having regard to other texts.

There are many limiting texts of Vrihaspati and other sages, in the Chapter (of this work) relating to (the action called) Non-delivery of Gifts, such as—"Co-heirs joint or separated are equal with respect to immoveables : for, one is incompetent in all cases, to make a gift, a mortgage, or a sale ;"—and these texts may be seen there.

4. VRIHASPATI declares :—"If a particular share has been enjoyed by one, his that (share) shall not be altered : if one who has made an amicable partition raises a dispute again ; he shall be maintained by the king in (possession of) his own share, and shall be punished, should he persist."

If a particular share has been enjoyed by one who has made an amicable partition, that alone is his share, and it shall not be altered :— this has been declared, for the purpose of (securing) certainty, by the latter part of the text.

5. Thus, in the VIVA'DA-RATNA'KARA is finished, the subject of rights and liabilities of separated members.

विवादरत्नाकरे

दायभागः ।

विवादरत्नाकरे

दायभागः

CHAPTER I.

(1) अथ दायभागः। (2) तत्सङ्गतौ मनुः। एष स्त्रीपुंसयोरुक्तो धर्म्मो वो रतिसंहितः। आपद्यपत्यप्राप्तिश्च दायभागं निबोधत॥ (3) नारदः। विभागोऽर्थस्य पित्र्यस्य पुत्रैर्यत्र प्रकल्पते। दायभाग इति प्रोक्तं तद्विवादपदं बुधैः॥ यत्र यस्मिन् व्यवहारपदे, प्रकल्पते क्रियते। (4) मनुः। ऊर्द्ध्वं पितुश्च मातुश्च समेत्य भ्रातरः समम्। भजेरन् पैतृकं रिक्थम् अनीशास्ते हि जीवतोः॥ समं तुल्यं, नात्र विंशोद्धारादीति यावत्। ननु प्रमीतपितृकविभाग एव मनुना विंशोद्धारादीनां कथनात् कथं सममिति चेत्, न, तस्य गुणवज्ज्येष्ठादिविषयत्वात्। उदयकरस्तु सममिति कृतोद्धारधनाभिप्रायमिति व्याख्यातवान्। हलायुध-पारिजाताभ्यान्तु सममिति स्थाने सहेति पठितं, व्याख्यातञ्च पारिजातेन, सह परस्परम्। पैतृकमित्यत्र एकशेषं कृत्वा तद्धितप्रत्ययः, तेन मातृधनस्यापि ग्रहणमिति हलायुधः। पैतृकमित्युपादानेऽपि पैतामहादिधनमपि विवक्षितम्, द्रव्ये पितामहोपात्ते इत्यादि-वाक्येन तत्रापि भागस्य बोधनादित्यपरे। द्वयमपि चेदं विवक्षितं, परन्तु भूतपूर्व्वगत्या मातृधने तु दुहितृतदन्वयाभावे पुत्रभागान्वय इति बोद्धव्यम्। (5) देवलः। पितर्य्युपरते पुत्रा विभजेयुर्धनं पितुः। अस्वाम्यं हि भवेदेषां निर्द्दोषे पितरि स्थिते॥ निर्द्दोषे पातित्यादिदोषरहिते। (6) नारदः। पितर्य्यूर्द्ध्वं गते पुत्रा विभजेयुर्धनं पितुः। मातुर्दुहितरोऽभावे दुहितॄणां तदन्वयः॥ मातुर्धनं दुहितरो विभजेरन्, दुहितॄणामभावे तदन्वयो दुहित्रन्वयो विभजेदित्यर्थः। पितर्य्यूर्द्ध्वं गते इत्येतावतैव विभागे सिद्धे पुत्रग्रहणं क्षेत्रजादीनामप्यवबोधार्थं, ततश्च द्वादशपुत्राणामन्यतरस्मिन्नपि विद्यमाने नान्यस्य धनभाक्त्वं, पितुरिति वचनं भ्रातॄणां मध्ये यद्येकस्य विद्याधनादि विभजेत्, तदा तस्य विभागो नास्तीति बोधनार्थम्,

दुहितुः सान्निध्यात्तत्पदेन तस्या एव परामर्शौचित्यात्। लक्ष्मीधरस्वरसोऽप्येवम्। प्रकाशपारिजातौ तु तदन्वयो दुहित्रन्वयः पुत्रपौत्रादिरित्याहतुः। (7) शङ्खलिखितौ। अत ऊर्द्ध्वं मृक्थभागो न जीवति पितरि पुत्रा ऋक्थं विभजेरन्, यद्यपि स्यात्पश्चादधिगतं तैरनर्हा एव पुत्राः॥ अर्थधर्म्मयोरस्वातन्त्र्यात्पितरि निर्द्दोषे, पश्चादधिगतं पितृनिरपेक्षैः पुत्रैः समर्थैर्विद्यादिभिर्मिलित्वा अर्ज्जितम्। (8) अथ मनुः। ज्येष्ठ एव तु गृह्णीयात्पित्र्यं धनमशेषतः। शेषास्तमुपजीवेयुर्यथैव पितरं तथा॥ ज्येष्ठेन जातमात्रेण पुत्री भवति मानवः। पितॄणामनृणश्चैव स तस्मात्सर्व्वमर्हति॥ यस्मिन्नृणं सन्नयति येन चानन्त्यमश्नुते। स एव धर्म्मजः पुत्रः कामजानितरान्विदुः॥ पितेव पालयेत्पुत्राञ्ज्येष्ठो भ्रातॄन्यवीयसः। पुत्रवच्चापि वर्त्तेरञ्ज्येष्ठभ्रातरि धर्म्मतः॥ ज्येष्ठः कुलं वर्द्धयति विनाशयति वा पुनः। ज्येष्ठः पूज्यतमो लोके ज्येष्ठः सद्भिरगर्हितः॥ यो ज्येष्ठो ज्येष्ठवृत्तिः स्यान्मातेव स पितेव सः। अज्येष्ठवृत्तिर्यस्तु स्यात् स संपूज्यस्तु बन्धुवत्॥ (9) तथा। न चादत्त्वा कनिष्ठेभ्यो ज्येष्ठः कुर्व्वीत यौतकम्॥ ज्येष्ठएव तु गृह्णीयादिति सकलज्येष्ठगुणवाञ्ज्येष्ठो विभाज्यपितृधने पितृवत्स्वतन्त्रः स्यात् इत्यर्थः। तमुपजीवेयुस्तत्कृतवृत्त्या वर्त्तेरन्। पुत्रीभवति कृतापत्योत्पत्तिशास्त्रार्थो भवतीत्यर्थः। मात्रग्रहणान्न संस्कारापेक्षा। अनृणः, त्रिभिरृणैरृणवाञ्जायते इति श्रुत्या यदृणत्रयं बोधितं, तत्रैकस्मादुत्तीर्णो भवतीत्यर्थः। सन्नयति सङ्गमयति। आनन्त्यं सुखानां, तेनानन्तं सुखमित्यर्थः, अश्नुते प्राप्नोति ऋणमुक्तः सन्नित्यर्थः। कामजानित्यर्थवादमात्रम्। कनीयसां भागबोधनेन भागाभावाबोधकत्वात्। पितेव पालयेत्, न तु विप्रलभेत। पुत्रवच्चापि वर्त्तेरन्, न तत्र द्वेषं कुर्य्युरित्यर्थः। कुलं वर्द्धयति, सम्यग्व्यापारेण कनिष्ठपरिपालनेन कुलवृद्धिः। विनाशयतीति योग्यतामात्रम्। ज्येष्ठस्य वृत्तिः, स्नेहेन कनीयसां भरणपालनादि। बन्धुवत् प्रत्युत्थानाभिवादनैर्मातुलादिवत् पूजनीयो नावज्ञाचरणेन। यौतकं, तेभ्यः पृथक्कृत्य कल्पितं द्रव्यं, मिश्रणे अमिश्रणे च युधातुपाठात्। हलायुधस्तु यौतकं भार्य्यालङ्कारादीत्याह। (10) नारदः। बिभृयाद्वेच्छतः सर्व्वाञ्ज्येष्ठोभ्राता यथा पिता। भ्राता शक्तः कनिष्ठो वा शक्त्यपेक्षा कुले स्थितिः॥ (11) शङ्खलिखितौ। कामं वसेयुरेकतः संहता वृद्धिमाचक्षीरन्॥ संहता अन्योन्यालम्बनतया वृद्धिमाचक्षीरन् वृद्धिं स्फुटां कुर्व्वीरन्, वृद्धियुक्ता भवन्तीति यावत्। (12) मनुः। एवं सह वसेयुर्वा पृथग्वा धर्म्मकाम्यया। पृथग्विवर्द्धते धर्म्मस्तस्माद्धर्म्म्या पृथक्क्रिया॥ पृथगित्यादि, मध्यगधनस्य स्वेच्छया अविनियोज्यत्वात् निरपेक्षस्वत्वास्पदद्रव्य-साध्य-यागाद्य-

नुष्ठानाभावात् तत्सिद्धयर्थोऽयं न्यायप्राप्तो विभाग उच्यते। पृथग्वा धर्म्मकाम्ययेति, न पुनः, अविभागादधर्म्मः कलञ्जभक्षणादिवत्, विभागाच्च धर्म्मो ज्योतिष्टोमादिवदिति। (13) वृहस्पतिः। एकपाकेन वसतां पितृदेवद्विजार्च्चनम्। एकं भवेत्, विभक्तानां तदेव स्याद्गृहे गृहे॥ एकपाकेनेत्यत्राविभागे सतीति विवक्षितम्। (14) हारीतः। जीवति पितरि पुत्राणामर्थादानविसर्गाक्षेपेषु न स्वातन्त्र्यं, कामदाने प्रोषिते चार्त्तिं गते वा ज्येष्ठ एवार्थांश्चिन्तयेत्॥ अर्थादानं पितृनैरपेक्ष्येण साधारणधनग्रहणम्, अर्थार्जनमिति पारिजातः। विसर्गो दानं, आक्षेपः ऋणिकहस्तात्तद्धनग्रहणम्। कामदाने काममात्रादेवार्थदातरि। प्रकाशकारेण तु कामं दीने इति पठित्वा काममिति सन्निहितपित्रनुज्ञामाहेति, दीने विक्षिप्ते इति विवृतम्। (15) शङ्खलिखितौ। पितर्य्यशक्ते कुटुम्बस्य व्यवहारं ज्येष्ठः कुर्य्यादनन्तरो वा कार्य्यज्ञस्तदनुमतेन, नत्वकामे पितरि ऋक्थभागो, वृद्धे विपरीतचेतसि दीर्घरोगिणि वा ज्येष्ठएव पितृवदर्थान् पालयेदितरेषां, ऋक्थमूलं हि कुटुम्बम्, अस्वतन्त्राः पितृमन्तो मातर्य्यप्येवमवस्थितायाम्॥ अनन्तरोऽनुजः, तदनुमतेन ज्येष्ठानुज्ञया, विपरीतचेतसि वातादिदोषेण भ्रान्तचेतसि, ऋक्थमूलं धनमूलं कुटुम्बं कुटुम्बभरणम्, अस्वतन्त्रा दानाद्यनधिकारिणः, मातर्य्येवं गुणवत्यां जीवन्त्याम् अस्वतन्त्राः पुत्रा इत्यन्वयः। (16) इति विवादरत्नाकरे दायभागतरङ्गः।

CHAPTER II.

(1) अथ जीवत्पितृकविभागः। (2) तत्र मनुविष्णू। पैतृकन्तु पिता द्रव्यमनवाप्यं यदाप्नुयात्। न तत् पुत्रैर्भजेत्सार्द्धम् अकामः स्वयमर्जितम्॥ पैतृकं पितृक्रमागतम्, अनवाप्यं पित्रा आप्तुमशक्यं, न तत् पुत्रैः समम् अनिच्छन् विभजेत् स्वयमर्जितत्वात्। (3) याज्ञवल्क्यः। भूर्या पितामहोपात्ता निबन्धो द्रव्यमेव वा। तत्र स्यात्सदृशं स्वाम्यं पितुः पुत्रस्य चोभयोः॥ निबध्यते इति निबन्धः आकरादौ नियतं लभ्यं, सदृशं स्वाम्यं, नात्रांशाधिक्यं नवा पितुरिच्छया दानम्। (4) व्यासः। क्रमागते गृहक्षेत्रे पिता पुत्राः समांशिनः। पैतृके न विभागार्हाः सुताः पितुरनिच्छतः॥ (5) वृहस्पतिः। द्रव्ये पितामहोपात्ते स्थावरे जङ्गमे तथा। सममंशित्वमाख्यातं पितुः पुत्रस्य चैव हि॥ पैतामहं हृतं

पित्रा स्वशक्त्या यदुपार्ज्जितम् । विद्याशौर्य्यादिनाप्तञ्च तत्र स्वाम्यं पितुः स्मृतम् ॥ प्रदानं स्वेच्छया कुर्य्याद्भागञ्चैव ततो धनात् । तदभावे तु तनयाः समांशाः सम्प्रकीर्त्तिताः ॥ हृतं, परैरपहृतं यत् अशक्त्या पितामहेन नोद्धृतं, स्वशक्त्या च पित्रोद्धृतं तत्, विद्याशौर्य्यादिनाप्तञ्च, पितैव कुर्य्यादित्यर्थः । (6) अथ पुत्रा विभजेरन्नित्यधिकारे नारदः । मातुर्निवृत्ते रजसि प्रत्तासु भगिनीषु च । निवृत्ते वापि रमणे पितर्य्युपरतस्पृहे ॥ प्रत्तासु विवाहितासु, निवृत्ते रमणे रतिसामर्थ्ये निवृत्ते, उपरतस्पृहे विषयस्पृहाविच्छेदवति, प्रकाशे तु निरपेक्षे च रमणे, निरस्ते चापि रमणे इति पाठद्वयं वाक्यभेदपुरस्कारेण लिखितम्, तदपि तदीयार्थव्याख्यानेन फलतोऽविरुद्धम् । हलायुधस्तु रमणादिति पठितवान्, तत्रापि फलाविशेष एव । (7) बृहस्पतिः । पित्रोरभावे भ्रातॄणां विभागः संप्रदर्शितः । मातुर्निवृत्ते रजसि जीवतोरपि शस्यते ॥ अत्रापि निवृत्ते चापीति विवक्षितम् । (8) गौतमः । ऊर्द्ध्वं पितुः पुत्रा ऋक्‌थं विभजेरन् निवृत्ते रजसि मातुर्जीवति पितरि चेच्छति ॥ (9) शङ्खलिखितौ । जीवति वा पितरि ऋक्‌थभागोऽनुमतः प्रकाशं वा मिथो वा धर्म्मतः ॥ अनुमतः पित्रनुमतः, प्रकाशं मध्यस्थसमक्षं, मिथस्तदसमक्षम् । (10) बौधायनः । पितुरनुमत्या दायविभागः ॥ (11) अथ हारीतः । जीवन्नेव वा विभज्य वनमाश्रयेत्, वृद्धाश्रमं वा गच्छेत्, स्वल्पेन वा संविभज्य भूयिष्ठमादाय वसेत् यद्युपदश्येत् पुनस्तेभ्यो गृह्णीयात्, क्षीणांश्च विभजेत् ॥ वनमाश्रयेत्, आश्रमान्तरं परिगृह्णीयात् । वेदसन्न्यासित्वेन पुत्रैश्वर्य्ये वासो वृद्धाश्रम इति प्रकाशकारः । वृद्धाश्रमः, चतुर्थाश्रम इति हलायुधपारिजातौ, तन्मते वनमाश्रयेदित्यनेन वानप्रस्थाश्रममाश्रयेदिति विवक्षितम् । वस्तुतस्तु वाकारोऽनास्थायाम्, तेन वनगमनवृद्धाश्रमगमनत्वाभिमतादन्योऽपि स्थितिप्रकारोलभ्यते, तत्र वा वसेत् । वस्तुतो वेदसन्न्यासी गृहस्थाश्रममेव स्वातन्त्र्येण वाञ्छति, तं प्रति स्वल्पेनेत्यादि बोद्धव्यम् । उपदश्येदुपक्षीयेत । (12) अत्र नारदः । पितैव वा स्वयं पुत्रान्विभजेद्वयसि स्थितः । ज्येष्ठं वा श्रेष्ठभागेन यथा वास्य मतिर्भवेत् ॥ वाशब्दोविकल्पार्थः, पिता वा पुत्रा वा विभजेयुः । वयसि स्थितः, पूर्व्वविशेषेण न हीनतया असमर्थ इत्यर्थः । अतएव गौतमः, विभक्तजः पित्र्यमेवेति,—विभागोत्तरकालं पुत्रोत्पत्तौ विभागमाह । श्रेष्ठः प्रशस्ततमोऽधिक इत्यर्थः । यथा वास्य पितुर्मतिर्भवति समाधिकभागेषु, तथा विभजेत् । (13) विष्णुः । पिता चेत् पुत्रान् विभजेत्, तस्य स्वेच्छा स्वयमुपात्तेऽर्थे ॥ पितृ:ऽव्यानुपश्लेषार्जितधनविषयमेतत् । (14) याज्ञवल्क्यः । विभागञ्चेत्पिता कुर्य्यात् स्वेच्छया

विभजेत्सुतान्। ज्येष्ठं वा श्रेष्ठभागेन सर्व्वे वा स्युः समांशिनः॥ एतदपि स्वार्जितधनविषयं, पूर्व्वपुरुषार्जिते पितापुत्रयोः समांशित्वाभिधानात्। (15) अत्रैव समं विभागमाश्रित्य विशेषमाह। यदि कुर्य्यात्समानंशान् पत्न्यः कार्य्याः समांशिकाः। न दत्तं स्त्रीधनं यासां भर्त्रा वा श्वशुरेण वा॥ यदि पिता पुत्रान् समांशान् कुर्य्यात्, तदा स्वपत्न्योऽपि समांशिकाः कार्य्याः। एवञ्च पुत्राणां विषमांशपक्षे पत्न्योऽपि विषमांशा बोद्धव्याः, न तु पुत्रादिपत्न्यः, पितुर्विभाजकत्वात् तत्प्रातियोगिकपत्नीत्वस्यैवावगमात्। यदि तु कस्याश्चित् पत्न्याः भर्त्रा श्वशुरेण वा धनं न दत्तं, तदा ता अपि तावद्धनवत्यः कार्य्या इत्यर्थः। अत्र पत्नीनामपुत्राणामपीति हलायुधः। दत्ते स्त्रीधने अर्द्धं वक्ष्यतीति प्रकाशः। (16) नारदः। द्वावंशौ प्रतिपद्येत विभजन् आत्मनः पिता॥ प्रतिपद्येत लभेत, विभजन् विभागं कुर्व्वाणः। (17) बृहस्पतिः। जीवद्विभागी तु पिता गृह्णीतांशद्वयं स्वयम्॥ एतच्च शङ्खपर्य्यालोचनया एकपुत्रत्वे द्रष्टव्यम्। (18) तथाच पित्रधिकारे शङ्खलिखितौ। स यद्येकपुत्रः स्यात्, द्वौ भागावात्मनः कुर्य्यात्, द्विपदचतुष्पदेषु रूपमधिकम्॥ रूपमधिकमिति, वस्तुस्वरूपमधिकं गृहीत्वा अंशद्वयं गृह्णीयादित्यर्थः। (19) तथा। वृषभो ज्येष्ठाय, गृहं यवीयसे, अन्यच्च पितुरवस्थानात्॥ अस्यार्थः। नानापुत्रवत्त्वे ज्येष्ठकनिष्ठयोर्गुणवत्त्वे ज्येष्ठाय वृषभो दातव्यः, गृहं कनिष्ठाय, पितुरनिच्छयापि, अन्यथा नियमानर्थक्यापत्तेः। यत्तु याज्ञवल्क्येन, सर्व्वे वा स्युः समांशिनः, इत्युक्तं, तत्सर्व्वेषां तुल्यरूपत्त्वे पितुरिच्छया समांशित्वं न्यूनाधिकांशित्वञ्चेत्यविरोध इति हलायुधः। पारिजातस्तु एकपुत्रः ज्येष्ठपुत्र इत्याह। भाष्यकारस्तु पुत्रशब्दं न पठितवान्, यद्येकाकी स्यादिति पठितवान्, यद्येकाकी पत्नीविरहितोऽपि स्यात् तदाप्यंशद्वयं गृह्णीयात्, सपत्नीकश्चेत् तामप्यपरेणांशेन तोषयेत्। रूपमधिकं, द्विपदचतुष्पदमध्ये एकम् अंशद्वयाधिकं गृह्णीयात्, ज्येष्ठयवीयसोर्गुणवत्त्वे चासावधिकविधिः पितुरनिच्छयापि, अन्यथा नियमानर्थक्यापत्तेः, याज्ञवल्क्योक्तसमांशित्वञ्च सर्व्वेषां गुणवत्त्वेन। उत्कर्षाभावे पितुरिच्छया समांशित्वं न्यूनाधिकांशित्वञ्चेत्यविरोध इत्याह। अन्यत्रेति पितृवासगृहवर्ज्जमित्यर्थः। (20) बौधायनः। पुत्रेभ्यो दायं विभजेदिति श्रुतिः, समः सर्व्वेषामविशेषात्, वरं वा रूपमुद्धरेज्ज्येष्ठः, तस्मात् ज्येष्ठं पुत्रं धनेन निरवसाययन्तीति श्रुतिः, दशानां वैकमुद्धरेत् ज्येष्ठः, समम् इतरे विभजेरन्॥ वरं वा रूपमुद्धरेज्ज्येष्ठः, यावन्ति वस्तूनि तेषु एकं वरं गृह्णीयाज्ज्येष्ठ इत्यर्थः। अत्र श्रुतिं हेतुमाह तस्मादित्यादि, ज्येष्ठं पुत्रं

धनेनोद्धरणलक्षणेन, निरवसायन्ति इतरपुत्रेभ्यः पृथक् कुर्व्वन्ति, पश्चान्तरं दशानां वेति दशानां गवादीनां सजातीयानां एकमुद्धरेत्पितुरनिच्छयापि, सोऽयं विकल्पो ज्येष्ठगुणतारतम्याद्व्यवस्थितः। (21) आपस्तम्बः। एकधनेन ज्येष्ठं तोषयित्वा जीवन् पुत्रेभ्यो विभजेत्समं, क्लीवमुन्मत्तं पतितं परिहाप्य॥ जीवन्नेव यः प्रजोत्पत्तावसमर्थ इत्यर्थः। एकधनेन उत्कृष्टाश्वादिना, क्लीवमित्यादिना द्विभागानधिकारिणः सर्व्वएवाभिमताः। ज्येष्ठवित्ताल्पत्व-भूयस्त्वापेक्षया गुणाधिक्ये सति मन्तव्यमिति व्यवस्था। (22) अत्र मनुः। भ्रातॄणामविभक्तानां यद्युत्थानं भवेत्सह। न तत्र विषमं भागं पिता दद्यात् कथञ्चन॥ उत्थानं धनार्जनानुकूलव्यापारः। (23) नारद-बृहस्पति-याज्ञवल्क्याः। समन्यूनाधिका भागाः पित्रा येषां प्रकल्पिताः। तथैव ते पालनीया विनेयाः स्युरतोऽन्यथा॥ (24) नारदः। पित्रैव तु विभक्ता ये समन्यूनाधिकैर्धनैः। तेषां स एव भागः स्यात्सर्वस्यैव पिता प्रभुः॥ पूर्व्वं सम्भूयोत्थाने भ्रातॄणां मिलित्वा धनार्ज्जने विषमभागनिषेधनम्, इदन्तु पितुरर्जिते विषमविभागविधानम्, इत्यविरोधः। (25) इति विवादरत्नाकरे जीवत्पितृकविभागतरङ्गः।

CHAPTER III.

(1) अथ प्रमीतपितृकविभागः। (2) तत्र मनुः। ज्येष्ठस्य विंश-उद्धारः सर्वद्रव्याच्च यद्वरम्। ततोऽर्द्धं मध्यमस्य स्यात्तुरीयन्तु यवीयसः॥ ज्येष्ठश्चैव कनिष्ठश्च संहरेतां यथोदितम्। येऽन्ये ज्येष्ठकनिष्ठाभ्यां तेषां स्यान्मध्यमं धनम्। सर्वेषां धनजातानामाददीताग्र्यमग्रजः। यच्च सातिशयं किञ्चिद्दशतः, प्राप्नुयाद्वरम्॥ गुणवज्ज्येष्ठादिविषयोऽयमुद्धारः। अत्रेदृशी विषयव्यवस्था, यदा बहवः पुत्रा एकमातृका गुणवन्तः, किन्तु यथाक्रमं गुण-ह्रासः, तदा ज्येष्ठस्य मध्यकाञ्चनाद्विंशो भाग उद्धारः कर्त्तव्यः, सर्व्वद्रव्याच्च यद्वरं धनं तद्दातव्यम्। मध्यमस्य ततोऽर्द्धञ्चत्वारिंशत्तमो भागो मध्यमञ्च धनम्। एवं कनीयसस्तुरीयमशीतितमो भागो हीनञ्च द्रव्यं दातव्यम्। यदा तु ज्येष्ठकनिष्ठावेव गुणवन्तौ, तदा तयोर्यथोक्त उद्धारो दातव्यः, ये तु मध्यमा निर्गुणास्तेषां मध्यमं धनम्। मध्यमस्य गुणवतो यदुद्धाररूपमुक्तं चत्वारिंशत्तमो भागः, स समं विभज्य दातव्यः। यदा तु बहवो मध्यमा अतिगुणवन्तस्तदा

प्रत्येकं चत्वारिंशत्तमो भाग उद्धृत्य दातव्यः। यदि ज्येष्ठो गुणातिशयवान्, अन्ये निर्गुणास्तदा सर्व्वधनापेक्षया यच्छ्रेष्ठं द्रव्यं, यच्च समानजातीयापेक्षया सातिशयं पद्मरागादि, सर्वेषां गोमहिष्यादीनां दशतो दशसु दशसु एकं श्रेष्ठमुद्धृत्य ज्येष्ठो गृह्णीयादिति। (3) यत्र ज्येष्ठोऽधिकगुणोऽपरे तु मध्यमगुणास्तत्र, विशेषमाह गौतमः। विंशतिभागो ज्येष्ठस्य मिथुनमुभयतोदद्युक्तो रथो गोवृषः। काणखोरकूटवण्डा मध्यमस्यानेकाश्चेदविर्धान्यायसी गृहमनोयुक्तं चतुष्पदां चैकैकं यवीयसः सममितरत्सर्व्वम्॥ सर्वस्मात् पितृधनाद्विंशतितमो भागो ज्येष्ठस्य, मिथुनं गोमिथुनमुभयतोदन्ता अश्वरासभादयः एषामन्यतमसजातीयाभ्यां युक्तो रथः, गोवृषः सेकसमर्थो वृषः, अयमुद्धारः सति सम्भवे ज्येष्ठस्य, काणखोरकूटवण्डा मध्यमस्यानेकाश्चेदिति, खोरो वृद्धः, कूटः शृङ्गविकलः, वण्डो बालविरहितः वेंड़े इति यस्य प्रसिद्धिः, अयं मध्यमस्योद्धारो ह्यनेकाश्चेद्यद्येषामपि भवन्तीत्यर्थः। अविर्धान्यायसी गृहमनोयुक्तं चतुष्पदाञ्चैकैकं यवीयस इति, अविर्मेषी व्रीहिलौहयोः समासेन निर्द्देशादानुरूप्येण किञ्चिद्देयम्। गृहमेकम्, अनः शकटं, युक्तं बलीवर्द्दयुक्तं, चतुष्पदां गवादीनाञ्चैकैकं कनिष्ठस्योद्धारः। सममितरत्, उद्धृतातिरिक्तं सममेव विभजनीयमित्यर्थः। एवमन्यत्रापि यत्र उद्धारे गुरुलघुभावस्तत्र भ्रातॄणां ज्येष्ठमध्यमकनिष्ठानां गुणवत्त्वाद्यपेक्षया व्यवस्था द्रष्टव्या। लोके तु ज्येष्ठमात्रपुरस्कारेण च मध्यमकनिष्ठोद्धारस्थानादायैव ज्येष्ठस्य विंशोद्धारो दृश्यते। (4) हारीतः। विभजिष्यमाणे गवां समूहे वृषभमेकधनं वरिष्टं वा ज्येष्ठाय दद्युर्देवतागृहञ्च, इतरे निष्क्राम्य कुर्य्युः, एकस्मिन्नेव दक्षिणं ज्येष्ठायानुपूर्व्वमितरेषाम्॥ एकधनमुत्कृष्टधनम्, देवता विष्ण्वादिप्रतिमा, गृहं पैतृकम्, निष्क्राम्य कुर्य्युर्गृहान्तराणीति शेषः। यदा गृहान्निष्क्राम्य गृहान्तरकरणासम्भवः, तदा दक्षिणं श्रेष्ठं ज्येष्ठाय भवेदिति शेषः। आनुपूर्व्यमनुपूर्व्वता, तेन मध्यमाय मध्यमं, कनिष्ठाय ततोऽपि हीनमित्यर्थः। हरिहरस्तु देवतागृहपदेन दुर्गादिपूजामण्डपं व्याख्याय तज्ज्येष्ठाय दत्त्वा अन्ये मण्डपान्तरं कुर्य्युरित्याह। (5) आपस्तम्बः। देशविशेषे सुवर्णं कृष्णा गावः कृष्णं भौमं ज्येष्ठस्य मिथः पितुः परिभाण्डञ्च॥ कृष्णं भौमं भूमिभवं तिलमाषादि, परिभाण्डं भोजनपात्रादि। (6) बौधायनः। असति पितरि चतुर्णां वर्णानां गोश्वाजावयो ज्येष्ठांशो यथासंख्येन॥ एतच्च ज्येष्ठस्य भ्रातुः किञ्चिद्गुणवत्त्वे। (7) देवलः। पुत्राणां मध्यमो दायः समानानामपीष्यते। ज्येष्ठस्य दशमं भागं न्यायवृत्तस्य निर्द्दिशेत्॥ मध्यमो दायो मध्यमं धनं विंशोऽंशः, एतच्च

ज्येष्ठे वेदसमन्विते, अन्येषु निर्गुणेषु मन्तव्यमिति हलायुधपारिजातौ। अन्ये तु यदा ज्येष्ठोऽग्निवेदसम्पन्नोऽन्येऽपि गुणवन्तस्तदा ज्येष्ठस्य दशमो भागः, अन्येषां पुत्राणां मध्यमो भागो, मध्यमं धनं विंशो भागः प्रत्येकमिति प्रथमखण्डार्थः। यदा अग्निवेदवान् ज्येष्ठः, अन्येऽपि निर्गुणाः, तदा ज्येष्ठस्य दशमो भागो निर्गुणभ्रातॄणान्तु पूर्ब्बवच्चत्वारिंशत्तमो भाग एव विभज्य दातव्य इति द्वितीयखण्डार्थः। (8) इति विवादरत्नाकरे प्रमीतपितृकविभागतरङ्गः।

CHAPTER IV.

(1) अथानेकमातृकभ्रातृविभागः। (2) तत्र मनुः। पुत्रः कनिष्ठो ज्येष्ठायां कनिष्ठायाञ्च पूर्ब्बजः कथं तत्र विभागः स्यादिति चेत्संशयो भवेत्॥ एकं वृषभमुद्धारं संहरेत् स तु पूर्ब्बजः। ततोऽपरेऽज्येष्ठवृषास्तदूनानां स्वमातृतः॥ पूर्ब्बजसजातीयमातृप्रभवनानापुत्रविषय एवायं संशयः। नानावर्णानां दायविभागस्याग्रे वक्ष्यमाणत्वात्, पूर्ब्बजशब्देन पूर्ब्बोढ़ायां जातः कनीयानेवोच्यते, ततोऽपरेऽज्येष्ठवृषास्तदूनानां स्वमातृत इत्यग्रिमखण्डात्। ततो ज्यष्ठवृषात् अपरे अज्येष्ठवृषाः अश्रेष्ठवृषास्तदूनानां ज्येष्ठपुत्रात्कनीयसः ऊनानां तन्मातृकनिष्ठमातृकाणामित्यर्थः। (3) मातृतो ज्यैष्ठमभिधाय तत्रैव विशेषमाह। ज्येष्ठस्तु जातो ज्येष्ठायां हरेद्वृषभषोड़शाः। ततः स्वमातृतः शेषा भजेरन्निति धारणा॥ वृषभः षोड़शो यासां गवां ताः, तथा तस्यात्यन्तसाजात्यस्यान्तरङ्गत्वादुद्धारः। शेषा मातुरज्येष्ठत्वेन कारणेन अश्रेष्ठमेकैकं वृषभं हरेरन्। एतच्च परमतमुक्तं मनुना, स्वमतन्तु, सदृशस्त्रीषु जातानां पुत्राणामविशेषतः। न मातृतो ज्यैष्ठ्यमस्ति जन्मतो ज्यैष्ठ्यमुच्यते,—इत्यादिना जन्मतो ज्यैष्ठ्यमस्तीति दर्शितमिति प्रकाशकारः। हलायुधस्तु अस्यार्थः, यदा ज्येष्ठायां कनिष्ठः, कनिष्ठायाञ्च ज्येष्ठो भवति, तदा योऽसौ कनिष्ठायां पूर्ब्बजातः, स एकं श्रेष्ठवृषमुद्धारं गृह्णीयात्। तस्माद्वृषात् येऽन्येऽश्रेष्ठवृषाः, ते तदूनानां पूर्ब्बजातकनिष्ठानां स्वमातृतः स्वमातृक्रमेण यथापकर्षं प्रत्येकमेकैकशो दातव्याः, परिशिष्टं समं विभजनीयम्। यदा तु ज्येष्ठायामेव ज्येष्ठो भवति तदाविशेषमाह ज्येष्ठस्त्वित्यादिना। वृषभः षोड़शो यासां गवां तास्तथा। अन्ये पुनः स्वमातृक्रमेण पूर्ब्बोक्तमेकैकं वृषभ-

मुद्धारं गृह्णीयुः। (4) अत्रैव गौतमः। वृषभोऽधिको ज्येष्ठस्य, वृषषोड़शा ज्यैष्ठिनेयस्य समधा वा ज्यैष्ठिनेयेन यवीयसा॥ ज्येष्ठः मन्वनुसारात् कनीयसीपुत्रः प्रथमं जातोऽपेक्षितः। ज्यैष्ठिनेयस्तु ज्येष्ठायां जातो ज्येष्ठः, समधा समप्रकारेण, एतच्च सर्व्वेषां तुल्यरूपत्वे द्रष्टव्यम्। (5) शङ्खलिखितौ। वृषभोऽधिको ज्येष्ठाय, गृहं यवीयसे॥ अत्रापि ज्येष्ठो मन्वनुसारात् कनीयसीपुत्र एव द्रष्टव्यः। (6) गौतमः। प्रतिमातृबान्धववर्गे भागविशेषः॥ अस्यार्थः, यदा बह्वीषु समानजातीयासु स्त्रीषु समसंख्या बह्वः पुत्रा भवन्ति, तदा भ्रातृभागस्य दुःशकत्वात्, मातृभागमादाय तैः स्ववर्गे सोदर्य्यभ्रात्रादिरूपे विभागविशेषो विंशोद्धाररूपः कर्त्तव्यः। (7) तदाह बृहस्पतिः। यद्येकजाता बह्वः समाना जातिसंख्यया। सापत्न्याः, तैर्विभक्तव्यं मातृभागेन धर्म्मतः। सवर्णा भिन्नसंख्या ये पुम्भागस्तेषु विद्यते॥ (8) विष्णुः। सवर्णाः पुत्राः समानान् अंशान् आदद्युः, ज्येष्ठाय श्रेष्ठमुद्धारञ्च दद्युः॥ एतच्च पुत्राणां भिन्नसंख्यकत्वे। (9) मनुः। उद्धारो न दशस्वस्ति सम्पन्नानां स्वकर्म्मसु। यत्किञ्चिदेव देयं स्यात् ज्यायसे मानवर्द्धनम्॥ अस्यार्थः, अध्ययनादितुल्येषु, दशतश्चाप्नुयाद् वरम्, इत्युद्धारो न कर्त्तव्यः। एतच्चोपलक्षणं, सर्व्वेषामेवोद्धाराणामिह प्रतिषेधः, यत्किञ्चिदेवेति वचनात्, किन्तु जन्ममात्रनिबन्धनज्येष्ठनिमित्तकं किञ्चिन्मानवर्द्धनं दातव्यम्। यदा गुणवत्त्वे न तेषां परस्परं विशेषो भवति, तदा,—तदूनानां स्वमातृतो,—ज्येष्ठस्तु जातो ज्येष्ठायाम्—इति च मन्तव्यमिति लिखित्वोक्तवान्। यत् कैश्चिदुक्तं,—तदूनानां स्वमातृत इति ज्येष्ठस्तु जातो ज्येष्ठायामिति च,—पूर्व्वपक्षमुक्त्वा, सदृशस्त्रीषु इत्यादिना सिद्धान्तितम्, अन्यथा विरोधादिति, तदपहस्तितम्, गुणाचारादिति विशेषेण व्यवस्थायाः प्रतिपादितत्वादिति। युक्तञ्चैतत्, सति सिद्धान्तत्वे पूर्व्वपक्षितत्वस्य व्यवस्थापनानर्हत्वात्, लक्ष्मीधरेण ज्येष्ठापुत्रस्य कनीयस एव ज्येष्ठत्वप्रयुक्तोद्धारव्यवस्थापनाच्च, पारिजातस्याप्येवं परिग्रहाच्च। (10) तथा जन्मज्येष्ठस्य चाह्वानं सुब्रह्मण्यास्वपि स्मृतम्। यमयोश्चैव गर्भेषु जन्मतो ज्येष्ठता मता॥ सुब्रह्मण्या नाम मन्त्रविशेषो ज्योतिष्टोमे छन्दोगैर्निगद्यते। प्रयोगबहुत्वात् बहुवचनं तत्र पठ्यते, प्रथमपुत्रेण पितरं व्यपदिश्याहूयते,—अमुकस्य पिता अमुकस्य पितामहो यजत इति। तच्च जन्मज्येष्ठतया विहितं नाटसूत्रे, यथा ज्येष्ठं स्त्रीपुंसां ये जीवेयुरिति वचनात्। (11) देवलः। वाहर्वर्णेषु चारित्रयात् यमयोः पूर्व्वजन्मतः। यस्य जातस्य यमयोः पश्यन्ति प्रथमं मुखम्। सन्ताने पितरश्चैव तस्मिन् ज्यैष्ठं प्रतिष्ठितम्॥

(12) मनुः । यो ज्येष्ठो विनिकुर्वीत लोभात् भ्रातॄन् यवीयसः । सोऽज्येष्ठः स्यात्, अभागश्च, नियन्तव्यश्च राजभिः ॥ विनिकुर्व्वीत वञ्चयेत् । अज्येष्ठो ज्येष्ठवत् न पूज्यः । (13) तथा । एवं समुद्धृतोद्धारे समान् अंशान् प्रकल्पयेत् । उद्धारेऽनुद्धृते त्वेषाम् इयं स्यात् अंशकल्पना । एकाधिकं हरेज्ज्येष्ठः पुत्रोऽध्यर्द्धं ततोऽनुजः । अंशमंशं यवीयांस इति धर्म्मो व्यवस्थितः ॥ एकाधिकं एकेनांशेनाधिकं द्वौ अंशौ इति यावत्, ततोऽनुजः पुनरध्यर्द्धं अर्द्धांशसहितम् एकम् अंशं गृह्णीयात्, कनीयांसस्तु प्रत्येकम् एकैकम् अंशं, यदा विनोद्धारं विभागस्तदा । एतच्च, यदा ज्येष्ठतदनुजौ गुणविद्यातिशयसम्पन्नौ, अन्ये तु निर्गुणाः, तदा मन्तव्यम् । जन्मविद्यागुणज्येष्ठो द्व्यंशं दायादवाप्नुयादिति, ज्येष्ठमधिकृत्य वृहस्पतिवचनात्, तदनुजे च न्यायसाम्यात् । विंशोद्धारादि च, यदा सर्व्वे गुणाचारादियुक्ताः, परस्परं गुणाचारादौ च किञ्चिद्वैषम्यं, तदा बोद्धव्यम् । (14) गौतमः । द्व्यंशी वा पूर्व्वजः स्यात् एकैकम् इतरेषाम् ॥ इदञ्च, ज्येष्ठस्यैव गुणातिशययुक्तत्वे अन्येषां निर्गुणत्वे । (15) तथा । एकैकं वा धनं रूपवत् काम्यं पूर्व्वतः पूर्व्वों लभेत दशतः पशूनाम् ॥ समानजातीयान् दशतो दश दश पशून् पूर्व्वः पुर्व्वोलभेत इत्यर्थः । (16) नैकशफद्विपदानाम् ॥ अश्वादीनाम् एकशफानां स्त्र्यादीनाञ्च द्विपदानां न दश दश गृह्णीयादित्यर्थः । एतच्च, सर्व्वेषां समत्वे धनबहुत्वे च, मन्तव्यम् । (17) वशिष्ठः । अथ भ्रातॄणां दायभागः, द्व्यंशं हरेज्ज्येष्ठो गवाश्वस्य चैकम् दशमं, अजादयो गृहञ्च कनिष्ठस्य, कार्ष्णायसं गृहोपकरणानि मध्यमस्य ॥ द्व्यंशमिति, द्वावंशौ ज्येष्ठोहरेत्, गवाश्वस्येति दशसु गोषु अश्वेषु च एकैकं श्रेष्ठं गृह्णीयात् । इदञ्च वशिष्ठवचनं ज्येष्ठस्य सातिशयगुणवत्त्वे इतरयोश्च गुणवत्त्वे । (18) नारदः । ज्येष्ठायांशोऽधिकोदेयः कनिष्ठायाऽवरः स्मृतः । समांशभागाः शेषाः स्युरप्रत्ता भगिनी तथा । क्षेत्रजेषु च पुत्रेषु तद्वत् जातेषु धर्म्मतः ॥ प्रकाशकारेण तु वाक्यमिदं, कनिष्ठायावर इति स्थाने श्रेष्ठाय तु वर इति पठितं, व्याख्यातञ्चाग्रे प्रथमोत्पन्नस्यांशद्वयम्, श्रेष्ठः कुटुम्बकर्म्मण्युपयुक्तः, तस्मै वरं श्रेष्ठं किञ्चित् देयमिति । अप्रत्ता कुमारी भगिनी, तथा अंशभागिनीत्यर्थः, भागश्च इत्थम् औरसे क्षेत्रजे च इत्यग्रे व्यक्तीभविष्यति, औरसेषु पुत्रेषु तदुक्तं, क्षेत्रजेष्वाह,—क्षेत्रजेषु पुत्रेषु तद्वत् जातेषु धर्म्मतः, तद्वत् विभागो यथा औरसेषु उक्तः, किम्भूतेषु जातेषु धर्म्मतः, स्वं क्षेत्रं क्लीवादिभिर्यदान्यस्मै सकुल्याय सवर्णाय वा दीयते, तदा च ततो जातो धर्म्मतो जात इत्युच्यते, तेषु अप्यधिको ज्येष्ठांशो देय इति । कथं पुनरेकस्य क्षेत्रजाताना-

मनेकेषां सम्भवः, उच्यते यमजोत्पन्नविषयमेतत्। (19) कीदृशाय ज्येष्ठाय अधिकोऽंशो देय इत्यत्राह वृहस्पतिः। जन्मविद्यागुणज्येष्ठो द्व्यंशं दायात् अवाप्नुयात्। समांशभागिनस्त्वन्ये तेषां पितृसमस्तु सः॥ (20) उशनाः। वर्णानामनुलोमानां विभागोऽयं प्रदर्शितः। समत्वेनैकजातानां विभागस्तु विधीयते॥ सर्व्वेषां पुत्राणां निर्गुणत्वेन तुल्यानां, तथा कस्यचित् गुणवत्त्वेऽपि सर्व्वे चेत् नानाविधधनार्जकाः, तदा समएव भाग इत्यर्थः। (21) याज्ञवल्क्यः। विभजेरन् सुताः पित्रोरूर्द्ध्वम् ऋक्थम् ऋणं समम्॥ (22) तथा। सामान्यार्थसमुत्थाने विभागस्तु समः स्मृतः। अनेकपितृकाणान्तु पितृतो भागकल्पना॥ येन चैषां स्वयमुत्पादितं स द्व्यंशमेव हरेदित्यस्य वशिष्ठवचनस्यापवादोऽयं सामान्येति। यदा सामान्यार्थस्य कृषिबाणिज्यादिना सम्यक् उत्थानं संवर्द्धनं केनचित् कृतं भवति, तदा तत्र समएव भागो न संवर्द्धनकर्त्तुरंशद्वयमित्यर्थः। वशिष्ठवचनन्तु तदितरविषयतया व्यवस्थाप्यम्। अनेकभ्रातृणां ये पुत्राः, तेषां समविषमसंख्यकानामपि, पैतामहे धने विभज्यमाने, पितृणां योऽंशः, सएव तेषां, न प्रत्येकम् अंशं कल्पयेदित्यर्थः। (23) अत्रैव वृहस्पतिः। समवेतैस्तु यत् प्राप्तं सर्व्वे तत्र समांशिनः। तत् पुत्रा विषमसमाः समभागहराः स्मृताः॥ अविभक्तपितृकाः विषमसमाः पुत्राः। (24) कात्यायनः। अविभक्ते मृते पुत्रे तत्सुतं रिक्थभागिनम्। कुर्व्वीत जीवनं येन लब्धं नैव पितामहात्॥ लभेतांशं स पित्र्यन्तु पितृव्यात् तस्य वा सुतात्। स एवांशस्तु सर्व्वेषां भ्रातृणां न्यायतो भवेत्॥ लभेत तत् सुतो वापि निवृत्तिः परतो भवेत्। अस्यार्थः। यदा भ्रातृणां मध्ये कश्चिदेको न विद्यते, तदा तत्सुतस्य तु भागोन निवर्त्तते इति। (25) देवलः। अविभक्तविभक्तानां कुल्यानां वसतां सह। भूयो दायविभागः स्यात् आचतुर्थादिति स्थितिः॥ अयमर्थः। अविभक्तानामेव वा, विभक्तानां सहवसतां संसृष्टानां वा पुनर्विभागो भ्रातृ-तत्सुत-तत्सुत-पर्य्यन्तमेव, तत्सुतात् चतुर्थात् निवर्त्तते इति। (26) तथा। तावत् कुल्याः सपिण्डाः स्युः पिण्डभेदस्त्वनन्तरम्। सममिच्छन्ति पिण्डानां दायार्थस्य विभाजनम्॥ एतच्च यदा स्वविषयो विभागार्थिना अभुज्यमानोऽपरेण तु तद्देशस्थितेन भुज्यमानस्तदा। (27) वशिष्ठः। अथ भ्रातृणां दायविभागो याश्चानपत्याः स्त्रियस्तासाञ्चापुत्रलाभात्॥ स्त्रियोऽत्र भ्रातृजायाः, ता यदि शङ्कितपुत्राः, तदा तासामपि भागो दातव्यः। पुत्रानुत्पत्तौ भागो भ्रातृणामेव, तासाञ्च भरणमात्रं कार्य्यमित्यर्थः। (28) विष्णुः। मातरः पुत्रभागानुसारभागहारिण्यः अनूढ़ाश्च दुहितरः॥ मातर इति बहु-

अन्धोऽचिकित्स्यरोगाद्या भर्त्तव्यास्तु निरंशकाः ॥ तत्सुतः पातित्याद्यनन्तरोत्पन्नः, जड़ो विकलान्तःकरणः, अचिकित्स्यरोगोऽप्रतिक्रियकुष्ठादिः, आदिशब्देनान्ये ऋष्यन्तरोक्ता अनंशा भरणीया ग्राह्याः । (9) क्लीवादीनामनंशताप्राप्तौ तत्पुत्राणामपि निरंशत्वप्रसक्तौ अयमेवाह । औरसाः क्षेत्रजास्तेषां निर्द्दोषा भागहारिणः । सुतास्त्वेषां प्रभर्त्तव्या यावन्न भर्त्तृसात्कृताः ॥ (10) क्लीवादिपरिणीतपत्नीः प्रत्याह । अपुत्रा योषितश्चैषां भर्त्तव्याः साधुवृत्तयः । निर्वास्या व्यभिचारिण्यः प्रतिकूलास्तथैव च ॥ प्रतिकूला इत्यत्र प्रातिकूल्यं विषप्रयोगादिकारित्वं विवक्षितं, न तु कलहमात्रकारित्वम् । (11) नारदः । पितृद्विट् पतितः षण्डो यश्च स्यादपपात्रितः । औरसा अपि नैतेऽंशं लभेरन् क्षेत्रजाः कुतः । दीर्घतीव्रामयग्रस्ता जड़ोन्मत्तान्धपङ्गवः । भर्त्तव्याः स्युः कुलस्यैते तत्पुत्रास्त्वंशभागिनः ॥ पितरं यो द्वेष्टि स पितृद्विट्, द्वेषश्च पितरि जीवति मारणादिफलः, मृते तु तदुद्देशेनोदकाद्यदानरूपः । अपपात्रितः राजबधादिदोषेण कृतघटापवर्जनः, प्रकाशकृता तु औपपातकीति पठित्वा उपपातकैर्युक्त इति विवृतम् । दीर्घं राजयक्ष्मादि, तीव्रं कुष्ठादि, भर्त्तव्याः पोषणीयाः । कुलस्य भ्रात्रादेः । (12) देवलः । मृते पितरि न क्लीवकुष्ठ्युन्मत्तजड़ान्धकाः । पतितः पतितापत्यं लिङ्गी दायांशभागिनः ॥ तेषां पतितवर्ज्जेभ्यो भक्तवस्त्रं प्रदीयते । तत्पुत्राः पितृदायांशं लभेरन् दोषवर्ज्जिताः ॥ मृते मृतेऽपीत्यर्थः । लिङ्गी अतिशयेन कपटव्रतचारी । (13) अत्र विष्णुः । पतितक्लीवाचिकित्स्यरोगविकलास्त्वभागहारिणः, ऋक्थग्राहिणस्ते भर्त्तव्याः, तेषां चौरसा, न तु पतितस्य ॥ पतनीये कर्म्मणि कृते अनन्तरोत्पन्नाः प्रतिलोमासु स्त्रीषु उत्पन्नाश्चाभागिनस्तत्पुत्राः पैतामहेऽप्यर्थे, ऋक्थग्राहिणोऽंशग्राहकस्य । (14) बौधायनः । अतीतव्यवहारान् ग्रासाच्छादनैर्बिभृयुः । अन्धजड़क्लीवव्यसनिव्याधितांश्चाकर्म्मिणः पतिततज्जातवर्ज्जम् ॥ अतीतव्यवहारान् अप्राप्तव्यवहारान्, अकर्म्मिणो धर्म्मयागादिषु नाधिकारिणः । तथाचाहुः । यज्ञार्थं द्रव्यमुत्पन्नं तस्माच्च विनियोजयेत् । स्थानेषु धर्म्मयुक्तेषु न स्त्रीमूर्खविधर्म्मिषु ॥ पतित-तदपत्यैः सह सर्व्वव्यवहारनिषेधात् न भरणमपि । (15) वशिष्ठः । अनंशास्त्वाश्रमान्तरगताः ॥ आश्रमान्तरं गृहस्थाश्रमात् । (16) गौतमः । जड़क्लीवौ तु भर्त्तव्यौ, अपत्यं जड़स्य भागार्हं, शूद्रापुत्रवत् प्रतिलोमासु ॥ अर्हपदात् यदासावधिकारी भवति, तदा भागी, न तु जड़ापत्यत्वमात्रेणेति द्योत्यते । शूद्रापुत्रवदिति प्रतिलोमासु स्त्रीषु जातानामपि शुश्रूषमाणानां शूद्रापुत्रवज्जीवनं देयमित्यर्थः ।

(17) कात्यायनः। अक्रमोढ़ासुतश्चैवं सगोत्रात् यश्च जायते। प्रव्रज्यावसितश्चैव न ऋक्थं तेषु चार्हति। अक्रमोढ़ासुतस्त्वृक्थी सवर्णश्च यदा पितुः। असवर्ण-प्रसूतश्च क्रमोढ़ायाश्च यो भवेत्। प्रतिलोमप्रसूता या तस्याः पुत्रो न ऋक्-थभाक्। ग्रासाच्छादनमत्यर्थं देयं तद्बन्धुभिर्मतम्। बन्धूनामप्यभावे तु पित्र्यं द्रव्यं तदाप्नुयात्। अपित्र्यं तद्धनं प्राप्तं दापनीया न बान्धवाः॥ अक्रमोढ़ासुतोऽत्र नानावर्णानां कन्यानां विवाहे यः क्रमः शास्त्रीयः, तदु-ल्लङ्घनेन विवाहितायाम् असवर्णायाम् उत्पन्नः, अग्रे अनेनैवाक्रमोढ़ासुते सवर्ण-जाते अक्रमोढ़ासुतस्त्वृक्थीत्यनेन भागग्राहकत्वविधिः। सगोत्रात् यस्तु जायते सगोत्रायां परिणीतायां यो जायते, प्रव्रज्यावसितः प्रव्रज्यां गृहीत्वा तत्र भ्रष्टः, अक्रमोढ़ासुतस्त्विति अक्रमोढ़ासुतोऽपि सवर्ण एव स्यात् तदा ऋक्थी भाग-ग्राहक एव, एवमसवर्णप्रसूतोऽपि क्रमोढ़ायां जातो भागग्राहक एव। प्रति-लोमप्रसूता या इति अपकृष्टवर्णेनोत्कृष्टवर्णा या परिणीता तत्पुत्रो न ऋक्थभाक्, ग्रासाच्छादनमिति तस्यैव यदि बान्धवाः सन्ति तदा तैः ग्रासा-च्छादनमत्यर्थं देयं, बन्धूनाम् अभावे तु स्वयमेव तद्धनं गृह्णीयात्। यदा तु बान्धवैरपि अपित्र्यमेव धनं प्राप्तं, तदा ग्रासाच्छादनमपि न ते तस्य दापयितव्या इति। (18) बृहस्पतिः। असंस्कृता भ्रातरस्तु ये स्युस्तत्र यवीयसः। संस्कार्य्याः पूर्व्वजैस्ते वै पैतृकान्मध्यगाद्धनात्॥ यवीयसोयवीयांसः आर्षत्वान्नम् दीर्घयोरभावादित्येके। अन्ये तु यवीयसः कनिष्ठस्य मध्यगादि-त्याहुः। फलतश्च न कश्चित् विशेषः। (19) व्यासः। असंस्कृतास्तु ये तत्र पैतृकादेव तद्धनात्। संस्कार्य्या भ्रातृभिर्ज्येष्ठैः कन्यकाश्च यथाविधि॥ कन्यकासंस्कारः परिणयरूपः। (20) नारदः। येषान्तु न कृताः पूर्व्वैः संस्कारविधयः क्रमात्। कर्त्तव्या भ्रातृभिस्तेषां पैतृकादेव तद्धनात्। अविद्यमाने पित्रर्थे स्वांशात् उद्धृत्य वा पुनः। अवश्यकार्य्याः संस्कारा भ्रातृणां पूर्व्वसंस्कृतैः॥ अत्र संस्कारविधयो जातकर्म्माद्युपनयान्ताः। (21) देवलः। कन्याभ्यश्च पितृद्रव्यं देयं वैवाहिकं वसु। अपुत्रस्य च कन्या स्वं धर्म्मजा पुत्रवद्धरेत्॥ (22) याज्ञवल्क्यः। असंस्कृतास्तु संस्कार्य्या भ्रातृभिः पूर्व्व-संस्कृतैः। भगिन्यश्च निजादंशाद्दत्त्वांशन्तु तुरीयकम्॥ (23) विष्णुः। अनूढ़ानाञ्च कन्यानां वित्तानुरूपेण संस्कारं कुर्य्यात्॥ (24) मनुः। स्वेभ्यः स्वेभ्यस्तु कन्याभ्यः प्रदद्युर्भ्रातरः पृथक्। स्वात् स्वात् अंशात् चतुर्भागं पतिताः स्युरदित्सवः॥ अत्र निजादंशादुद्धृत्य चतुर्थो भागो दातव्य इति नार्थः, किन्तु यज्जातीयपुत्रस्य यो भागः, तच्चतुर्थोऽंशो यो भवति, तं परिकल्प्य कन्यायै

संस्कारार्थं दद्यादित्यर्थो विवक्षितः। तेन ब्राह्मणीपुत्राणां चतुर्षु अंशेषु, क्षत्रियाणां त्रिषु, समुदायात्, चतुर्थमंशं दद्युरित्यर्थो भवति। अत्र चानेकवाक्यगतचतुर्थांश-दर्शनात् चतुर्थांशस्यैव दानं, प्रयोजनन्तु संस्कारः। चतुर्थांशदानविधिर्विष्णोरपि तयैव दिशा नेतव्यः। कल्पतरुप्रकाशमिताक्षरा अप्येवम्। विष्णुवाक्यदर्शनात् चतुर्थांशदानम् उपलक्षणम्, यावता संस्कारो भवति, तावत्येव तात्पर्य्यमिति हलायुधादिमतम्। युक्तञ्चैतत् कर्त्तव्यसंस्कारस्यौचित्यात्। (25) कात्यायनः। कन्यकानान्त्वदत्तानां चतुर्थो भाग इष्यते। पुत्राणाञ्च त्रयो भागाः स्वाम्यं स्वल्पधने स्मृतम्॥ स्वाम्यं स्वल्पधने स्मृतमिति यदा चतुर्थभागरूपे धनेऽल्पता, संस्कारस्त्वधिकधननिर्व्वाह्यः, तदा यावता धनेन संस्कारो भवति, तावति धने कन्यकानां स्वाम्यं प्रभुत्वम्। तेन तावद्धनमेव स्वांशादाकृष्यापि भ्रात्रा संस्कारार्थं देयमिति। मातुश्च वैवाहिकं स्त्रीधनं जीवन्त्यामपि मातरि। (26) शङ्खलिखितौ। विभज्यमाने दायेभ्यः स्वकन्यालङ्कारं वैवाहिकं स्त्री-धनञ्च कन्या लभते। स्वकन्यालङ्कारं स्वकीयनूपुरादि कन्या लभते॥ (27) बौधायनः। मातुरलङ्कारं दुहितरः साम्प्रदायिकं लभेरन् अन्यद्वा॥ मातुरल-ङ्कारं वैवाहिकं कन्या लभते, यदि चालङ्कारादन्यदपि वैवाहिकं मातुर्भवति तदा तदपि कन्या लभते इत्यर्थः। (28) अर्हति स्त्रीत्यनुवृत्तौ पुनर्बौधायनः। न दायं निरिन्द्रिया अदाया हि स्त्रियो मता इति श्रुतिः॥ निरिन्द्रिया निःसत्त्वा इति प्रकाशः, अदाया अनंशा इत्यर्थः। एतच्च विहितांशस्त्री-व्यतिरिक्तविषयम्। (29) इति विवादरत्नाकरे विभागानधिकारितरङ्गः।

CHAPTER VI.

(1) अथ विभाज्यम्। (2) तत्र कात्यायनः। पैतामहञ्च पित्र्यञ्च यत्किञ्चित् स्वयमर्ज्जितम्। दायादानां विभागे तु सर्व्वमेतद्विभज्यते। ऋक्थं प्रीतिप्रदत्तन्तु दत्त्वा शेषं विभाजयेत्। आचतुर्थात्तु तद्ग्राह्यं क्रमेणैव तु तत्सुतैः॥ स्वयमर्ज्जितम्, असाधारणप्रयोजकरूपव्यतिरेकेणेति शेषः। ऋक्थं प्रीतिप्रदत्तञ्चेति, पित्रा यत् ऋक्थं कस्मैचित् प्रीत्या दातुं प्रतिश्रुतं तत् प्रीतिप्रदत्तं, तद्दत्त्वा अवशिष्टं विभजनीयम्। आचतुर्थादिति,— त्रयाणामुदकं कार्य्यं त्रिषु पिण्डः प्रवर्त्तते— इति वचनात्, यो यस्य पिण्ड-

दानेनोपकरोति, स तस्य विभज्य धनं गृह्णीयादित्यर्थः। हलायुधस्तु, यस्मै प्रतिश्रुतं तम् आरभ्य चतुर्थत्वं विवक्षितमित्याह। (3) नारदः। यच्छिष्टं पितृदायेभ्यो दत्त्वर्णं पैतृकन्तु यत्। भ्रातृभिस्तत् विभक्तव्यम् ऋणी न स्यात् यथा पिता॥ पितृदायोऽत्र पित्रा अन्यस्मै प्रतिश्रुतं धनम्। प्रकाशकारस्तु पितृदानेभ्य इति पाठं पुरस्कृतवान्, अर्थोऽत्रापि स एव। (4) कात्यायनः। भ्रात्रा पितृव्यमातृभ्यां कुटुम्बार्थम् ऋणं कृतम्। विभागकाले देयं तत् ऋक्थिभिः सर्व्वमेव तु। तदृणं धनिने देयं नान्यथैव प्रदापयेत्। भावितञ्चेत् प्रमाणेन विरोधात् परतो यदा॥ तदृणमित्यादि, यदृणं भ्रात्रादिभिः कृतं, विरोधात् विवादात् सन्दिग्धीभूतं, तदेव धनिने देयं यदि विवादात् परतो धनिना प्रमाणेन साधितं भवेत्, नान्यथेत्यर्थः। (5) तथा। पित्रं पितृणसम्बद्धम् आत्मीयञ्चात्मना कृतम्। ऋणम् एवंविधं शोध्यं विभागी बन्धुभिः सह॥ पित्रं पित्रा कृतं, पितृणसम्बद्धं पितृऋणं दातुम् आत्मना कृतं, आत्मीयं कुटुम्बार्थं पूर्व्ववाक्योक्तभ्रात्रादिव्यतिरिक्तविषयं, आत्मना कृतं कुटुम्बार्थमेव। (6) तथा। धर्म्मार्थं प्रीतिदत्तञ्च यदृणं स्वनियोजितम्। तत् दृश्यमानं विभजेत्, न दानं पैतृकात् धनात्॥ यतः स्वयम् असाधारणेन साधारणधनं धर्म्मार्थं दत्तं, प्रीत्या च यत् दत्तम्, ऋणञ्च यत् स्वयमुत्तमर्णत्वेन अन्यस्मै दत्तं, तत् ज्ञायमानं, विभक्तव्यं, यतः पैतृकात् धनात् असाधारणेन दानं नोचितमिति कल्पतरुः। प्रकाशपारिजातौ तु, यदृणमेकेन साधारणमसाधारणधर्म्मार्थं कृतं, यदृणं कृत्वा अन्यस्मै प्रीत्या दत्तं, यच्च स्वनियोजितं स्वभोगार्थं कृतं, तत् त्रयमपि तथा निश्चीयमानमपि, विभजेत् पृथक् कुर्य्यात्, येन कृतं तेनैव तत् देयं, न पैतृकात् धनात् सर्व्वैः देयमित्यर्थ इत्याहतुः। वस्तुतस्तु सर्व्वमेतत् विवक्षितमिति सर्व्वार्थपरतयैव वाक्यमिदं व्याख्यातुमुचितमिति। (7) तथा। दृश्यमानं विभज्येत गृहं क्षेत्रं चतुष्पदम्। गूढ़द्रव्याभिशङ्कायां प्रत्ययस्तत्र कीर्त्तितः॥ प्रत्ययो दिव्यम्। (8) एतदेव स्पष्टयति। गृहोपस्करवाह्यास्तु दोह्याभरणकर्म्मिणः। दृश्यमाना विभज्यन्ते कोषं गूढ़ेऽब्रवीत् भृगुः॥ गृहोपस्कर उदूखलादिः, कर्म्मिणो दासादयः, सुप्रसिद्धम् अन्यत्। (9) मनुः। अजाविकञ्चैकशफं न जातु विषमं भजेत्। अजाविकञ्च विषमं ज्येष्ठस्यैव विधीयते॥ विषमाणाम् अजाविकैकशफानां न मूल्यादिना समो विभागः करणीयः, किन्तु ज्येष्ठेनैव ते ग्राह्या इत्यर्थः। (10) इति विवादरत्नाकरे विभाज्यतरङ्गः।

CHAPTER VII.

(1) अथाविभाज्यम् । (2) तत्र मनुः । विद्याधनन्तु यद्-यस्य तत् तस्यैव धनं भवेत् । मैत्रम् औद्वाहिकञ्चैव माधुपर्किकमेव च ॥ विद्याधनम् औद्वाहिकञ्च अग्रे वक्ष्यते । मैत्रं मित्रात् लब्धं, माधुपर्किकं मधुपर्ककाले पूज्यतया लब्धं, तस्यैव भवेत् अविभाज्यं भवेदित्यर्थः । (3) याज्ञवल्क्यः । क्रमादभ्यागतं द्रव्यं हृतम् अभ्युद्धरेत्तु यः । दायादेभ्यो न तत् दद्यात् विद्यया लब्धमेव च ॥ क्रमादभ्यागतं पितृक्रमात् आगतं यत्किञ्चित् अन्यैर्हृतम् असामर्थ्यादिना पूर्व्वपुरुषेणानुद्धृतं यो द्रव्यम् अंशिनां मध्ये एक उद्धरति, तत् अंश्यन्तरेभ्यो न दद्यात् । अत्र च अंश्यन्तराणाम् अनुज्ञयेति मिताक्षराकारः । यच्च संहितायां हारीतः । पूर्व्वनष्टान्तु यो भूमिम् एक एवोद्धरेत् श्रमात् । यथा भागं लभन्तेऽन्ये दत्त्वांशन्तु तुरीयकमिति वाक्यं लिखति स्म, तच्च स्मृतिमहार्णव-कामधेनु-कल्पतरु-पारिजात-प्रभृत्यलिखनात् अयुक्तमेव । (4) व्यासः । विद्याप्राप्तं शौर्य्यधनं यच्च सौदायिकं भवेत् । विभागकाले तत् तस्य नान्वेष्टव्यं तद्रिक्थिभिः ॥ शौर्य्यधनं युद्धादिलब्धं, सौदायिकम्—ऊढ़या कन्यया वेत्यादिना कात्यायनेन अग्रे वक्ष्यते । (5) गौतमः । स्वयमर्जितम् अवैद्याय वैद्यो नाकामो दद्यात् ॥ स्वयमर्जितं विद्ययेति शेषः । वैद्यो विद्यावान् । (6) कात्यायनः । नाविद्यानान्तु वैद्येन देयं विद्याधनात् क्वचित् । समविद्याधिकानान्तु देयं वैद्येन तद्धनम् ॥ (7) नारदः । वैद्योऽविद्याय नांशन्तु प्रदद्याद्वै स्वतो धनात् । पैत्रं द्रव्यं समाश्रित्य न चेत् तेन तदाहृतम् ॥ अत्र चेदमभिप्रेतं, यदा साधारणधनेनैव ग्रासाच्छादनाद्युपयोगं कृत्वा समधिगतविद्यः साधारणधनानाश्रयेण विद्यया धनं प्राप्नोति, तदाऽविद्याय न देयं, साधारणधनाश्रयेण तु विद्ययार्जितम् अविद्यायापि देयम् । यदा तु विद्यार्जनकाले साधारणधनोपयोगो नास्ति तदा अर्जनकाले साधारणधनोपयोगेऽपि विदुषा न कस्यचिद्देयम्, किन्तु विदुष एव तद्धनं, पितृद्रव्यानुपम्भेषार्जितस्याविभाज्यत्वम् उक्त्वा पृथग्विद्यालब्धस्यापि व्यासेनाविभाज्यत्वप्रतिपादनात् । अतएव पुनरग्रे विद्याधनस्य यदविभाज्यत्वं वक्ष्यते तदसाधारणधनोपम्भेषेनैव उपात्तविद्यया धनार्जनकालेऽपि साधारणधनोपयोगे द्रष्टव्यमिति : हलायुधनिबन्धोऽप्येवमेव । प्रकाशकारादयस्तु विद्याधनादीनां बोधकवचनानि

पितृधनोपश्लेषविरहपराण्येवेत्याहुः, तच्च न उभयोपादानानुपपत्तेः। (8) विभजेदित्यनुवृत्तौ पुनर्नारदः। शौर्य्यभार्य्याधनं हित्वा यच्च विद्याधनं भवेत्। न विभाज्यानि तान्याहुः प्रसादो यश्च पैतृकः। मात्रा च स्वधनं दत्तं यस्मै स्यात् प्रीतिपूर्व्वकम्। तस्याप्येष विधिर्दृष्टो मातापीष्टे यथा पिता॥ स्वधनपदोपादानात् स्त्रीधनविषयमिदम्। (9) व्यासः। पितामहेन यद्दत्तं पित्रा वा प्रीतिपूर्व्वकम्। तस्य तन्नापहर्त्तव्यं मात्रा दत्तञ्च यद्भवेत्॥ (10) याज्ञवल्क्यः। पितृद्रव्याविनाशेन यदन्यत् स्वयमर्जितम्। मैत्रम् औद्वाहिकञ्चैव दायादानां न तद्भवेत्॥ अन्यन्मैत्रादिव्यतिरिक्तमपि। (11) मनुविष्णू। अनुपघ्नन् पितृद्रव्यं श्रमेण यदुपार्जितम्। स्वयमीहितलब्धं तत् नाकामो दातुमर्हति॥ (12) व्यासः। अनाश्रित्य पितृद्रव्यं स्वशक्त्याप्नोति यद्धनम्। दायादेभ्यो न तद्दद्यात् विद्यालब्धञ्च यद्भवेत्॥ (13) अथ कात्यायनः। परभक्तप्रदानेन प्राप्तविद्यो यदन्यतः। तया प्राप्तन्तु यद्वित्तं विद्याप्राप्तं तदुच्यते। उपन्यस्ते च यल्लब्धं विद्यायां पणपूर्व्वकम्। विद्याधनन्तु तद्विद्याद्विभागे न विभज्यते। शिष्यादार्त्विज्यतः प्रश्नात्सन्दिग्धप्रश्ननिर्णयात्। स्वज्ञानशंसनाद्वादाल्लब्धं प्राध्ययनाच्च यत्। विद्याधनन्तु तत् प्राहुर्विभागे न विभज्यते। शिल्पेष्वपि हि धर्म्मोऽयं मूल्याद्यच्चाधिकं भवेत्। विद्यापणकृतञ्चैव याज्यतः शिष्यतस्तथा। एतद्विद्याधनं प्राहुः सामान्यं यदतोन्यथा। परं निरस्य यल्लब्धं विद्यया पणपूर्व्वकम्। विद्याधनन्तु तद्विद्यान्न विभाज्यं बृहस्पतिः। विद्याप्रतिज्ञया लब्धं शिष्यादाप्तञ्च यद्भवेत्। ऋत्विङ्न्यायेन यल्लब्धमेतद्विद्याधनं भृगुः॥ प्राध्ययनात् प्रकृष्टाध्ययनात्। मूल्याद्यच्चाधिकं भवेदिति उचितमूल्यात्पुरुषबुद्ध्या यदधिकं लभ्यते, तदपि तस्यासाधारणमेवेत्यर्थः। विद्यापणकृतमिति, अत्राध्याये अत्र वादस्थाने वा अप्रमादिना इदं वक्तव्यमित्यनेन रूपेण यल्लब्धं, तदप्यसाधारणमित्यर्थः। विद्याप्रतिज्ञयेति अहमेवेमां विद्यामधीये इति प्रतिज्ञा, तया लब्धम्। (14) अथ यादृशं शौर्य्यधनमविभाज्यं तदाह। आरुह्य संशयं यच्च प्रसभं कर्म्म कुर्व्वते। तस्मिन् कर्म्मणि तुष्टेन प्रसादः स्वामिना कृतः। तत्र लब्धन्तु यत्किञ्चित् धनं शौर्य्येण तत् भवेत्। ध्वजाहृतं भवेत् यत् तु विभाज्यं नैव तत् स्मृतम्। संग्रामादाहृतं यत्तु विद्राव्य द्विषतां बलम्। स्वाम्यर्थे जीवितं त्यक्त्वा तत् ध्वजाहृतम् उच्यते॥ (15) अथ यादृशमौद्वाहिकम् असाधारणं तदाह। यल्लब्धं लाभकाले तु सजात्या कन्यया सह। कन्यागतन्तु तद्वित्तं शुल्कं वृद्धिकरं स्मृतम्। वैवाहिकन्तु तत् विद्यात् भार्य्यया यत् सहागतम्। धनमेवंविधं सर्व्वं विज्ञेयं

कर्म्मसाधकम् ॥ (16) शङ्खलिखितौ। न वास्तुविभागो नोदपात्रालङ्कारानुयुक्तस्त्रीवाससाम् अपां प्रचारवर्त्मनाम् अविभागश्चेति प्रजापतिः ॥ वास्तुगृहं, उदपात्रं लौहवारिभाजनं, अलङ्कारोऽङ्गन्यस्तएव, अनुयुक्तमुपभुक्तं, तेन एकोपभोगविषयस्त्रीवाससां न विभाग इति शाप्यते। अपां प्रचारवर्त्मनां जलप्रचरणमार्गाणाम्। (17) मनुविष्णू। वस्त्रं पत्रम् अलङ्कारं कृतान्नम् उदकं स्त्रियः। योगक्षेमप्रचारञ्च न विभाज्यं प्रचक्षते ॥ पत्रशब्दो लेख्यनिविष्टधनपरः,—धनं पत्रनिविष्टमिति कात्यायनवचनात्,—ऋणमपास्य लेखितमिति वृहस्पतिवचनाच्च। हलायुधस्तु पत्रं वाहनमित्याह। कृतान्नं शक्वादि। तण्डुलादीति पारिजाते। स्त्रियः संयुक्ताः,—अविभागः स्त्रीषु संयुक्तास्विति गौतमवचनात्। योगक्षेमं मन्त्रिपुरोहितादि तद्धेतुत्वात्। प्रचारो गवादीनां प्रचरणमार्गः, योगक्षेमं पितृक्रमेण राजकुलादावुपजीव्यमिति प्रकाशः। हलायुधस्तु योगो-योगहेतुर्नौकादिः, क्षेमः क्षेमहेतुर्दुर्गादीत्याह। (18) व्यासः। अविभाज्यं सगोत्राणाम् आसहस्रकुलादपि। याज्यं क्षेत्रञ्च पत्रञ्च कृतान्नम् उदकं स्त्रियः ॥ क्षेत्रं वास्तुक्षेत्रं, पत्रं वाहनमिति प्रकाशकारः। (19) कात्यायनः। धनं पत्रनिविष्टन्तु धर्म्मार्थं यन्निरूपितम्। उदकञ्चैव दाराश्च निबन्धो यः क्रमागतः। धृतं वस्त्रम् अलङ्कारो नानुरूपञ्च यद्भवेत्। यथाकालोपयुक्तानि तथा योज्यानि बन्धुभिः। गोप्रचारश्च रथ्या च वस्त्रं यच्-चाङ्गयोजितम्। प्रयोज्यं न विभज्येत शिल्पार्थञ्च वृहस्पतिः। देशस्य जातेः सङ्घस्य धर्म्मो-ग्रामस्य यो भृगुः। उदितः स्यात् स तेनैव दायभागं प्रकल्पयेत् ॥ धृतं वस्त्रं बहुमूल्यम्, अङ्गयोजितम् अबहुमूल्यं विवचितम्। धर्म्मार्थं यन्निरूपितं सर्व्वसाधारणधर्म्मार्थं यद्व्यवस्थापितं देवाराधनाय घण्टादि। निबन्धः पूर्व्वं व्याख्यातः। नानुरूपञ्च यद्भवेत् यत्र साक्षाद्विभागो न सम्भवो। प्रयोज्यं प्रयुक्तमृणमिति हलायुधः। प्रयोज्यं प्रयोगार्हं पुस्तकादि, तन्न विभज्येत मूर्खादिभिरिति पारिजातः। शिल्पार्थं तूलिकादि। (20) अथ वृहस्पतिः। वस्त्रादयोविभाज्या यैरुक्तन्तैर्न विचारितम्। धनं भवेत्समृद्धानां पत्रालङ्कारसंश्रितम्। मध्यस्थितम् अनाजीव्यं दातुं नैकस्य शक्यते। युक्त्या विभजनीयं तत् अन्यथानर्थकं भवेत्। विक्रीय वस्त्राभरणम् ऋणम् उद्ग्राह्य लेखितम्। कृतान्नञ्चाकृतान्नेन परिवर्त्त्य विभज्यते। उद्धृत्य कूपवाप्यम्भस्त्वनुसारेण गृह्यते। यथाभागानुसारेण सेतुः क्षेत्रं विभज्यते। एकां स्त्रीं कारयेत् कर्म्म यथांशेन गृहे गृहे। बह्व्यः समांशतो देया दासानामप्ययं विधिः। योगक्षेमवतो लाभः समत्वेन विभज्यते।

प्रचारश्च यथांशेन कर्त्तव्य ऋक्थिभिः सदा॥ मध्यस्थितमनाजीव्यं मध्यगं सदनुपयुक्तं, दातुं नैकस्य शक्यते, एकस्मै दातुमशक्यं, योगक्षेमवतो विभागयोगक्षेमवतो मन्त्रिपुरोहितादेः। अत्र वस्त्रादीनां बहुमूल्यानां स्वरूपतो विभाज्यत्वमुक्तम्, अतो मन्वादीनामविभाज्यत्ववचनम् अल्पमूल्यवस्त्रादौ स्वरूपत एव निषेधकं, बहुमूल्येषु उक्तातद्विभागप्रकारव्यतिरिक्तप्रकारेण विभागनिषेधकं द्रष्टव्यमित्यविरोधः। प्रकाशकारस्त्वल्पमूल्यमङ्गसंयुक्तं यत्, तन्न विभजनीयम्, समृद्धन्तु धनं पत्रालङ्कारहस्त्यादिसंश्रितं यत् तत् विभजनीयमेव, तस्य विभागप्रकार उक्तो मध्यस्थितमनाजीव्यमित्यादिनेत्याह। (21) इदानीं यद्विधविद्याधनादीनामपि विभागोऽर्हति तदाह कात्यायनः। कुले विनीतविद्यानां भ्रातॄणां पितृतोऽपि वा। शौर्य्यप्राप्तन्तु यद्वित्तं विभाज्यं तद् बृहस्पतिः॥ कुले पितामहपितृव्यादिभ्यः पितृत एव वा शिक्षितविद्यानां भ्रात्रादीनां यद्विद्याशौर्य्यप्राप्तं धनं, तद्विभजनीयमेवेत्यर्थः। (22) नारदः। कुटुम्बं बिभृयाद्-भ्रातुर्यो विद्याम् अधिगच्छतः। भागं विद्याधनात् तस्मात् स लभेताश्रुतोऽपि सन्॥ अश्रुतः अविद्यः। (23) मनुः। यत् किञ्चित् पितरि प्रेते धनं ज्येष्ठोऽधिगच्छति। भागो यवीयसां तत्र यदि विद्यानुपालिनः॥ यत्किञ्चित्पितरि प्रेते असाधारणविद्यादिना ज्येष्ठो धनमर्जयति, तत्र ज्येष्ठार्जिते ज्येष्ठस्यांशद्वयम्, एकैकस्तु भागः कनिष्ठानां, यदि ते विद्याभ्यासरता इत्यर्थः। (24) अविद्यानान्तु सर्व्वेषामीहातो यद् धनं भवेत्। समस्तत्र विभागः स्याद्-अपित्र्य इति धारणा॥ यदा सर्व्व एव भ्रातरोऽविद्वांसः कृष्यादिना धनमर्जयन्ति, तदा तस्मिन् अपित्र्ये धने सम एव विभागः, न तु तत्र बहुतरम् अनेनोपात्तम् इत्युद्धारादि कर्त्तव्यमित्यर्थः। (25) स्वयमर्जितमित्यनुवृत्तौ गौतमः। अविद्याः समं विभजेरन्॥ अविद्यास्तद्धनासाधारणप्रयोजकविद्याशून्याः। (26) वशिष्ठः। येन चैषां स्वयमुत्पादितं स्यात्, स द्व्यंशमेव हरेत्॥ यदा बहूनां मध्ये साधारणधनमाश्रित्य एव कृष्यादिनार्जयति, तदा तस्य द्वावंशौ, शेषाणामेकैकः। (27) व्यासः। साधारणं समाश्रित्य यत्किञ्चिद्वाहनायुधम्। शौर्य्यादिनाप्नोति धनं भ्रातरस्तत्र भागिनः। तस्य भागद्वयं कार्य्यं शेषास्तु समभागिनः॥ एतत्परिभाषितविद्याशौर्य्यादिधनव्यतिरिक्तविद्याशौर्य्यादिधनाभिप्रायेण द्रष्टव्यमिति। (28) इति विवादरत्नाकरेऽविभाज्यतरङ्गः।

CHAPTER VIII.

(1) **अथ स्त्रीधनकृत्यम्।** (2) तत्र मनुः। न निर्हारं स्त्रियः कुर्य्युः कुटुम्बाद्बहुमध्यगात्। स्वकादपि च वित्ताद्धि स्वस्य भर्त्तुरनाज्ञया॥ कुटुम्बशब्देनात्र कुटुम्बधनं साहचर्य्यादभिमतम्। तेन बहुमध्यगात् धनात् स्त्रीभिर्धनिनाम् अननुमत्या निर्हारो धनस्य निष्कृष्य हरणं न कार्य्यम्। तथा स्वकादपि कुटुम्बान्तरापेक्षया भर्त्तुरसाधारणधनादपि निष्कृष्य हरणं धनस्वामिनाम् अननुमत्या न कार्य्यमित्यर्थः। (3) मनुविष्णू। पत्यौ जीवति यः स्त्रीभिरलङ्कारो धृतो भवेत्। न तं भजेरन् दायादा भजमानाः पतन्ति ते॥ पत्युरनुज्ञातेनाप्यदत्तोऽप्यलङ्कारो यो मण्डनार्थं धृतः, सोऽपि दायादैर्न हर्त्तव्य इति मेधातिथिरिति प्रकाशः। (4) अत्रापस्तम्बः। अलङ्कारो भार्य्याया ज्ञातिधनञ्चेत्येके॥ ज्ञातिधनञ्चेति विवाहे यद्धनं यौतकाख्यं लब्धं तदपि भार्य्याया एवेत्यर्थः। (5) नारदः। भर्त्त्रा प्रीतेन यद्दत्तं स्त्रियै तस्मिन् मृतेऽपि तत्। सा यथाकामम् अश्नीयात् दद्याद्वा स्थावरादृते॥ (6) यावत् भर्त्त्रा दत्तं धनं स्त्रीस्वातन्त्र्यविषयं तावत् दर्शयति व्यासः। द्विसहस्रपणो दायः स्त्रियै देयो धनस्य तु। यच्च भर्त्त्रा धनं दत्तं सा यथाकामम् आप्नुयात्॥ द्वे सहस्रे पणानां परिमाणम् अस्येति द्विसहस्रपण इति वचनात्, अल्पे धने अल्पदानमेवेति—स्वेच्छादेयं स्वयंप्राप्तमिति वचनात्, साधारणधनाभिप्रायमेतदिति वदन्ति। प्रकाशस्तु या अयोग्यभर्त्तृका भर्त्तव्यत्वेन श्रुताः पृथक्क्रियन्ते, ताभ्यः पणसहस्रद्वयाधिकमदेयमिति। (7) कात्यायनः। ऊढ़या कन्यया वापि पत्युः पितृगृहेऽथवा। भ्रातुः सकाशात् पित्रोर्वा लब्धं सौदायिकं स्मृतम्। सौदायिकं धनं प्राप्य स्त्रीणां स्वातन्त्र्यम् इष्यते। यस्मात् तदानृशंस्यार्थं तैर्दत्तं तत्प्रजीवनम्। सौदायिके सदा स्त्रीणां स्वातन्त्र्यं परिकीर्त्तितम्। विक्रये चैव दाने च यथेष्टं स्थावरेष्वपि॥ पत्युर्गृह इति सम्बन्धः। भ्रातुः सकाशात् पित्रोर्वेत्युपलक्षणम्। तेन ऊढ़या अनूढ़या वा, पतिगृहे पितृगृहे वा, स्वमातुः स्वपितुर्वा, तत्कुल्येभ्यो वा, यल्लब्धं तत् सौदायिकम्। आनृशंस्यम् अदारुणता, तेन यस्मादियं वित्ताभावात् दारुणा न भवतु, एतदर्थं तैः पित्रादिभिर्दत्तं तत् प्रजीवनमिति लभ्यते। तदेवं सौदायिके धने स्थावरसाधारणं स्त्रीणां स्वातन्त्र्यं, भर्त्तृदत्ते तु स्थावरादन्यस्मिन् स्थितम्। (8) तथा। भर्त्तृदायं मृते पत्यौ

विन्यसेत् स्त्री यथेष्टतः। विद्यमाने तु संरक्षेत् क्षपयेत् तत्कुलेऽन्यथा। अपुत्रा शयनं भर्त्तुः पालयन्ती गुरौ स्थिता। भुञ्जीतामरणात् क्षान्ता, दायादा ऊर्द्ध्वम् आप्नुयुः॥ अत्र भर्त्तृदायो भर्त्तृसम्बन्धेन स्त्रीस्वत्वाश्रयो धनं, तच्च द्विधा,—मृते भर्त्तरि अभिकार्थ्यन्तराभावात् स्त्रीस्वत्वाश्रयः, जीवत्येव भर्त्तरि तत्सम्बन्धेन वा स्त्रीस्वत्वाश्रयः। तत्र प्रथमे, स्त्री स्थावरात् अन्यत् यथेष्टं विन्यसेत् विनियुञ्जीत, गुरुसमीपे स्थिता भर्त्तुः शय्यां पालयन्ती समयं क्षपयेत्। स्थावरम् अधिकृत्याह, भुञ्जीतामरणात्, अग्रे दायादा आप्नुयुः। द्वितीये त्वाह, विद्यमाने तु संरक्षेत्, व्यये भर्त्तुरनुज्ञां पालयन्ती तद्वनरक्षां कुर्य्यात्, इति प्रकाशानुसारः। हलायुधपारिजातौ तु भर्त्तृदायं, भर्त्तृदत्त-स्त्रीधनम्, आहतुः। तदत्रापुत्रसंक्रान्ते स्त्रीस्वत्वाश्रयेऽपि धने आकाङ्क्षायाः सत्त्वात्प्रकाशस्वरसो बलीयान्, प्रकरणानुरोधस्य, आकाङ्क्षाया बलवत्त्वात्, निर्हारनिषेधवत्, त्यज्यतेऽपीति। (9) मनुः। वशापुत्रासु चैवं स्याद्रक्षणं निष्कुलासु च। पतिव्रतासु च स्त्रीषु विधवास्वातुरासु च। जीवन्तीनान्तु तासां ये तद्धरेयुः स्वबान्धवाः। ताञ्छिष्याच्चौरदण्डेन धार्म्मिकः पृथिवीपतिः॥ वशा बन्ध्या, अपुत्राः प्रणष्टपुत्राः, निष्कुलाः प्रणष्टमातापितृकुलाः। (10) देवलः। वृत्तिराभरणं शुल्कं लाभश्च स्त्रीधनं भवेत्। भोक्त्री च स्वयमेवेदं पतिर्नार्हत्यनापदि। वृथा मोक्षे च भोगे च स्त्रियै दद्यात् सवृद्धिकम्। पुत्रार्त्तिहरणे वापि स्त्रीधनं भोक्तुमर्हति॥ वृत्तिवृत्त्यर्थं दत्तधनं, लाभो बन्धुभ्य-लब्धं, शुल्कं विवाहार्थितया कन्यायै दत्तं धनम्। वृथा मोक्षे चेति, यदा आवश्यककार्य्यादिना धनमादाय वृथादानभोगौ करोति, तदा सवृद्धिकं धनं दद्यात्। पुत्रार्त्तिहरणार्थन्तु, स्त्रीधनं, विनापि स्त्रीसम्मत्या, ग्रहीतव्यम्। (11) कात्यायनः। न भर्त्ता नैव च सुतो न पिता भ्रातरो न च। आदाने वा विसर्गे वा स्त्रीधने प्रभविष्णवः। यदि ह्येकतरस्तेषां स्त्रीधनं हरते बलात्। स वृद्धिं प्रतिदाप्यः स्यात् दण्डञ्चैव समाप्नुयात्। तदेव यद्यनुज्ञाप्यः भक्षयेत् प्रीतिपूर्व्वकम्। मूलमेव स दाप्यः स्याद् यदा स धनवान् भवेत्। व्याधितं व्यसनस्थञ्च धनिकैर्वाऽपपीड़ितम्। दृष्ट्वा निसृष्टं यत् प्रीत्या दद्यादात्मेच्छया हि सः॥ व्याध्यादिना गृहीतं स्वाम्यादिकं दृष्ट्वा स्त्रिया यत् प्रीत्या धनं स्वामि-प्रभृतये दत्तम्, तत् स्वेच्छया स्वामिप्रभृतिभिर्देयमित्यनन्तरवाक्यार्थः। (12) याज्ञवल्क्यः। दुर्भिक्षे धर्म्मकार्य्ये च व्याधौ सम्प्रतिरोधके। गृहीतं स्त्रीधनं भर्त्ता न स्त्रियै दातुमर्हति॥ धर्म्मकार्य्ये अवश्यकर्त्तव्ये। व्याधाविति, यस्मिन् व्याधौ कार्य्यप्रतिरोधो भवति, तन्निर्हारार्थं स्त्रीधनं गृहीतं न स्त्रियै

दातव्यमित्यर्थः। (13) कात्यायनः। अथ चेत् स द्विभार्य्यः स्यात् न च तां भजते पुनः। प्रीत्या निसृष्टमपि चेत् प्रतिदाप्यः स तद्धनम्। ग्रासाच्छादन-वासानाम् आच्छेदो यत्र योषितः। तत्र स्वम् आददीत स्त्री विभाग-मृक्थिनस्तथा॥ लिखितस्येति धर्म्मोऽयं प्राप्ते भर्त्तृकुले वसेत्। व्याधिता प्रेतकाले तु गच्छेद्‌बन्धुकुलं ततः॥ अपकारक्रियायुक्ता निर्लज्जार्थविनाशिका। व्यभिचाररता स्त्री तु स्त्रीधनं न च सार्हति॥ यज्ञार्थं द्रव्यमुत्पन्नं तस्माद्‌द्रव्यं नियोजयेत्। स्थानेषु धर्म्मयुक्तेषु न स्त्रीमूर्खविधर्म्मिषु॥ भर्त्रा प्रतिश्रुतं देयम् ऋणवत् स्त्रीधनं सुतैः। तिष्ठेद्‌भर्त्तृकुले जातु न या पितृकुले वसेत्॥ यदा प्रीत्या यया भार्य्यया धनं दत्तं, तां पतिर्न भजते ऋतुकालादावपि, तथा ग्रासाच्छादनवासानामाच्छेदो वा भवति, तदा व्याध्याद्युपहतं पतिमालोक्य स्वधनं दत्तमपि तया बलाद्‌ग्राह्यं, तच्चाश्रमे तस्या लब्धं भवति, तदापि पत्यादि-सकाशाद्-ग्राह्यम् इत्ययं शास्त्रधर्म्मः। प्राप्ते च तत्र धने सा भर्त्तुः कुले एव वसेत्। बलवति व्याधौ तद्‌बन्धुकुलं गच्छेदिति, बन्धुकुलं तत इत्यन्तस्यार्थः। (14) इति विवादरत्नाकरे स्त्रीधनकृत्यतरङ्गः।

CHAPTER IX.

(1) अथ स्त्रीधनविभागनिर्णयः। (2) तत्र मनुः। जनन्यां संस्थिता-यान्तु समं सर्व्वे सहोदराः। भजेरन् मातृकं रिक्थं भगिन्यश्च सनाभयः॥ समं ज्येष्ठोद्धारादिशून्यम्, भगिन्योऽत्र अप्रत्ता अप्रतिष्ठिताश्च विवक्षिताः, अग्रिमबृहस्पतिवाक्यानुसारात् सनाभयः सहोदराः। (3) तथा। यास्तासां स्युर्दुहितरस्तासामपि यथांशतः। मातामह्या धनात् किञ्चित् प्रदेयं प्रीति-पूर्व्वकम्॥ तासां भगिनीनां यथांशतो धनबहुत्वाल्पत्वानुसारेण। (4) तथा। अन्वाधेयञ्च यद्दत्तं पत्या प्रीतेन चैव यत्। पत्यौ जीवति वृत्तायाः प्रजायास्तद्धनं भवेत्॥ अन्वाधेयलक्षणं वक्ष्यते। एतच्च वचनं, वृत्तायां जीवत्यपि पत्यौ एवंविधधनद्वये पतिसम्बन्धनिराकरणार्थम् आरब्धमिति हलायुधः। (5) बृहस्पतिः। स्त्रीधनं स्यादपत्यानां दुहिता च तदंशिनी। अप्रत्ता चेत् समूढ़ा तु लभते मानमात्रकम्॥ अपत्यानां पुत्राणां तदंशिनी

पुत्रांशसमांशिनी। अप्रत्ता अनूढ़ा। तेनैतद्वाक्यबलान्मनुवाक्येऽपि अनूढ़ानामेव भ्रातृभिः सह समांशित्वमिति बोद्धव्यम्। ऊढ़ानान्तु मानानुसारेण किञ्चिद्देयम्। (6) गौतमः। स्त्रीधनं दुहितॄणामप्रत्तानामप्रतिष्ठितानाञ्च॥ एतत् न पुत्रांशस्य व्यावृत्त्यर्थं किन्तु दुहितृवंशप्रतिपादनार्थम्। अप्रतिष्ठिता विवाहितानपत्या निर्धनभर्त्तृका दुर्भगा च। (7) मनुः। मातुस्तु यौतकं यत् स्यात् कुमारीभाग एव सः॥ यौतकमत्र परिणयनकाले पित्रादिभिः स्त्रियै दत्तम्। हलायुधस्तु यौतकं शाकसूपार्थं स्त्रियै दत्तं तया स्वकौशलेन विशेषितम्, तत्र न भ्रातॄणामूढ़ानाञ्च भागः, अनपत्यानां दुर्भगाणामूढ़ानाञ्च सम एवांश इति। (8) वशिष्ठः। मातुः पारिणाय्यं स्त्रियो विभजेरन्॥ पारिणाय्यं परिच्छद आदर्श-कङ्कणादि। (9) विभजेरन्नूर्द्ध्वमित्यनुवृत्तौ याज्ञवल्क्यः। मातुर्दुहितरः शेषमृणात्ताभ्य ऋतेऽन्वयः॥ ऋणात् मातॄणात्, शेषमवशिष्टं, तेन मातॄणं परिशोध्य यौतकं पारिणाय्यञ्च धनमवशिष्टम् अप्रत्ता अप्रतिष्ठिताश्च दुहितरो भजेरन् इति खण्डार्थः। ताभ्यो दुहितृभ्य ऋते विना तदन्वयः दुहितुः पुत्रादिः। ब्राह्मादिविवाहविषयमेतत्। (10) तथाच विवाहेष्वित्यनुवृत्तौ विष्णुः। सर्व्वेष्वेव प्रसूतानां तद्धनं दुहितृगामि॥ (11) मनुः। स्त्रियास्तु यद्भवेद्वित्तं पित्रा दत्तं कथञ्चन। ब्राह्मणी तद्धरेत् कन्या तदपत्यस्य वा भवेत्॥ यदा भर्त्ता स्वापत्यानि च न सन्ति, सपत्न्यश्च नानाजातीयाः तद्दुहितरश्च सन्ति, तदा ब्राह्मणी कन्या पितृदत्तं मातृसपत्नीधनमर्हति, तदभावे तदपत्यं वेत्यर्थः। पित्रा दत्तमिति स्त्रीधनमात्रोपलक्षणम् इत्यसहायमेधातिथिरिति प्रकाशकारः। (12) कात्यायनः। दुहितॄणामभावे तु ऋक्‌थं पुत्रेषु तद्भवेत्। बन्धुदत्तन्तु बन्धूनामभावे भर्त्तृगामि तत्। भगिन्यो बान्धवैः सार्द्धं विभजेयुः सभर्त्तृकाः। स्त्रीधनस्येति धर्म्मोऽयं विभागस्तु प्रकल्पितः॥ पारिणाय्यं यौतकं पितृदत्तञ्च धनं दुहितॄणामभावे पुत्रगामि। तदतिरिक्तस्त्रीधने पूर्व्वोक्ताः। अभावे पूर्व्वोक्तानां भर्त्तृगाम्येव धनमिति। (13) इति विवादरत्नाकरे स्त्रीधनविभागनिर्णयतरङ्गः।

CHAPTER X.

(1) अथाप्रजाधने विवाहविशेषेण व्यवस्था। (2) तत्र नारदः। स्त्रीधनं स्यादपत्यानां भर्त्तृगाम्यप्रजासु च। ब्राह्म्यादिषु चतुर्ष्वाहुः पितृगामीतरेषु च॥ चतुर्ष्विति न पञ्चमव्यवच्छेदार्थं, तेन ब्राह्मदैवार्षगान्धर्व्वप्रजापत्येषु अप्रजाया धनं तदपगमे भर्त्तृगामि, इतरेषु राक्षसासुरपैशाचेषु पितृगामि। विवाहकाललब्धस्त्रीधनविषयमिदम्। (3) तथाच मनुः। ब्राह्मदैवार्षगान्धर्व्व-प्राजापत्येषु यद्धनम्। अतीतायामप्रजसि भर्त्तुरेव तदिष्यते। यत्त्वस्याः स्याद्धनं दत्तं विवाहेष्वासुरादिषु। अतीतायामप्रजसि मातापित्रोस्तदिष्यते॥ अप्रजसि अनपत्यायाम्। (4) देवलः। सामान्यं पुत्रकन्यानां मृतायां स्त्रीधनं स्त्रियाम्। अप्रजायां हरेद्भर्त्ता माता भ्राता पितापि वा॥ हरेद्-भर्त्ता ब्राह्म्यादिषु, मातेत्यासुरादिषु, एवञ्च मनुनारदयोरपि देवलोक्तमादायात्र तात्पर्य्यमिति मन्तव्यम्। (5) अत्र गौतमः। भगिनीशुल्कं सोदर्य्याणा-मूर्द्ध्वं मातुः पूर्व्वञ्चैके॥ यो भगिन्या भर्त्तृगृहादासुरादिविवाहेष्वर्थो लब्धः, स ऊर्द्ध्वं मातुः, मातर्य्यतीतायां, सोदर्य्याणां पूर्व्वञ्चेति चशब्दोऽप्यर्थे, तेन मातुर्मरणात् पूर्व्वमपि भगिनीनामीदृशं सोदर्य्याणामित्येके। परमतमेतदित्यत्र हलायुधः। (6) याज्ञवल्क्यः। बन्धुदत्तं तथा शुल्कमन्वाधेयकमेव च। अप्रजायामतीतायां बान्धवास्तदवाप्नुयुः॥ शुल्कं यद्गृहीत्वा कन्या दीयते तदिह विवक्षितम्। अन्वाधेयकं स्त्रीधनलक्षणम्। बान्धवाः सोदराः। इदमप्यासुरादिविवाहविषयम्। (7) मनुः। अपुत्रायां मृतायान्तु पुत्रिकायां कथञ्चन। धनं तत्पुत्रिकाभर्त्ता हरेतैवाविचारयन्॥ एतच्च यदा अपुत्राया-स्तस्याः कुमारी न भवति भगिनी वा, तदा बोद्धव्यम्। (8) तथाच पैठीनसिः। प्रेतायां पुत्रिकायां न भर्त्ता तद्द्रव्यमर्हत्यपुत्रायां कुमार्य्या स्वस्रा वा तद्ग्राह्यम्॥ अत्र कुमार्य्या अभावे स्वस्रा ग्राह्यम्। (9) याज्ञवल्क्यः। दत्त्वा कन्यां हरन् दण्ड्यो व्ययं दद्याच्च सोदयम्। मृतायां सर्व्वमादद्यात् परिशोध्योभयव्ययम्॥ कन्यां वाचा दत्त्वा विना दोषमपहरन् राज्ञा दण्ड्यः, व्ययञ्च सवृद्धिकं वरस्य दापयितव्यः, कारणे त्वपहारी न दोषाय। यदाह। दत्तामपि हरेत् कन्यां श्रेयांश्चेद्वर आव्रजेत्॥ यदि तु दैवाद्वाग्दत्ता कन्या म्रियते, तदा यत् पूर्व्वसम्बन्धिनामुपचारार्थं पित्रा दत्तं, यच्च सम्बन्धिना अङ्गुरीयकादि दत्तं, तदुभयं परिशोध्य परिगण्यावशिष्टमाददात्। (10)

अर्हतीत्यनुवृत्तौ शङ्खः। स्वयं शुल्कं वोढ़ा॥ (11) बौधायनः। ऋक्थं मृतायाः कन्याया गृह्णीयुः सोदराः स्वयम्। तदभावे भवेन्मातुस्तदभावे पितुर्भवेत्॥ अथ कन्यानूढ़ाभिप्रेता। (12) वृहस्पतिः। मातृष्वसा मातुलानी पितृव्यस्त्री पितुः स्वसा। श्वश्रूः पूर्व्वजपत्नी च मातृतुल्याः प्रकीर्त्तिताः। यदासामौरसो न स्यात् सुतो दौहित्र एव वा। तत्सुतो वा धनं तासां स्वस्रीयाद्याः समाप्नुयुः॥ औरसादीनामभावे मातृष्वस्रादीनां स्वधनं स्वस्रीयाद्या आप्नुयुरित्यर्थः। (13) इति विवादरत्नाकरे अप्रजाधने विवाहविशेषेण व्यवस्थातरङ्गः।

CHAPTER XI.

(1) अथ स्त्रीधनलक्षणम्। (2) तत्र मनुकात्यायनौ। अध्यग्न्यध्यावाहनिकं दत्तञ्च प्रीतितः स्त्रियै। मातृभ्रातृपितृप्राप्तं षड़्विधं स्त्रीधनं स्मृतम्॥ अध्यग्नि, उद्वाहकाले येन केनचित् दत्तम्। अध्यावाहनिकं, पतिगृहं नीयमानायाः पृष्ठतो यन्नीयते तत्, भर्त्तृगृहाद्यदा पितृगृहं वाह्यते तदा श्वशुरादिभिर्द्दत्तमध्यावाहनिकमिति मेधातिथिः, तदपि ग्राह्यं न्यायसाम्यात्। दत्तञ्च प्रीतितः शीलधर्म्मनैपुण्यादिषु उत्पन्नप्रीतिना श्वशुरादिना दत्तञ्च। षड़्विधमिति न्यूनसंख्याव्यवच्छेदार्थं नत्वधिकव्यवच्छेदार्थम्। आधिवेदनिकस्यापि स्त्रीधनस्याधिकस्य याज्ञवल्क्येनाभिधानात्। (3) तथाच याज्ञवल्क्यः। पितृमातृपतिभ्रातृदत्तमध्यग्न्युपागतम्। आधिवेदनिकञ्चापि स्त्रीधनं परिकीर्त्तितम्॥ (4) लक्षितञ्च तेनैव। अधिविन्नस्त्रियै देयमाधिवेदनिकं समम्। न दत्तं स्त्रीधनं यस्यै दत्ते त्वर्द्धं प्रकीर्त्तितम्॥ यस्या उपरि विवाहः, साधिविन्ना। तथा अन्वाधेयस्याधिकस्य विष्णुना कथनात्। (5) तथाच विष्णुः। पितृमातृसुतभ्रातृदत्तम् अध्यग्न्युपागतम्। आधिवेदनिकं शुल्कम् अन्वाधेयकमिति स्त्रीधनलक्षणम्॥ (6) नारदः। अध्यग्न्यध्यावाहनिकं भर्त्तृदायस्तथैव च। भ्रातृदत्तं पितृभ्याञ्च षड़्विधं स्त्रीधनं स्मृतम्॥ अत्रापि नाधिकव्यवच्छेदे तात्पर्य्यम्। (7) देवलः। वृत्तिराभरणं शुल्कं लाभश्च स्त्रीधनं भवेत्॥ (8) कात्यायनः। प्राप्तं शिल्पैस्तु यद्वित्तं प्रीत्या चैव यदन्यतः। भर्त्तुः स्वाम्यं सदा तत्र शेषन्तु स्त्रीधनं भवेत्॥ उक्तप्रकाराति-

रिक्तं यत् स्त्रीधनं स्त्रियार्जितम्, तत्र स्त्रिया एव स्वाम्यमित्यर्थः। (9) तथा। विवाहकाले यत् स्त्रीभ्यो दीयते ह्यग्निसन्निधौ। तदध्यग्निकृतं सद्भिः स्त्रीधनं परिकीर्त्तितम्। यत् पुनर्लभते नारी नीयमाना हि पैतृकात्। अध्यावाहनिकं नाम स्त्रीधनं समुदाहृतम्॥ एतत् कात्यायनीयम् अध्यावाहनिकम्। (10) तथा। प्रीत्या प्रदत्तं यत् किञ्चिच्छ्वश्वा वा श्वशुरेण वा। पादवन्दनिकं यत् तल्लावण्यार्जितमुच्यते। विवाहात् परतो यत्तु लब्धं भर्त्तृकुलात् स्त्रिया। अन्वाधेयन्तु तत् प्रोक्तं यल्लब्धं स्वकुलात्तथा।, ऊर्द्धं लब्धं तु यत् किञ्चित् संस्कारात् प्रीतितः स्त्रिया। भर्त्तुः पित्रोः सकाशाद्वा अन्वाधेयन्तु तद्भृगुः। गृहोपस्कर-वाह्यानां दोह्याभरणकर्म्मिणाम्। मूल्यं लब्धञ्च यत् किञ्चित् शुल्कं तत् परिकीर्त्तितम्॥ गृहादिकर्म्मिभिः तत्कर्म्मकरणाय प्रेरणार्थं यद्धनं स्त्रियै उत्कोच-रूपतया दत्तं तच्छुल्कमित्यर्थः। सौदायिकञ्च पूर्व्वमेव प्रसङ्गादुक्तमिति नेह प्रकरणे दर्शितम्। (11) इति विवादरत्नाकरे स्त्रीधनलक्षणतरङ्गः।

CHAPTER XII.

(1) अथावलुप्तविभागः। (2) तत्र मनुः। ऋणे धने च सर्व्वस्मिन् प्रविभक्ते यथाविधि। पश्चाद्दृश्येत यत्किञ्चित् तत्सर्व्वं समतां नयेत्॥ (3) याज्ञवल्क्यः। अन्योऽन्यापहृतं द्रव्यं विभक्तैर्यत्र दृश्यते। तत् पुनस्ते समैरंशैर्विभजेरन्निति स्थितिः॥ अत्र चौत्सर्गत एव विभागे प्राप्ते वचनारम्भबलेन साधारणधनापहारे स्तेयदोषो न भवतीति विज्ञाप्यते इति हलायुधः। (4) कात्यायनः। प्रच्छादितन्तु यद्येन पुनरागत्य तत्समम्। भजेरन् भ्रातृभिः सार्द्धमभावे तु पितुः सुताः। अन्योऽन्यापहृतं यच्च दुर्विभक्तञ्च यद्भवेत्। पश्चात्प्राप्तं विभज्येत समभागेन तद्भृगुः। विभक्तेनैव यत् प्राप्तं धनं तस्यैव तद्भवेत्। हृतं नष्टञ्च यल्लब्धं प्रागुक्तञ्च पुनर्भजेत्। बन्धुनापहृतं द्रव्यं बलान्नैव प्रदापयेत्। बन्धूनामविभक्तानां भोगं नैव प्रदापयेत्॥ हृतं परेणापहृतम्। नष्टमदृश्यमानं यल्लब्धं प्रागुक्तं पैतामहम्। बलान्नैव प्रदापयेदित्यनेन छलादिना तद्ग्राह्यमित्यभिप्रेतम्। भोगं नैव प्रदापयेत्, तद्विभागकाले नासावधिकोपभोक्ता च भोगं दापयितव्य इत्यर्थः। (5) बृहस्पतिः। साधा-

रण-ऋणन्यासनिह्नवे छद्मना क्रियाम्। पार्श्वहानिकरीं कृत्वा बलान्नैव प्रदापयेत्। मायाविनो धृतधनाः क्रूरा लुब्धाश्च ये नराः। सम्प्रीत्या साधनीयास्ते स्वार्थहान्या छलेन वा॥ साधारणेति। साधारण-ऋणन्यासनिह्नवे केनचित् कृते, छद्मना पार्श्वहानिकरीं निह्नवकर्त्तृस्वत्वहानिकरीं क्रियां कृत्वा तन्निह्नुतमपहारकं दापयेन्न तु बलादित्यर्थः। (6) इति विवादरत्नाकरे अवलुप्तविभागतरङ्गः।

CHAPTER XIII.

(1) अथ नानावर्णानां विभागः। (2) तत्र मनुः। एतद्विधानं विज्ञेयं विभागस्यैकयोनिषु। बह्वीषु चैकजातानां नानास्त्रीषु निबोधत। ब्राह्मणस्यानुपूर्व्वेण चतस्रस्तु यदा स्त्रियः। तासां पुत्रेषु जातेषु विभागोऽयं प्रकीर्त्तितः। कीनाशो गोवृषो यानम् अलङ्कारश्च वेश्म च। विप्रस्यौद्धारिकं देयमेकांशश्च प्रधानतः। त्र्यंशं दायाद्धरेद्विप्रो द्वावंशौ क्षत्रियासुतः। वैश्याजोऽध्यर्द्धमेवांशमंशं शूद्रासुतो हरेत्॥ एकयोनिषु, सवर्णेषु, एकजातानामेकेनोत्पादितानाम्। बह्वीषु नानास्त्रीषु अनेकवर्णजातासु भार्य्यासु एकजातानामित्यन्वयः। कीनाशो हलवाहकः। यानमश्वादि। तेन कीनाशगोवृषयानालङ्कारवेश्मानि देयानि विप्रापुत्रस्य, तदंशत्रये एकः प्रधानतः सारतश्च कर्त्तव्य इत्यर्थः, गोवृषादीनि च सति सम्भवे। (3) अनुद्धृतोद्धारविभागमुररीकृत्याह। सर्व्वं वा ऋक्थजातन्तु दशधा प्रविभज्यते। धर्म्म्यं विभागं कुर्व्वीत विधिनानेन धर्म्मवित्। चतुरोऽंशान् हरेद्विप्रस्त्रीनंशान् क्षत्रियासुतः। वैश्यापुत्रो हरेद्द्व्यंशमंशं शूद्रासुतो हरेत्॥ विप्र इत्येकत्वस्याविवक्षितत्वादनेकेषु विप्रेष्वियमेव व्यवस्थेति। (4) नारदः। वर्णावरेष्वंशहानिरूढ़ाजातेष्वनुक्रमात्॥ वर्णावरा विप्रस्य क्षत्रियादयः। ऊढ़ा परिणीता, अंशहानिः क्षत्रियाया जातस्य त्रयोऽंशा इत्यादि। वर्णान्तरेष्विति क्वापि पाठः। तत्राप्ययमेवार्थः। (5) महाभारते भीष्म उवाच। क्षत्रियस्यापि भार्य्ये द्वे विहिते कुरुनन्दन। तृतीया वा भवेच्छूद्रा नतु दृष्टान्ततः स्मृता। अष्टधा तु भवेत् कार्य्यं क्षत्रियस्वं युधिष्ठिर। क्षत्रियाया हरेत् पुत्रश्चतुरोऽंशान् पितुर्धनात्। युद्धौपचारिकं

यत्तु पितुरासीद्धरेच्च तत्। वैश्यापुत्रस्त भागांस्त्रीञ्छूद्रापुत्रस्तथाष्टमम्। सोऽपि दत्तं हरेत् पित्रा नादत्तं हर्त्तुमर्हति। एकैव हि भवेद्भार्य्या वैश्यस्य कुरुनन्दन। द्वितीया वा भवेच्छूद्रा न तु दृष्टान्ततः स्मृता। पञ्चधा तु भवेत् कार्य्यं वैश्यस्वं भरतर्षभ। तयोरपत्ययोर्वक्ष्ये विभागञ्च नराधिप। वैश्यापुत्रेण हर्त्तव्याश्चत्वारोऽंशाः पितुर्धनात्। पञ्चमस्तु भवेदंशः शूद्रापुत्रस्य भारत। सोऽपि दत्तं हरेत् पित्रा नादत्तं हर्त्तुमर्हति॥ दृष्टान्तोऽत्र वेदः। तेन वेदेनाकथितापि रागतस्तृतीया शूद्रा क्षत्रियेण विवाहिता यदि स्यात्, तदा तु तत्पुत्रस्यैवांशइत्यर्थः। एवमुत्तरत्रापि। युद्धोपकरणं खड्गादि। (6) याज्ञवल्क्यः। चतुस्त्रिद्व्येकभागाः स्युर्वर्णशो ब्राह्मणात्मजाः। क्षत्रजातास्त्रिद्व्येकान्विशस्तु द्व्येकभागिनः॥ यत्र ब्राह्मणस्य चतस्रः, क्षत्रियस्य च तिस्रो-भार्य्यास्तत्रेदं वचनम्। वर्णशो ब्राह्मणात्मजाः वर्णे वर्णे ब्राह्मणात्मजा इत्यर्थः। अत्र च यत्र क्षत्रियवैश्यावधिकगुणौ, तत्र महाभारतोक्ता विभागव्यवस्था। मन्दगुणयोस्तु याज्ञवल्क्योक्ता व्यवस्थेत्यविरोधः। (7) विष्णुः। ब्राह्मणस्य चतुर्वर्णेषु ये पुत्रा भवेयुस्ते पैतृकमृक्थं दशधा विभजेयुः। तत्र ब्राह्मणीपुत्रश्चतुरोऽंशानादद्यात्, क्षत्रियापुत्रस्त्रीन्, द्वावंशौ वैश्यापुत्रः, शूद्रापुत्रस्त्वेकम्। अथ चेच्छूद्रापुत्रवर्ज्जं ब्राह्मणस्य पुत्रत्रयं भवेत्, तदा नवधा धनं विभजेयुः, वर्णक्रमेण च चतुस्त्रिद्विभागोक्तानंशानादद्युः। वैश्यवर्ज्जमष्टधा कृत्वा चतुस्त्रीनेकञ्च समादद्युः। क्षत्रियवर्ज्जं सप्तधा कृत्वा चतुरो द्वावेकञ्च। ब्राह्मणवर्ज्जं षड्धा कृत्वा त्रीन् द्वावेकञ्च। क्षत्रियवैश्यशूद्रेष्वप्येवमेव विभागः। अथ ब्राह्मणस्य ब्राह्मणक्षत्रियौ पुत्रौ स्यातां, तदा सप्तधा कृताद्धनात् ब्राह्मणश्चतुरोऽंशानादद्यात्, त्रीन् राजन्यः। ब्राह्मणस्य ब्राह्मणवैश्यौ चेत् पुत्रौ, तदा तद्धनात् षड्धा विभक्ताच्चतुरोऽंशान् ब्राह्मण आदद्यात्, द्वौ वैश्यासुतः। अथ ब्राह्मणस्य ब्राह्मणशूद्रौ पुत्रौ स्यातां, तदा तद्धनं पञ्चधा विभजेयातां, चतुरोऽंशान् ब्राह्मणस्त्वादद्यात्, एकं शूद्रः। अथ ब्राह्मणस्य क्षत्रियस्य वा क्षत्रियवैश्यौ पुत्रौ स्यातां, तदा तद्धनं पञ्चधा विभजेयातां, त्रीनंशान् क्षत्रियस्त्वादद्यात्, द्वावंशौ वैश्यः। अथ ब्राह्मणस्य क्षत्रियस्य वा क्षत्रियशूद्रौ पुत्रौ स्यातां, तदा तद्धनं चतुर्धा विभजेयातां, त्रीनंशान् क्षत्रियस्त्वादद्यात्, एकं शूद्रः। अथ ब्राह्मणस्य क्षत्रियवैश्ययोर्वा वैश्यशूद्रौ पुत्रौ स्यातां, तदा तद्धनं त्रिधा विभजेयातां, द्वावंशौ वैश्य आदद्यात्, एकं शूद्रः॥ (8) अथ शङ्खलिखितौ। अन्यवर्णस्त्रीषु जातानां दायादर्द्धार्द्धहानिर्वर्णक्रमेण॥ (9) विष्णुः। यदि ब्राह्मणीपुत्रौ द्वौ स्यातामेकः शूद्रापुत्रस्तदा ब्राह्मणीपुत्रावष्टौ

भागानादद्याताम्, एकं शूद्रापुत्रः, अथ शूद्रापुत्रावुभौ स्यातामेको ब्राह्मणीपुत्रः, तदा षड्धा विभज्य चतुरोऽंशान् ब्राह्मण आदद्यात्, द्वावंशौ शूद्रापुत्रौ, अनेन क्रमेणांशकल्पना अन्यत्रापि भवति ॥ (10) पुनर्विष्णुः । अथैकपुत्रा ब्राह्मणस्य ब्राह्मणक्षत्रियवैश्याः सर्व्वहराः, क्षत्रियवैश्यौ वा राजन्यस्य, वैश्यस्य वैश्यः, शूद्रः शूद्रस्य ॥ यदा ब्राह्मणस्य ब्राह्मण्यादिभार्य्यासु तिसृषु मध्ये एक एव पुत्रो ब्राह्मणः, क्षत्रियो, वैश्यो वा, तदा सर्व्वहरः स एव । एवं यदि क्षत्रियस्यापि भार्य्याद्वये क्षत्रिय एव, वैश्य एव वा, तदा स एव सर्व्वहरः । एवं वैश्यस्याप्येको वैश्यः सर्व्वहरः, शूद्रस्यैकः शूद्रः सर्व्वहरः । क्षत्रियवैश्ययोस्तृतीया द्वितीया भार्य्या अवैदिकतया नात्रोक्ताः, अवैधयोस्तु क्षत्रियवैश्यत्तीयद्वितीयपरिणययोरेवमेव नेयम् । (11) वशिष्ठः । यदि ब्राह्मणक्षत्रियवैश्याः पुत्राः स्युः, त्र्यंशं ब्राह्मण्याः पुत्रो हरेत्, द्व्यंशं राजन्यायाः पुत्रः, सममितरे विभजेरन् ॥ इतरे वैश्यापुत्राः । अत्र च विष्णुवशिष्ठौ विषमविभागवादिनौ भागिगुणोत्कर्षाभ्यामविरोधितया व्यवस्थाप्यौ । (12) मनुः । समवर्णासु वा जाताः सर्व्वे पुत्रा द्विजन्मनाम् । उद्धारं ज्यायसे दत्त्वा भजेरन्नितरे समम् ॥ यत्र द्विजन्मनां समवर्णासु नानास्त्रीषु बहवः, पुत्राः, तथा वाशब्दादसवर्णास्वपि नानास्त्रीषु बहवः पुत्रास्तदा ज्यायसे किञ्चिदुद्धारं दत्त्वा सममितरे विभजेरन् । (13) तथा । शूद्रस्यतु सवर्णैव नान्या भार्य्योपदिश्यते । तस्यां जाताः समांशाः स्युर्यदि पुत्रशतं भवेत् ॥ (14) बौधायनः । सवर्णापुत्रानन्तरापुत्रयोरनन्तरापुत्रश्चेद् गुणवान् ज्येष्ठांशं हरेद् गुणवानशेषाणां भर्त्ता भवति ॥ (15) बृहस्पतिः । विप्रेण क्षत्रियाजातो जन्मज्येष्ठो गुणान्वितः । भवेत् समांशो विप्रेण वैश्याजातस्तथैव च ॥ (16) गौतमः । ब्राह्मणस्य राजन्यापुत्रो गुणसम्पन्नो ज्येष्ठतुल्यभाक् ज्येष्ठांशहीनमन्यत् ॥ अन्यद्रवादि, ज्येष्ठांशहीनं ज्येष्ठांशरूप उद्धारो न करणीय इत्यर्थः । (17) तथा च राजन्यावैश्यापुत्रसमवाये, यथा स, ब्राह्मणीपुत्रेण ॥ यथा ब्राह्मणीपुत्रेण, क्षत्रियापुत्रस्तुल्यभाक् ब्राह्मणस्य, तथा ब्राह्मणीपुत्राभावे राजन्यावैश्यापुत्रयोस्तिश्चतोर्गुणवान् वैश्यापुत्रो राजन्यापुत्रेण कनिष्ठेन निर्गुणेन सह तुल्यांशः । ज्येष्ठांशहीनो ब्राह्मणीपुत्र इव राजन्यापुत्र इत्यर्थः (18) क्षत्रियाच्चेदिति ॥ एवं क्षत्रियस्य क्षत्रियावैश्यापुत्रावेवंविधौ यदा भवतस्तदायमेव विभागक्रमः । तथा वैश्यस्यापि वैश्याशूद्रापुत्रयोरेवमेव । एवं वौधायनस्यैवंविधे विषये ज्येष्ठांशहारित्वाभिधानं सवर्णपुत्रे निर्गुणे कनीयसि । सगुणे तु कनीयसि तुल्यांशत्वमित्यविरोधः । (19) बृहस्पतिः । न प्रतिग्रहभू-

देया चत्रियादिसुताय वै। यद्यप्यस्य पिता दद्यान्मृते विप्रासुतो हरेत्॥ (20) वृद्धमनुः। ब्रह्मदायागतां भूमिं हरेद्यो ब्राह्मणीसुतः। गृहं द्विजातयः सर्व्वे तथा चैतं क्रमागतम्॥ ब्रह्मदायागतां प्रतिग्रहयाजनादिलब्धां, द्विजातयस्त्रैवर्णिकाः। प्रतिग्रहलब्धामित्यत्र पारिजातः। (21) वृहस्पतिः। शूद्रायां द्विजातिभिर्जातो न भूमेर्भागमर्हति। सजातावाप्नुयात् सर्व्वमिति धर्म्मो व्यवस्थितः॥ (22) देवलः। निषाद एकपुत्रस्तु विप्रस्य स तृतीयभाक्। द्वौ सकुल्याः सपिण्डा वा स्वधादाताथ संहरेत्। कुल्याभावे स्वधादाता आचार्य्यः शिष्य एव वा। सर्व्वास्त्वापत्सु तान्वर्णान्तथैव प्रतिपादयेत्॥ निषादः शूद्रायां ब्राह्मणाज्जातः। तेन तृतीयो भागः शूद्रापुत्रस्य, द्वौ सपिण्डस्य, तदभावे सकुल्यस्य भवेत्, सकुल्याभावे तु आचार्य्यः शिष्यो वा हरेत्। सर्व्वास्त्वापत्सु सर्व्वेषां सपिण्डसकुल्यादीनामभावे सगोत्रान्तान्वर्णान्निषादपितृगोत्रान् प्रतिपादयेदित्यर्थः। सगुणनिषादविषयमेतदिति पारिजातः। (23) विष्णुः। द्विजातीनां शूद्रस्त्वेकपुत्रोऽर्द्धहरः। अपुत्रस्य ऋक्थस्य या गतिः सात्रार्द्धस्य द्वितीयस्य॥ द्विजातीनां ब्राह्मणव्यतिरिक्तानां चत्रियवैश्यानाम्, ब्राह्मणजे शूद्रापुत्रे देवलेन तृतीयांशस्योक्तत्वात्, द्वितीयस्यार्द्धस्य ब्राह्मणभागभूतस्य। (24) मनुः। यद्यपि स्यात् सपुत्रो वा यद्यपुत्रोऽथवा भवेत्। नाधिकं दशमाद्दद्यात् शूद्रापुत्राय धर्म्मतः। ब्राह्मणचत्रियविशां शूद्रापुत्रो न ऋक्थभाक्। यदेवास्य पिता दद्यात्तदेवास्य धनं भवेत्॥ सपुत्रः वर्तमानद्विजातिपुत्रः, अपुत्रस्तद्रहितः। अत्र लक्ष्मीधरः। यदा पिता प्रसन्नः शूद्रापुत्राय ददाति, तदा दशमांशमेव दद्यादिति। तेन तन्मते, शूद्रापुत्रो न ऋक्थभाक्, न पित्राऽदत्तऋक्थभागिति नेयम्। हलायुधपारिजाताभ्याञ्च प्रथमं वाक्यमत्यन्तनिर्गुणोढ़शूद्रापुत्रपरतया, द्वितीयञ्च निर्गुणानूढ़शूद्रापुत्रपरतया, भागनिषेधकमेव वर्णितम्। (25) वृहस्पतिः। अनपत्यस्य शुश्रूषुर्गुणवान् शूद्रयोनिजः। लभेताजीवनं शेषं सपिण्डाः समवाप्नुयुः॥ अपरिगृहीतास्वित्यधिकारादनूढ़ापुत्रविषयमेतत्। (26) अत्र गौतमः। शूद्रापुत्रोऽप्यनपत्यस्य शुश्रुषुश्चेल्लभेत वृत्तिमूलमन्तेवासिविधिना॥ अनूढ़शूद्रापुत्रोऽपि वर्णत्रयस्य अविद्यमानान्यद्विजातिपुत्रस्य वृत्तिमूलं कृष्यादिरूपं जीवनमूलं किञ्चिल्लभेत, यदि शुश्रूषुरन्तेवासिवदाराधनकर्त्ता स्यादित्यर्थः। (27) यत्तु तस्मै पित्रादत्तमपि देयमाहतुः शङ्खलिखितौ। न शूद्रापुत्रोऽर्थभागी, यदेवास्य पिता दद्यात् स एवास्य भागः, तस्य गोमिथुनञ्चापरं दद्यात् कृष्णायसं कृष्णधान्यं तिलवर्ज्जम्॥ (तदनूढ़ापुत्रविषयं)। (28) गौतमः। शूद्रापुत्रवत् प्रतिलो-

मासु। इतरवर्णजाताः शूद्रापुत्रवदन्तेवासिविधिना मूलमात्रभाजइत्यर्थः। (29) मनुः। दास्यां वा दासदास्यां वा यः शूद्रस्य सुतो भवेत्। सोऽनुज्ञातो हरेदंशमिति धर्म्मो व्यवस्थितः॥ दास्यां—ध्वजाहृतो भक्तदास इत्यादिलक्षणान्यतमलक्षणवत्यां, दासदास्यां—तथाविधलक्षणवद्दासदास्यां वाऽनूढ़ायां दासजातोऽनुज्ञातोऽपि तथा मतइति व्यवस्थितोधर्म्मः। परिचारकदास्यामिति कल्पतरुः। (30) याज्ञवल्क्यः। जातोऽपि दास्यां शूद्रेण कामतोऽंशहरो भवेत्। मृते पितरि कुर्य्युस्तं भ्रातरस्त्वर्द्धभागिनम्॥ कामतः पितुरिच्छया भागं लभते। यदि पितुरूर्द्धं परिणीतापुत्राः सन्ति, तदा स्वभागापेक्षयार्द्धभागग्राहकं दासीपुत्रं कुर्य्युरित्यर्थः। (31) परिणीतापुत्राभावे आह। अभ्रातृको हरेत् सर्व्वं दुहितॄणां सुतादृते॥ परिणीतासुताभावे परिणीतभार्य्यादुहितृपुत्राभावे च दासीपुत्रएव पितुरूर्द्धं सर्व्वं हरेत्। (32) इति विवादरत्नाकरे नानावर्णानां विभागतरङ्गः।

CHAPTER XIV.

(1) अथ विभक्तजविभागः। (2) मनुः। ऊर्द्धं विभागाज्जातस्तु पित्र्यमेव धनं हरेत्। संसृष्टास्तेन वा ये स्युर्विभजेत स तैः सह॥ पित्रा सह विभक्तेषु पुत्रेषु पश्चाज्जातो मृते पितरि पित्र्यंशं सर्व्वं हरेत्। जीवति पितरि पितृधनादंशमात्रम्। एवकारेण तु नापि विभक्तभ्रात्रंशमिति द्योतयति। (3) वृहस्पतिः। पित्रा सह विभक्ता ये सापत्ना वा सहोदराः। जघन्यजाश्च ये तेषां पितृभागहरास्तु ते। अनीशः पूर्व्वजः पित्रे भ्रातृभागे विभक्तजः॥ पूर्व्वजः विभागपूर्व्वजः विभक्त इति यावत्, असौ पितृभागे अनीशः, विभक्तजः विभक्तपितृजातः भ्रातृभागे अनीश इत्यर्थः। (4) तथा। पुत्रैः सह विभक्तेन पित्रा यत् स्वयमर्जितम्। विभक्तजस्य तत् सर्व्वमनीशाः पूर्व्वजाः स्मृताः। यथा धने तथर्णेऽपि दानाधानक्रयेषु च। परस्परमनीशास्ते मुक्ता शौचोदकक्रियाः॥ (5) याज्ञवल्क्यः। विभक्तेषु सुतो जातः

सवर्णायां विभागभाक्। दृश्याद्वा तद्विभागः स्याद् आयव्ययविशोधितात्॥ (6) मिश्राः। पितृविभक्ता अनन्तरोत्पन्नस्य विभागं दद्युः॥ एतद्द्वयमपि विभागसमयगर्भस्थ-विभागानन्तरोत्पन्न-विषयम्। अनेन विभागसमयगर्भस्थस्य विभागानन्तरजस्य विभक्तैः सद्भिः 'स्वभागादाकृष्य तद्भागपूरणं कर्त्तव्यमित्युक्त', तदन्यस्य विभागानन्तरजस्य विभक्तस्य पितुर्धनभागितेति मन्वादिमतं विभाग-समयोत्पन्नस्यास्पष्टतामादाय, स्पष्टगर्भायान्तु विभाग एव नास्तीति प्रकाश-कारः। हलायुधस्तु विष्णुवाक्यलिखनानन्तरं याज्ञवल्क्यं लिखित्वाह, अस्यार्थः सवर्णायामुत्पन्नो विभक्तजो यदि गुणवान्, तदा सर्व्वस्मात् दृश्यात् दृश्यरूपात् पूर्व्वविभक्तरूपात् भागं लभते, यदि तु मन्दगुणस्तदा दृश्यादेव परिदृश्यमानादेव भूम्यादेर्भूमिरूपधनात् उत्पन्नधान्यादिरूपात् भ्रातृकृतमृणं पातयित्वा अव-शिष्टभागं लभते इति। (7) इति विवादरत्नाकरे विभक्तजविभागतरङ्गः।

CHAPTER XV.

(1) अथ विभक्तागतविभागः। (2) तत्र बृहस्पतिः। कृतेऽकृते विभागे वा ऋक्थी यत्र प्रवर्त्तते। सामान्यञ्चेद् भावयति तत्र भागहरस्तु सः॥ भावयति विभावयति ममाप्यत्रांश इति। (3) तथा। ऋणं लेख्यं गृहं क्षेत्रं यस्य पैतामहं भवेत्। चिरकालप्रोषितोऽपि भागभागा-गतस्तु सः। गोत्रसाधारणं त्यक्त्वा योऽन्यदेशं समाश्रितः। तद्वंशस्यागतस्यांशः प्रदातव्यो न संशयः। तृतीयः पञ्चमश्चैव सप्तमो वापि यो भवेत्। जन्म-नामपरिज्ञाने लभेतांशं क्रमागतम्॥ यस्त्वाचतुर्थादविभक्तविभक्तानामित्यादि देवलोक्तनियमः, स सहवासादौ, अयन्तु दूरदुर्गमवासादावित्यविरोधः। (4) तथा। यं परम्परया मौलाः सामन्ताः स्वामिनं विदुः। तदन्वय-स्यागतस्य दातव्या गोत्रजैर्मही॥ (5) इति विवादरत्नाकरे विभक्तागतविभाग-तरङ्गः।

CHAPTER XVI.

(1) अथ पुत्रान्तरैर्विभागः। (2) तत्र मनुः। पुत्रिकायां कृतायान्तु यदि पुत्रोऽनुजायते। समस्तत्र विभागः स्यात् ज्यैष्ठता नास्ति हि स्त्रियाः॥ पुत्र औरसः। अनु पुत्रिकाकरणात्। स्त्रियः पुत्रिकात्मिकायाः। पुत्रिका च,—अपुत्रोऽनेन विधिनेत्यादिवाक्येन—पुत्रलक्षणप्रकरणे मनुना कथनीया। (3) बृहस्पतिः। एक एवौरसः पित्र्ये धने स्वामी प्रकीर्त्तितः। तत्तुल्या पुत्रिका प्रोक्ता भर्त्तव्यास्त्वपरे सुताः॥ (4) मनुः। एक एवौरसः पुत्रः पित्र्यस्य वसुनः प्रभुः। शेषाणामानृशंस्यार्थं प्रदद्यात्तु प्रजीवनम्॥ शेषाणां ये तत्र तत्रांशभागित्वेन निषिद्धास्तेषामानृशंस्यं दया, प्रजीवनं भरणम्। (5) तथा। यवीयाञ्ज्येष्ठभार्य्यायां पुत्रमुत्पादयेद् यदि। समस्तत्र विभागः स्यादिति धर्म्मो व्यवस्थितः॥ ज्येष्ठस्याविभक्तस्यापुत्रस्य भार्य्यायां कनिष्ठेन नियुक्तेनोत्पादितः पुत्रो मृते पितर्य्युत्पादकेन पितृव्येन सह विभजमानः सममंशं लभते, न तु पितृज्येष्ठताप्रयुक्तमुद्धारादिकमस्येत्यर्थः। (6) अत्रैव न्यायद्योतकं वाक्यम्। उपसर्जनं प्रधानस्य धर्म्मतो नोपपद्यते। पिता प्रधानं जनने तस्माद्धर्म्मेण तं भजेत्॥ उपसर्जनमप्रधानं क्षेत्रजः सः प्रधानस्यौरसस्य तुल्य इति धर्म्मतो नोपपद्यते, यतस्तत्र पिता जनकः पितृव्य एव प्रधानमिति प्रकाशकारः। लक्ष्मीधरस्तु उपसर्जनत्वमत्रोपसर्जनरित्याह, फलतस्तत्र न विशेषः। धर्म्मेण शास्त्रोदितेन। (7) तथा। धनं यो बिभृयाद्भ्रातुर्मृतस्य स्त्रियमेव च। सोऽपत्यं भ्रातुरुत्पाद्य दद्यात्तस्यैव तद्धनम्॥ विभक्तस्य भ्रातुरनपत्यस्य च प्रमीतस्य धनं स्त्रियञ्च यो धारयति, स क्षेत्रजोत्पादनधर्म्मेण तस्यामपत्यमुत्पाद्य तदपत्यस्यैव तद्धनं दद्यात्, न तु लोभेन भ्रातृधनं स्वयमेव गृह्णीयादित्यर्थः। (8) तथा। यद्येकरिक्थिनौ स्याताम् औरसक्षेत्रजौ सुतौ। यद् यस्य पैतृकं रिक्थं स तद्गृह्णीत नेतरः॥ क्षेत्रजोऽत्रानियुक्तादुत्पन्नः। पैतृकम्रिक्थं पित्रा तन्मात्रे पुत्रप्रतिसन्धानार्थं समर्पितम्। अन्ये तु, यो यस्य पिता, तद्धनं स गृह्णीयादिति, ऋज्वेव वदन्ति। (9) अनेकपितृकानान्तु पितृतो भागकल्पना। यद् यस्य पैतृकं रिक्थं स तद् गृह्णीत नेतरः॥ अनेकपितृकाणामेकस्यां योषिति बहुभिः संजातानाम्। (10) यदा व्याधिपरिचर्य्यया व्याधिचिकित्सापरिचर्य्यया वा, विधिना क्षेत्रज उत्पादिते, औषधादिसेवया

व्याध्यपगमे औरस उत्पन्नः, तदा किं क्षेत्रजस्य प्रतिसन्धानमात्रं वा भागो वा, विभागपक्षे कीदृशस्तस्य भाग इत्यत्र मनुः। षष्ठन्तु क्षेत्रजस्यांशं प्रदद्यात् पैतृकाद्धनात्। औरसो विभजन् दायं पित्र्यं पञ्चममेव वा॥ सोऽयं पञ्चम-षष्ठभागविकल्पः, क्षेत्रजस्य गुणवत्तागुणवत्ताभ्यां व्यवस्थितः। (11) तथा। औरसक्षेत्रजौ पुत्रौ पितृऋक्थस्य भागिनौ। दशापरे तु क्रमशो गोत्र-ऋक्थांशभागिनः॥ अत्राद्यमर्द्धं पूर्व्वोक्तविध्यनुवादः। दश दत्तकादयः क्रमशः पूर्व्वपूर्व्वाभावे गोत्रभागिनो ज्ञातिकार्य्यकारिण इत्यसहायाचार्य्यः। ऋक्थांशभागिनः पितृऋक्थांशभागिनः। एतच्चौरसपुत्रिकाक्षेत्रजानामभावे। (12) पुत्रं प्रकृत्य वशिष्ठः। तस्मिंश्चेत् प्रतिगृहीत औरसः पुत्र उत्पद्यते, स चतुर्थभागभागी स्यात्, यदि नाभ्युदयिकेषु प्रयुक्तं स्यात्॥ तस्मिन्ननौरसे पुत्रे, स प्रतिगृहीतः पुत्रः। यदि स्यात् प्रभूतं धनमिति शेषः। यदि नाभ्युदयिकेषु प्रयुक्तं स्यात्, यदि धनं नाभ्युदयिकेषु यज्ञादिषु प्रयुक्तं विनियुक्तं स्यादित्यर्थः। (13) कात्यायनः। उत्पन्ने त्वौरसे पुत्रे तृतीयांशहराः स्मृताः। सवर्णाः, असवर्णास्तु ग्रासाच्छादनभागिनः॥ औरसे पुत्रे जाते दत्तकादयस्तृतीयांशभागिनः सवर्णा इत्यर्थः। अत्र पूर्व्वपरिगृहीतपुत्रे चतुर्थांश उक्तः, अनेन तु तृतीयांशभागित्वम्। तदिदमगुणवत्त्वगुणवत्त्वाभ्यां व्यवस्थाप्यम्। एतद्वाक्याच्च, शेषाणामानृशंस्यार्थं प्रदद्यात्तु प्रजीवनमिति मनुवाक्येऽपि, असवर्णानामेव पुत्राणां भरणमात्रविधानम्। (14) अत्र वृहस्पतिः। क्षेत्रजाद्याः सुतास्त्वन्ये पञ्चषट्सप्तभागिनः॥ क्षेत्रजाद्याः क्षेत्रजकानीनपौनर्भवाः यथासंख्यं पञ्चषट्सप्तभागिन इत्यर्थः। (15) हारीतः। विभजिष्यमाण एकविंशं कानीनाय दद्यात्, विंशं पौनर्भवाय, एकोनविंश-मामुष्यायणाय, अष्टादशं क्षेत्रजाय, सप्तदशं पुत्रिकापुत्राय, इतरानौरसाय दद्युः॥ आमुष्यायणो गूढ़ोत्पन्नः। इतरान् षोड़शभागान्। (16) ब्रह्म-पुराणे। समग्रधनभोक्ता स्यादौरसोऽपि जघन्यजः। त्रिभागं क्षेत्रजो भुङ्क्ते, चतुर्थं पुत्रिकासुतः। कृत्रिमः पञ्चभागन्तु, षड़्भागं गूढ़सम्भवः। सप्तांशक-स्त्वापविद्धः, कानीनस्त्वाष्टमांशकम्। नवभागं सहोढ़स्तु, क्रीतो दशममश्नुते। पौनर्भवस्तु परतो, द्वादशं स्वयमागतः। त्रयोदशं स्वभागन्तु शूद्रो भुङ्क्ते पितुर्धनात्॥ (17) वृहस्पतेः कानीने षड़ंशवादो, हारीतस्य तत्रैव विंश-भागवादः, ब्रह्मपुराणस्य तत्रैवाष्टमभागवादः, अतिगुणवत्त्वनिर्गुणत्वमध्यमगुण-वत्त्वेनैवाविरोधनीयः। पौनर्भवे वृहस्पतेः सप्तमांशवादः, ब्रह्मपुराणीयः पौन-र्भवे एकादशभागवादः, तत्रैव हारीतोक्तविंशभागवादः, अतिगुणवत्त्वगुणवत्त्व-

निर्गुणत्वैरविरोधनीयः। तथा चेत्रजोऽपि न गूढ़ोत्पन्नानामित्युक्तम्। अत्र च त्रयोदशसु पुत्रेष्वन्यतम उत्पन्नः पितुः किं लभते, इत्याकाङ्क्षायां ब्रह्मपुराणम्। विभजिष्यमाण इत्यादि हारीतवाक्यं, षट्सु दायादेषु विकल्प इत्यादि (§ 20) शङ्खलिखितवचनञ्च, मृते पितरि षण्णां सवर्णानां दायादानां विभागबोधकम्। तत्र प्रथममौरसापेक्षया षण्णां मन्दगुणत्वे, द्वितीयन्तु औरसेन सह समानगुणवत्त्वे। (18) पुनः शङ्खलिखितौ। रासभोऽधिको ज्येष्ठस्य, तस्याभावे चेत्रजपुत्रिकासुतयोः, तयोरप्यभावे त्रयाणामितरेषां, तेषामभावे सवर्णानामदायादानां सर्व्वऋक्थग्रहणम्। अत्र अदायादानामपि पूर्व्वपूर्व्वाभावे ऋक्थग्रहणं बोद्धव्यम्। (19) तथा अपविद्धः सहोढ़ो दत्तः क्रीतः शूद्रापुत्र उपनतश्च स्वयमित्यदायादाः षड़ेव पुत्रास्तेषां सारानुसारतोऽत्र महर्षीणां परस्परविरुद्धभागग्रहणवादो निर्गुणत्वगुणवत्त्वतदधिकगुणवत्त्वैरविरोधनीय इति। (20) शङ्खलिखितौ। षट्सु दायादेषु विकल्पः, औरसः चेत्रजः पुत्रिकापुत्रः पौनर्भवः कानीनो गूढ़ोत्पन्नश्चेति षट् पुत्रा बन्धुदायादाः पितृपितामहानामिकगोत्राः रिक्थपिण्डौ सापिण्ड्यञ्च तेषाम्, अर्थं दशधा कुर्य्यात्, द्वौ भागौ पितुः, द्वावौरसस्य, त्रीन् चेत्रजपुत्रिकापुत्रयोः, एकैकमितरेषाम्। एतेभ्यः प्रजीवनम्॥ विकल्पोंऽशव्यवस्था। बन्धुदायादाः गोत्रपिण्डोदकभाज ऋक्थभाजश्च। एतदेव विकृतं पितृपितामहानामित्यादिना। अनेन दशधा कृते साधारणेऽर्थे, द्वौ भागौ पितुः, द्वावौरसस्य, सार्द्धः सार्द्धौ भागः चेत्रजस्य पुत्रिकापुत्रस्य चोक्तः। एक एको भागः पौनर्भवकानीनगूढ़जेभ्यो देयः। एतेभ्यः प्रजीवनमेतच्च दायादेषु पुत्रेषु षट्सु सत्सु। (21) गौतमः। पुत्रा औरसचेत्रजदत्तापविद्धकृत्रिमगूढ़ोत्पन्ना ऋक्थभाजः कानीनसहोढ़पौनर्भवपुत्रिकापुत्रस्वयंदत्तक्रीता गोत्रभाजश्चतुर्थांशिनः औरसाद्यभावे॥ गोत्रभाजः गोत्रं भजन्ते पिण्डोदकदानक्रियादिभिः पुत्रकार्य्यं कुर्व्वन्तीति तथोच्यन्ते। एतच्च कानीनादीनां गोत्रमात्रभाक्त्ववचनमौरसादीनामेकतरस्यापि सम्भवेऽंशहरत्वप्रतिषेधार्थम्। चतुर्थांशिन औरसाद्यभावे पितरि सति, असति तु पितरि औरसाद्यभावक्रमेण सर्व्वऋक्थग्राहका एव। एतच्चतुर्थांशभागित्वमेषां गुणवत्त्वे, ब्रह्मपुराणञ्चामीषां मन्दगुणत्वे, इत्यविरोधः। शङ्खलिखितवाक्ये पौनर्भवकानीनयोरंशहारित्वाभिधानं, गौतमीयञ्च तन्निषेधनं, सवर्णासवर्णविषयत्वेन व्यवस्थाप्यम्। असवर्णास्तु ग्रासाच्छादनभागिन इति कात्यायनवाक्यात्। एवं शङ्खलिखितयोरपि अपविद्धे दत्ते चादायादत्वाभिधानं, गौतमस्य तत्रैव दायादत्वाभिधानमप्येवं विषयव्यवस्थयैव विबोधनीयम्। (22) सहोढ़-

दत्तकक्रीतस्वयमुपागतापविद्धशूद्रापुत्रानभिधाय, औरसादीन् परामृश्य, पुनर्वशिष्ठः । यस्य तु पूर्ब्वेषां वर्गाणां न कश्चिद्दायादः स्याद् एते तस्य भागं हरेयुः ॥ (23) हारीतः । षड्बन्धुदायादाः, साध्व्यां स्वयमुत्पादितः, क्षेत्रजः, पौनर्भवः, कानीनः, पुत्रिकापुत्रो, गूढ़ोत्पन्नश्चेति बन्धुदायादाः । दत्तः, क्रीतोऽपविद्धः, सहोढ़ः, स्वयमुपागतः, सहसादृष्टश्चेत्यबन्धुदायादाः ॥ गोत्रभाक्त्वेन बन्धुत्वं दायादत्वञ्च । लक्ष्मीधरस्तु बन्धुदायानाददते इति बन्धुदायादा इत्याह । तात्पर्य्यञ्च पूर्ब्बषट्कोत्तरषट्कयोः प्राधान्याप्राधान्ययोः समानम् । (24) मनुः । पुत्रान् द्वादश यानाह नृणां स्वायम्भुवो मनुः । तेषां षड्बन्धुदायादाः षड़दायादबान्धवाः । औरसः क्षेत्रजश्चैव दत्तः कृत्रिम एव च । गूढ़ोत्पन्नोऽपविद्धश्च दायादा बान्धवाश्च षट् । कानीनश्च सहोढ़श्च क्रीतः पौनर्भवस्तथा । स्वयंदत्तश्च शौद्रश्च षड़दायादबान्धवाः ॥ (25) बौधायनः । औरसं पुत्रिकापुत्रं क्षेत्रजं दत्तकृत्रिमौ । गूढ़ञ्चैवापविद्धञ्च ऋक्थभाजः प्रचक्षते । कानीनञ्च सहोढ़ञ्च क्रीतं पौनर्भवं तथा । स्वयंदत्तञ्च शौद्रञ्च गोत्रभाजः प्रचक्षते ॥ (26) औरसपुत्रिकापुत्रक्षेत्रजकानीनगूढ़ोत्पन्नापविद्धसहोढ़पौनर्भवदत्तकस्वयमुपागतकृत्रिमक्रीतानभिधाय देवलः । एते द्वादश पुत्रास्तु सन्तत्यर्थमुदाहृताः । आत्मजाः परजाश्चैव लब्धा याद्दच्छिकास्तथा । तेषां षड्बन्धुदायादाः पूर्ब्बेऽन्ये पितुरेव षट् । विशेषश्चापि पुत्राणामानुपूर्ब्ब्याद् विशिष्यते । सर्ब्वे चानौरसस्यैते पुत्रा दायहराः स्मृताः । औरसे पुत्रउत्पन्ने तेषु ज्यैष्ठं न विद्यते । तेषां सवर्णा ये पुत्रास्ते तृतीयांशभागिनः । हीनास्तमुपजीवेयुर्ग्रासाच्छादनसम्भृताः ॥ (27) औरसक्षेत्रजपुत्रिकापुत्रपौनर्भवकानीनगूढ़ोत्पन्नसहोढ़दत्तक्रीतस्वयमुपागतापविद्धयत्रक्कचनोत्पादितानभिधाय विष्णुः । एतेषां पूर्ब्बः पूर्ब्बः श्रेयान्, स एव दायहरः, स चान्यान् बिभृयात् ॥ (28) नारदः । औरसः क्षेत्रजश्चैव पुत्रिकापुत्र एव च । कानीनश्च सहोढ़श्च गूढ़ोत्पन्नस्तथैव च । पौनर्भवोऽपविद्धश्च दत्तः क्रीतः कृतस्तथा । स्वयञ्चोपागतः पुत्रा द्वादशैते प्रकीर्त्तिताः । तेषां षड्बन्धुदायादाः षड़दायादबान्धवाः । पूर्ब्बः पूर्ब्बः स्मृतो ज्यैष्ठो जघन्यो यो य उत्तरः । क्रमादेते प्रवर्त्तन्ते मृते पितरि तद्धने । ज्यायसो ज्यायसोऽभावे जघन्यो यो य आप्नुयात् ॥ (29) औरसपुत्रिकापुत्रक्षेत्रजकानीनपौनर्भवदत्तकक्रीतकृत्रिमस्वयन्दत्तसहोढ़ापविद्धानभिधाय याज्ञवल्क्यः । पिण्डदोऽंशहरश्चैषां पूर्ब्बाभावे परः परः ॥ (30) अत्र चैकस्यैव केनचित् बन्धुदायादत्वमुक्तं केनचिदबन्धुदायादत्वं यदुक्तं, तत् सगुणनिर्गुणत्वे अपेक्ष्याविरोधनीयम् । यापि यथा पूर्ब्ब-

श्रेष्ठत्वज्ञापनार्थं द्वादशानामुपक्रमणे पौर्व्वापर्य्यवैकल्पिकोक्तिः, सा पूर्व्वोक्तस्य सगुणत्वे पश्चादुक्तस्य निर्गुणत्वे ज्ञेया। एवमन्यत्राप्यनयैव दिशाऽविरोध-ऊहनीयः। (31) मनुः। न भ्रातरो न पितरः पुत्रा ऋक्थहराः स्मृताः॥ तथा। श्रेयसः श्रेयसोऽभावे पापीयानृक्थमर्हति। बहवश्चेत्तु सदृशाः सर्व्वे ऋक्थस्य भागिनः॥ सदृशा गुणवत्तया तदुपाधिना वा। (32) शङ्ख-लिखितौ। श्रेयसः श्रेयसोऽभावे पापीयानृक्थमर्हति॥ श्रेयसः श्रेयसः औरसादेरभावे पापीयान् न्यूनः क्षेत्रजादिरिति तात्पर्य्यार्थः। (33) वृहस्पतिः। दत्तोऽपविद्धः क्रीतश्च कृतः शौद्रस्तथैव च। जातिशुद्धाः कर्म्मशुद्धा मध्यमास्ते सुता मताः। क्षेत्रजो गर्हितः सद्भिस्तथा पौनर्भवः सुतः। कानीनश्च सहोढ़श्च गूढ़ोत्पन्नस्तथैव च॥ (34) हारीतः। शूद्रापुत्राः स्वयंदत्ता ये चैते क्रीतकास्तथा। सर्व्वे ते शौद्रिकाः पुत्राः काण्डपृष्ठा न संशयः। स्वकुलं पृष्ठतः कृत्वा यो वै परकुलं व्रजेत्। तेन दुश्चरितेनासौ काण्डपृष्ठो न संशयः। आपन्नतोऽभ्युपगतो यश्च स्याद्वैष्णवीसुतः। सर्व्वे ते मनुना प्रोक्ताः काण्ड-पृष्ठास्त्रयः सुताः॥ वैष्णवी अत्र शूद्रा। (35) इति विवादरत्नाकरे पुत्रान्तर-विभागतरङ्गः।

CHAPTER XVII.

(1) अथौरसपुत्रलक्षणम्। (2) तत्र वशिष्ठः। द्वादश त्वेव पुत्राः पुराणदृष्टाः, स्वयमुत्पादितः स्वे क्षेत्रे संस्कृते औरसः प्रथमः॥ (3) विष्णुः। अथ द्वादश पुत्रा भवन्ति, स्वे क्षेत्रे स्वयमुत्पादितः प्रथमः॥ (4) मनुः। संस्कृतायान्तु भार्य्यायां स्वयमुत्पादयेत्तु यम्। तमौरसं विजानीयात्पुत्रं प्रथम-कल्पितम्॥ (5) देवलः। संस्कृतायान्तु भार्य्यायां स्वयमुत्पादितो हि यः। औरसो नाम पुत्रः स प्रधानं पितृवंशधृक्॥ (6) याज्ञवल्क्यः। औरसो धर्म्मपत्नीजः॥ (7) आपस्तम्बः। सवर्णामपूर्व्वां शास्त्रविहितां यथर्त्तु गच्छतः पुत्रास्तेषां कर्म्मभिः सम्बन्धः दायेनाव्यतिक्रमश्च॥ अपूर्व्वां न पूर्व्वः पतिर्यस्याः, वाग्दत्तापि या न भवतीत्यर्थः इति प्रकाशकारः। शास्त्रविहितां शास्त्रेण पाणिग्रहणकर्म्मणा विहितां संस्कृतां, कर्म्मभिरग्नि-होत्रादिभिः, दायेनाव्यतिक्रमः सम्पूर्णदायेनाव्यतिक्रमस्तेषामेव कर्त्तव्य

इत्यर्थः। (8) बौधायनः। सवर्णायां संस्कृतायां स्वयमुत्पादितमौरसं विद्यादिति। अथाप्युदाहरन्ति, अङ्गादङ्गात् सम्भवसि हृदयादभिजायसे। आत्मा वै पुत्रनामासि स जीव शरदः शतमिति॥ सवर्णा द्विजस्य द्विजा, शूद्रस्य शूद्रा, नतु ब्राह्मणस्य ब्राह्मणी, क्षत्रियस्य क्षत्रिया, अन्यथा ब्राह्मणपरिणीतक्षत्रियापुत्रादेर्द्वादशपुत्रान्तर्भावो न स्यादिति पारिजातः। (9) शङ्खलिखितौ। ब्राह्मणस्तु सवर्णायाः पाणिं गृह्णीयात्, तस्यां पितामहानां तनवोऽनुसृयन्ते, पुत्रोपचारेणात्मानं सम्मन्त्रयेत् एवं ह्याह अङ्गादङ्गादित्यादि, आधत्त पितरो गर्भं कुमारं पुष्करस्रजम्। यथेह पुरुषस्यात्मा तथा त्वमभिजायसे। आत्मा पुत्र इति प्रोक्तः पितुर्मातुरनुग्रहात्। पुन्नाम्नस्त्रायसे यस्मात् पुत्रस्तेनासि संज्ञितः॥ (10) इति विवादरत्नाकरे औरसपुत्रलक्षणतरङ्गः।

CHAPTER XVIII.

(1) अथ क्षेत्रजः। (2) तत्रौरसानन्तरं वशिष्ठः। तदभावे नियुक्तायां क्षेत्रजो द्वितीयः॥ नियुक्तायां, पत्या वा गुरुभिर्वा, द्वितीयः औरसादीषन्न्यूनः। (3) विष्णुः। नियुक्तायां सपिण्डेनोत्तमवर्णेन वोत्पादितः क्षेत्रजो द्वितीयः॥ (4) मनुः। यस्तल्पजः प्रमीतस्य क्लीवस्य व्याधितस्य वा। स्वधर्मेण नियुक्तायां स ज्ञेयः क्षेत्रजः सुतः॥ तल्पो भार्य्या। व्याधितस्य वेत्यत्र व्याधिरप्रतिकार्य्यो विवक्षितः। स्वधर्मेण घृताभ्यक्तत्वादिना। (5) याज्ञवल्क्यः। क्षेत्रजः क्षेत्रजातस्तु सगोत्रेणेतरेण वा॥ सगोत्रेण स्वकुलोद्भवेन, इतरेण उत्कृष्टवर्णेन। (6) बौधायनः। मृतस्य च प्रसूतो यः क्लीवस्य व्याधितस्य वा। अन्येनानुमते स्वक्षेत्रे, स क्षेत्रजः, स एव द्विपिता द्विगोत्रश्च, द्वयोरपि स्वधारिक्थभाग्भवति॥ अन्येनापुत्रेण देवरादिना प्रसूतो य इत्यन्वयः। द्विपितेति कपोऽभावः समासान्तविधेरनित्यत्वात्, स द्विगोत्रो, द्वयोरपि गोत्रभाक्। स्वधा पितृकर्म्म। (7) याज्ञवल्क्यः। अपुत्रेण परक्षेत्रे नियोगोत्पादितः सुतः। उभयोरप्यसावृक्थी पिण्डदाता प्रकीर्त्तितः॥ यदा तु स्वयं पुत्रवान् देवरादिः क्षेत्रिपुत्रार्थं प्रवृत्तः, तदा क्षेत्रिण एव पुत्रो न वीजिनः। यत्र तु सपुत्रोऽपि

आवयोरपत्यमिह समानं भविष्यतीति संविद्रूपं क्रियाभ्युपगममाश्रित्योत्पादयति तत्र द्वयोरप्यसौ पुत्रो भवतीति। (8) आह मनुः। क्रियाभ्युपगमार्थेन वीजार्थं यत् प्रदीयते। तस्येह भागिनौ दृष्टौ वीजी क्षेत्रिक एव च॥ (9) नारदकात्यायनौ। क्षेत्रिकानुमते वीजं यस्य क्षेत्रे प्रजायते। तदपत्यं द्वयोरेव वोजिक्षेत्रिकयोर्मतम्॥ (10) शङ्खलिखितौ। मन्त्रसंस्कारकर्त्तुरपत्यमित्यङ्गिरसो, वीजिक्षेत्रिकयोरनुमते यद्वीजं प्रकीर्य्यते तद्-द्विधा शस्त्रमित्युशना॥ मन्त्रसंस्कारकर्त्तुः पाणिग्राहकस्य। तद्-द्विधा द्वयोरपि, शस्यं क्षेत्रफलम्। (11) हारीतः। जीवति क्षेत्रजमाहुरस्वातन्त्र्यात् मृते द्व्यामुष्यायणमनूप्तवीजत्वात्, नावीजं क्षेत्रं फलति, नाक्षेत्रं वीजं प्ररोहति, इत्युभयदर्शनादुभयोरपत्यमित्येके। तेषामुत्पादयितुः प्रथमपिण्डो भवति, द्वौ पिण्डौ निर्वपेन्निर्व्वापेऽथवैकपिण्डे द्वावनुकीर्त्तयेत्। द्वितीये पुत्रः, तृतीये पौत्रः, लेपिनश्च त्रीन्वाचक्षाण आसप्तमादित्येके॥ जीवति क्षेत्रजमन्यजमपि भर्त्तुरेव, कुतः अस्वातन्त्र्यात्, स्त्रिया इति शेषः। मृते च भर्त्तरि,—अपुत्रा शयनं भर्त्तुरित्यादिदर्शनात् यद्यप्यस्वातन्त्र्यं स्त्रिया अविशिष्टं, तथापि द्व्यामुष्यायणं द्वयोरपत्यमित्याहुः, कुतः अनूप्तवीजत्वात् क्षेत्रस्येति शेषः। जीवति हि वीजवप्तास्तोति न परस्परफलयोगोऽपत्यस्य कारणमित्याह नावीजमिति उभयोर्वीजिक्षेत्रिणोः। निरूप्यते अस्मिन्निति निर्वापः, पितृयज्ञः। एकपिण्डे द्वाविति एकैकस्मिन् पिण्डे द्वाविति वीप्सा मन्तव्या। यदि द्विपिता स्यादेकस्मिन् पिण्डे द्वौ द्वावुपलक्षयेदित्यापस्तम्बानुसारात्। द्वितीये पुत्र इत्यादि, पुत्रो द्वितीयमारभ्येत्यर्थः। लेपिनश्च त्रीनाचक्षाणो द्वौ द्वावनुकीर्त्तयेत्। (12) नारदः। द्व्यामुष्यायणका दद्युर्द्वाभ्यां पिण्डोदके पृथक्। ऋक्थादर्द्धं समादद्युर्वीजिक्षेत्रिकयोस्तथा॥ यत्र वीजिन औरसोऽस्ति, क्षेत्रिणोऽपि कथञ्चित्पश्चादौरसो जातः, तद्विषयमिदम्। अपुत्रयोस्तु द्वयोरपि कृत्स्नमर्थं गृह्णीयात्। (13) बौधायनः। अथाप्युदाहरन्ति। द्विपितुः पिण्डदानं स्यात् पिण्डे पिण्डे च नामनी। त्रयश्च पिण्डाः षण्णां स्युरेवं कुर्व्वन्न मुह्यति॥ न मुह्यति न दुष्यतीत्यर्थः। (14) इति विवादरत्नाकरे क्षेत्रजतरङ्गः।

CHAPTER XIX.

(1) अथ पुत्रिका-तत्पुत्रौ। (2) तत्र वशिष्ठः। तृतीयः पुत्रिका विज्ञायते, अभ्रातृका हि पुंसः पितॄनभ्येति प्रतीचीनं गच्छति पुत्रत्वम्॥ तृतीयः पुत्रः पुत्रिका औरसपुत्रतुल्या तत्कार्य्यकारित्वात् प्रतीचीनं गच्छति प्रत्यावृत्तं पुत्रत्वं पितृवंशाभिमुखं गच्छतीत्यर्थः। (3) शङ्खलिखितौ। पुत्रिका पुत्रवदिति प्रचेतसः। तस्यापत्यं पुत्रिकासुतो मातामहपितामहाभ्यां पिण्डदः। पुत्रदौहित्रयोर्लोके न विशेषोऽस्त्यनुग्रहे। तस्मात्तु संशयान्नेहो-पेयादभ्रातृकां स्त्रियम्॥ अनुग्रहे पुन्नामनरकोद्धारे। संशयादियं पुत्रत्वेन परिगृहीता न वेत्याकारात्। (4) औरसानुवृत्तौ याज्ञवल्क्यः। तत्समः पुत्रिकासुतः॥ (5) देवलः। तत्तुल्यः पुत्रिकापुत्रो दायादः सोऽथवा भवेत्। पितुर्मातामहस्यापि निरपत्यस्य पुत्रवत्॥ (6) विद्यादित्यनुवृत्तौ बौधायनः। अभ्युपगम्य दुहितरि जातं पुत्रिकापुत्रमन्यं दौहित्रम्॥ अभ्युपगम्य संविदम्—अस्यां यो जायते पुत्रः स मे पुत्र इत्याकारां कृत्वा, दौहित्रं दुहितुरपत्यं पुत्रिका-पुत्रसंज्ञकं पुत्रं विद्यात्। अन्यमिति औरसापेक्षया। अस्यामिति कल्पतरौ पाठः, स तु सुगम एव। (7) मनुः। दौहित्रो ह्यखिलं ऋक्थमपुत्रस्य पितु-र्हरेत्। दौहित्र एव तु हरेदपुत्रस्याखिलं धनम्॥ अपुत्रस्य औरसपुत्रशून्यस्य, उत्तरार्द्धोऽनुवाद इति प्रकाशः। हेतुवन्निगदोऽयमिति मनुटीकायामुदय-करः। (8) औरसानुवृत्तौ देवलः। तत्तुल्यः पुत्रिकापुत्रो दायादः सोऽथवा भवेत्। स एव दद्यात्पिण्डन्तु पित्रे मातामहाय च। पौत्रदौहित्रयोर्लोके न विशेषोऽस्ति धर्म्मतः। तयोर्हि मातापितरौ सम्भूतौ तस्य देहतः। अकृता वा कृता वापि यं विन्देत् सदृशात् सुतम्। पुत्री मातामहस्तेन दद्यात् पिण्डं हरेत् धनम्॥ दौहित्रोऽत्र कृताकृतपुत्रिकासुतः। (9) कृतदुहित्रधिकारे बृहस्पतिः। यथा पितृधने स्वाम्यं तस्याः सत्स्वपि बन्धुषु। तथैव तत्सुतो-ऽपीष्टे मातृमातामहे धने॥ (10) शङ्खलिखितौ। स्त्रीधनं कन्या लभते, तदपत्यस्य च द्रव्यं कन्याभाग एव। तच्छब्देन कन्यामातुः परामर्षः। तत्पुत्रस्योत्तरकालजन्मनोऽपुत्रस्यातीतस्य धनं कन्याभाग एव पुत्रिकाभाग एव, तस्याः सोदरतुल्यत्वादिति भावः। (11) मनुः। अपुत्रोऽनेन विधिना सुतां कुर्व्वीत पुत्रिकाम्। यदपत्यं भवेदस्यां तन्मम स्यात् स्वधाकरम्॥ स्वधाकरं

भ्राद्धादिकरम्। (12) वशिष्ठः। अभ्रातृकां प्रदास्यामि तुभ्यं कन्यामलङ्कृताम्। अस्यां यो जायते पुत्रः स मे पुत्रो भवेदिति॥ (13) गौतमः। पितोत्सृजेत् पुत्रिकामनपत्योऽग्निं प्रजापतिञ्चेष्ट्वास्मदर्थमपत्यमिति संवाद्याभिसन्धिमात्रात् पुत्रिकेत्येकेषाम्॥ अग्निं प्रजापतिञ्चेष्ट्वेति, आग्नेयीं प्राजापत्याञ्चेष्टिं कृत्वा एकाग्निमपि स्मार्त्तं यागमावसथ्ये, तदभावे पूजामात्रमपीति हरिहरः। संवाद्य परिभाष्य, अभिसन्धिमात्रात्—एतञ्च पूर्व्वविध्यनुवादता। (14) बृहस्पतिः। अग्निं प्रजापतिञ्चेष्ट्वा क्रियते गौतमोऽवदत्। अन्ये त्वाहुरपुत्रस्य चिन्तिता पुत्रिका भवेत्॥ चिन्तितेयमेव पुत्रिकेत्यनुध्याता। (15) विष्णुः। यस्त्वस्याः पुत्रः स मे पुत्रो भवेदिति या पित्रा दत्ता सा पुत्रिका। पुत्रिकाविधिना अप्रतिपादितापि भ्रातृहीना पुत्रिकैव॥ (16) ब्रह्मपुराणे। अपुत्रेण तु या कन्या मनसा पुत्रवत् कृता। राजाग्निबान्धवेभ्यश्च समर्च्चं वाथ कुत्रचित्। प्राग्गर्भमथवा शुल्कमुक्ता दत्ता वराय या। मृते पितरि वा दत्ता सा विज्ञेया तु पुत्रिका। पित्र्यादंशात् समं भागं लभते तादृशी सुता॥ (17) मनुः। मातुः प्रथमतः पिण्डं निर्व्वपेत् पुत्रिकासुतः। द्वितीयन्तु पितुस्तस्यास्तृतीयन्तु पितुः पितुः॥ अस्या इत्यनुषङ्गः। (18) इति विवादरत्नाकरे पुत्रिका-तत्पुत्रतरङ्गः।

CHAPTER XX.

(1) अथ पौनर्भवः। (2) तत्र विष्णुः। चतुर्थः पौनर्भवः॥ (3) मनुः। या तु पत्या परित्यक्ता विधवा वा स्वयेच्छया। उत्पादयेत् पुनर्भूत्वा स पौनर्भव उच्यते॥ उत्पादयेत् सवर्णादिति शेषः। पुनर्भूत्वा पुरुषान्तरेणात्मानं विवाह्येत्यर्थः। (4) याज्ञवल्क्यः। अक्षतायां क्षतायां वा जातः पौनर्भवः सुतः॥ (5) कात्यायनः। क्लीवं विहाय पतितं या पुनर्लभते पतिम्। तस्यां पौनर्भवो जातो व्यक्तमुत्पादकस्य सः॥ (6) इति, विवादरत्नाकरे पौनर्भवतरङ्गः।

CHAPTER XXI.

(1) अथ कानीनः। (2) तत्र वशिष्ठः। कानीनः पञ्चमः। यं पितृगृहे स्वयमसंस्कृता कामादुत्पादयेत् स कानीनो मातामहस्सुतो भवतीत्याहुः। अत्राप्युदाहरन्ति, अप्रदत्ता सुता यस्य पुत्रं विन्देत तुल्यतः। पुत्री मातामहस्तेन दद्यात् पिण्डं हरेद्धनम् ॥ कामात् स्वच्छन्दात्, अप्रदत्ता असंस्कृता, तुल्यतः समानजातीयात्। (3) बौधायनः। असंस्कृतामनतिसृष्टां यामुपगच्छेत्, तस्यां यो जातः स कानीनः ॥ असंस्कृता परिणयसंस्कारशून्या, अनतिसृष्टा अदत्ता। (4) ब्रह्मपुराणे। अदत्तायान्तु यो जातः सवर्णेन पितुर्गृहे। स कानीनः सुतस्तस्य यस्मै सा दीयते पुनः ॥ (5) नारदः। कानीनश्च सहोढ़श्च गूढ़ायां यश्च जायते। तेषां वोढ़ा पिता ज्ञेयस्ते च भागहराः स्मृताः ॥ सहोढ़ो गर्भजातः। अत्रापुत्रो यदि मातामहस्तदा तस्य पुत्रः कानीनः सहोढ़श्च। सपुत्रश्चेत्तदा वोढुः, उभयोरपुत्रत्वे चोभयोरिति पारिजातः। (6) इति विवादरत्नाकरे कानीनतरङ्गः।

CHAPTER XXII.

(1) अथ गूढ़ोत्पन्नः। (2) तत्र विष्णुः। गूढ़ोत्पन्नः षष्ठः, यस्य तल्पजस्तस्यासौ ॥ (3) मनुः। उत्पद्यते गृहे यस्य न च ज्ञायते कस्य सः। स गृहे गूढ़-उत्पन्न स्तस्य स्याद्यस्य तल्पजः ॥ तल्पजो भार्य्याजातः। वीजिनोऽपरिचयान्मातृजातीयएव चासौ, हीनजातीयसङ्गमशङ्काभावे चैवं, तच्छङ्कायां कार्य्यानुपयुक्तः प्रतिलोमज एव जायत इति। (4) इति विवादरत्नाकरे गूढ़ोत्पन्नतरङ्गः।

CHAPTER XXIII.

(1) अथ सहोढ़ः। (2) तत्र विष्णुः। सहोढ़ः सप्तमः। गर्भिणी या संस्क्रियते तस्याः पुत्त्रः। स तु पाणिग्राहस्य॥ तत्र प्रकाशकृता गर्भिण्याः कन्यात्वं पुरस्कृत्य,—पाणिग्रहणिका मन्त्राः कन्यास्वेव प्रतिष्ठिता इति संस्कार आक्षिप्तः। आथर्व्वणीयकेन विधिना पुनःसंस्कारविधिः श्रुतावस्तीत्यन्ये इति सिद्धान्तदृश्य(लिखितम्। वस्तुतस्तु पाणिग्रहणिकमन्त्रजसंस्कृतातिरिक्त-होमादिकर्म्मसंस्काराभिप्रायं संस्क्रियते-पदमिति। (3) मनुः। या गर्भिणी संस्क्रियते ज्ञाताज्ञातापि वा सती। वोढुः स गर्भो भवति सहोढ़ इति चोच्यते॥ (4) इति विवादरत्नाकरे सहोढ़तरङ्गः।

CHAPTER XXIV.

(1) अथ दत्तकः। (2) तत्र विष्णुः। दत्तश्चाष्टमः, स च मात्रा पित्रा वा यस्य दत्तः॥ तस्य स्यादिति शेषः। (3) मनुः। माता पिता वा दद्यातां यमद्भिः पुत्त्रमापदि। सदृशं प्रीतिसंयुक्तौ स ज्ञेयो दत्त्रिमः सुतः। उपपन्नो गुणैः सर्व्वैः पुत्त्रो यस्य तु दत्त्रिमः। स हरेत्रैव तद्रिक्थं संप्राप्तोऽप्यन्यगोत्रतः। गोत्ररिक्थे जनयितुर्न हरेद्दत्त्रिमः सुतः। गोत्ररिक्थानुगः पिण्डो व्यपैति ददतः स्वधा॥ आपदि प्रतिग्रहीतुः पुत्त्राभावे, सदृशं सवर्णम्। मेधातिथिस्तु न जातितः, किन्तु कुलानुरूपैर्गुणैरित्याह। प्रीतिसंयुक्तौ भयाद्युपाधिरहितौ। गुणैर्जातिविद्याचारैः। पुत्त्रत्वादेव रिक्थहरत्वे प्राप्ते,—उपपन्नो गुणैरिति वचनं, पश्चाज्जाते चौरसे सगुणस्य दत्त्रिमस्यांशप्राप्त्यर्थं, निर्गुणस्य भरणमात्रप्राप्त्यर्थञ्च। गोत्रमार्षेयं काश्यपादि प्रसिद्धम्। उत्सर्गतो गोत्ररिक्थानुयायित्वात् पिण्डदानमपि निवर्त्तते। स्वधाशब्दः श्राद्धादिपरः। (4) वशिष्ठः। शुक्रशोणितसम्भवः पुत्त्रो मातापितृनिमित्तकस्तस्य दान-विक्रयत्यागेषु मातापितरौ प्रभवतः। न त्वेकं पुत्त्रं दद्यात् प्रतिगृह्णीयाद्वा, स हि

सन्तानाय पूर्व्वेषाम्। न तु स्त्री दद्यात् प्रतिगृह्णीयाद्वा अन्यत्रानुज्ञानाद्भर्त्तुः। पुत्रं प्रतिग्रहीष्यन् बन्धूनाहूय राजनि चावेद्य निवेशनस्य मध्ये व्याहृतिभिर्हुत्वाऽदूरबान्धवमसन्निकृष्टमेव प्रतिगृह्णीयात्, सन्देहे चोत्पन्ने दूरबान्धवं शूद्रमिव स्थापयेत्। विज्ञायते ह्येकेन बहूंस्त्रायत इति॥ दानवद्विक्रयपरित्यागावपि न कार्य्यौ। विक्रय आपदि, भरणासामर्थ्ये त्यागः। सन्तानोच्छेदे हि पिण्डोदकक्रियानिवृत्तिर्महान्दोष इति प्रकाशः। पितुर्मातुश्च द्वयोरपि प्रत्येकमपि दानेऽधिकारः। इयांस्तु विशेषः, यत् सति पितरि, तदनुज्ञाना-न्मातुर्दातृत्वमसति तदभावेऽपि। बन्धूनाहूय दत्तकस्यांशप्राप्त्यर्थं स्वदायादान् सन्निधाप्य। अदूरबान्धवं सन्निहितात्मीयभातुलादिकम्, एतन्नामजात्यादिज्ञापनार्थं तस्य बान्धवस्याभावे तदसन्निकृष्टमपि प्रमाणान्तरेण दृढ़ेन नामगोत्रज्ञापनात् प्रतिगृह्णीयात्। असन्निकृष्टमेव इत्येवकारोऽप्यर्थः। सन्देहे चोत्पन्ने इति अथ कथञ्चिददूरस्थबान्धवं गृहीतवतो ब्राह्मणादी संशयः स्यात्, तदा शौद्रपुत्रमिव भरणमात्रोपयुक्तं कृत्वा स्थापयेत्। एकेन बहूंस्त्रायते, यतः कथञ्चिदेकेन पुत्रेण बहून् पूर्व्वजांस्त्रायते। तस्मादसन्दिग्धजात्यादिकमेव परिगृह्णीयादित्यर्थः। (5) इति विवादरत्नाकरे दत्तकतरङ्गः।

CHAPTER XXV.

(1) अथ क्रीतः। (2) तत्र विष्णुः। क्रीतश्च नवमः॥ (3) बौधायनः। मातापित्रोर्हस्तादन्यतरस्य वा योऽपत्यार्थं गृह्यते स क्रीतः॥ (4) मनुः। क्रीणीयाद्यस्त्वपत्यार्थे मातापित्रोर्यमन्तिकात्। स तु क्रीतः सुतस्तस्य सदृशोऽसदृशोऽपि वा॥ सदृशः सवर्णः, तदभावे असदृशः असवर्ण इति पारिजातः। प्रकाशकारस्तु सत्यामप्यसदृशस्मृतौ न हीनजातीयेनोत्तमजातीयः पुत्रत्वेन ग्राह्यः, उत्तमेन न हीनोऽपि पुत्रत्वेन ग्राह्यः। सदृशासदृशोक्तिस्तु गुणापेक्षया सजातीयेष्वेवेति मेधातिथिरित्याह। (5) इति विवादरत्नाकरे क्रीततरङ्गः।

CHAPTER XXVI.

(1) अथ स्वयमुपागतः। (2) तत्र विष्णुः। स्वयञ्चोपागतो दशमः। स च यस्योपगतः॥ तस्येति शेषः। (3) मनुः। मातापितृविहीनो यस्त्यक्तो वा स्यादकारणात्। आत्मानं स्पर्शयेद्यस्तु स्वयं दत्तस्तु स स्मृतः॥ अकारणादनपराधात्, आत्मानं स्पर्शयेत् अहन्ते पुत्र इति आत्मानं दद्यात्। (4) इति विवादरत्नाकरे स्वयमुपागततरङ्गः।

CHAPTER XXVII.

(1) अथापविद्धः। (2) तत्र विष्णुः। अपविद्धस्त्वेकादशः। स मात्रा पित्रा वा परित्यक्तो येन गृहीतः॥ तस्य पुत्र इति शेषः। (3) मनुः। मातापितृभ्यामुत्सृष्टं तयोरन्यतरेण वा। यं पुत्रं परिगृह्णीयादपविद्धस्तु स स्मृतः॥ उत्सृष्टं त्यक्तम्। त्यागश्चात्यन्तदुर्गत्या भरणासामर्थ्येन, केनचिद्वा दोषयोगेन। परिग्रहश्च पुत्रधिया न तु जीवितवासनया। (4) वशिष्ठः। अपविद्धः पञ्चमोऽयं, मातापितृभ्यान्तु त्यक्तं गृह्णीयात् पुत्रत्वेनेति॥ पञ्चमत्वेनोक्तिरुत्तरपुत्रषट्के पञ्चमत्वमादायेति। (5) इति विवादरत्नाकरे अपविद्धतरङ्गः।

CHAPTER XXVIII.

(1) अथ कृत्रिमः। (2) तत्र मनुः। सदृशं यं प्रकुर्व्वीत गुणदोषविचक्षणम्। पुत्रं पुत्रगुणैर्युक्तं स विज्ञेयस्तु कृत्रिमः॥ तत्रापि सदृशः सदृशगुण इति मेधातिथिः। गुणदोषविचक्षणं मातापित्रोरौर्द्ध्वदेहिककरणे गुणोऽकरणे दोषस्तद्विचक्षणम्। पुत्रगुणैः शुश्रूषादिभिर्युक्तम्। (3) बौधायनः। सदृशं सकामं यं कुर्य्यात् स कृत्रिमः॥ सकामं सह कामेन वर्त्तत इति, अस्याहं पुत्रो भविष्यामि यदि मामयं पुत्रत्वेन ग्रहीष्यतीति मन्यमानं

सदृशं सवर्णम्। (4) अत्र याज्ञवल्क्यः। कृत्रिमः स्यात् स्वयं कृतः॥ (5) तथा। सजातीयेष्वयं प्रोक्तस्तनयेषु मया विधिः॥ सति सवर्णे इति शेषः। कानीनगूढ़ोत्पन्नसहोढ़पौनर्भवाणां सवर्णत्वं जनकद्वारेण न स्वरूपतः तेषां सवर्णत्वजातिलक्षणाभावादिति प्रकाशः। (6) इति विवादरत्नाकरे कृत्रिमपुत्रतरङ्गः।

CHAPTER XXIX.

(1) अथ शूद्रापुत्रः। (2) तत्र विष्णुः। यत्रक्वचनोत्पादितस्तु द्वादशः॥ यत्रक्वचन ऊढ़ायामनूढ़ायां वा शूद्रायाम्। (3) वशिष्ठः। शूद्रापुत्र एव षष्ठो भवतीत्याहुः॥ षष्ठत्वमत्राप्युत्तरषट्कापेक्षया, औरसापेक्षया द्वादशत्वमेव। आहुरिति विप्रतिपत्तिसूचकम्। सा च धनग्रहणविषया, मनुर्हि शौद्रमादायेदमाह। अतो गुणवदगुणवत्त्वापेक्षया विकल्पः। (4) मनुः। यं ब्राह्मणस्तु शूद्रायां कामादुत्पादयेत् सुतम्। स पारयन्नेव शवस्तेन पारशवः स्मृतः॥ पारयन् पितृत्वाभिमतस्य किञ्चिदुपकुर्व्वन् शवः न्यूनोपकारकत्वात्। (5) बौधायनः। द्विजातिप्रवराच्छूद्रायां जातः कामात्पारशव इति॥ (6) अत्र मनुः। क्षेत्रजादीन् सुतानेतानेकादश यथोदितान्। पुत्रप्रतिनिधीनाहुः क्रियालोपान्मनीषिणः। य एतेऽभिहिताः पुत्राः प्रसङ्गादन्यवीजजाः। यस्यैते वीजतो जातास्तस्य ते, नेतरस्य तु॥ पुत्रप्रतिनिधीनौरसपुत्रिकापुत्रप्रतिनिधीनेतदभावे तत् कार्य्यकारिण आहुः अग्रिमवृहस्पतिवाक्यानुसारात्। अत्र हेतुः क्रियालोपात् क्रियाया अपत्यमुत्पादयितव्यमिति विधेर्लोपाल्लोपप्रसङ्गात्। नित्यो ह्ययं विधिः, स यथाकथञ्चिदुपपाद्यते इति अग्रिमवाक्ये यस्यैते इत्यादिखण्डेन तेषां मुख्यत्वनिषेधेन प्रतिनिधित्वमेव द्योत्यते। नेतरस्य मुख्यातिदेशः। (7) वृहस्पतिः। पुत्रास्त्रयोदश प्रोक्ता मनुना येऽनुपूर्व्वशः। सन्तानकारणं तेषामौरसः पुत्रिका तथा। आज्यं विना यथा तैलं सद्भिः प्रतिनिधीकृतम्। तथैकादश पुत्रास्तु पुत्रिकौरसयोर्विना॥ (8) ब्रह्मपुराणे। दत्तकश्च स्वयंदत्तः कृत्रिमः क्रीत एव च। अपविद्धश्च ये पुत्रा भरणीयाः सदैव हि। भिन्नगोत्राः पृथक्-पिण्डा भिन्नवंशकराः स्मृताः। सूतके मृतके वापि त्र्यहाशौचस्य भागिनः। अपि वस्त्रान्न-

दातॄणां क्षेत्रवीजवतान्तथा ॥ एतेन एषां प्रसङ्गात् त्र्यहाशौचभागित्वम् उक्तम्। (9) तथा। शूद्रो दासः पारशवो विप्राणां विद्यते क्वचित्। राज्ञान्तु शापदग्धानां नित्यं क्षत्रवतान्तथा। अथ संग्रामशीलानां कदाचिद्वा भवन्ति ते॥ एतेनैषां पुत्राणामसम्भवशङ्का निराक्रियते। (10) तथा। औरसो यदि वा पुत्रस्त्वथवा पुत्रिकासुतः। विद्यते तत्र तेषान्तु विज्ञेयाः क्षेत्रजादयः। एकादश पृथग्गोत्रा वंशमात्रकरास्तु ते। श्राद्धादि दासवत् सर्व्वं तेषां कुर्व्वन्ति नित्यशः॥ पुत्रिका चासौ सुतश्चेति पुत्रिका-सुतः। क्षेत्रजादय इत्यनेन औरसपुत्रिकाभ्यामन्ये पुत्रा उच्यन्ते। औरसो यदि पुत्रो यदि वा पुत्रिका, तदा क्षेत्रजादयो वंशमात्रकरा इत्यन्वयः। दासवत्, दासेतिकर्त्तव्यतया। (11) तथा। गूढ़ोत्पन्नश्च कानीनः सहोढ़ः क्षेत्रजस्तथा। पौनर्भवश्च वैश्यानां राजदण्डभयादपि। वर्जिताः पञ्च धनिनां शेषाः सर्व्वे भवन्त्यपि॥ अनेनाप्यमुख्यसुतानां वैश्यसम्भव उक्तः। तदेवं ब्राह्मणे राजनि वैश्ये चामुख्यपुत्रत्वं सम्भवत उक्तम्। (12) अथ शूद्रे प्रभुपरतन्त्रे स्वयं पुत्रोत्पादनं दुर्लभमित्याह। शूद्राणां दासवृत्तीनां पर-पिण्डोपजीविनाम्। परायत्तशरीराणां न क्वचित् पुत्र इत्यपि॥ तत् किं दासात् पुत्र एव नोत्पद्यते तत्राह। तस्माद्दासाच्च दास्याश्च जायते दास एव हि॥ दास एव प्रभुपरतन्त्रपुत्रो जायते, न तु पुत्रार्थक्रियायां क्वचित् स्वतन्त्र इत्यर्थः। (13) इति विवादरत्नाकरे शूद्रापुत्रतरङ्गः।

CHAPTER XXX.

(1) अथ पुत्रत्वविचारः। (2) तत्र वशिष्ठः। क्षेत्रिणः पुत्रो जनयितुः पुत्र इति विवदन्ते॥ (3) आपस्तम्बः। अप्रमत्ता रक्ष तन्तुमेतं मा च क्षेत्रे परवीजानि वाप्सुः जनयितुः पुत्रो भवति। साम्पराये मोघं वत्ता कुरुते तन्तुमेतमिति॥ अप्रमत्ताः प्रमादमनवधानमकुर्व्वन्तः, तन्तुं पुत्रपौत्रादिपर-म्पराम्। मा क्षेत्रे परस्य वीजानि वाप्सुः सिक्तानि भवन्तु। जनयितु-र्वीजिनः पुत्रो भवति उपकारक इति शेषः। साम्पराये पारलौकिकफले, मोघं निष्फलम्। (4) अथ गाथा वायुगीताः कीर्त्तयन्ति पुराविदः। यथा न वीजं वप्तव्यं पुंसा परपरिग्रहे॥ नश्यतीषुर्यथा विद्धः खे विद्धमनुविध्यतः।

तथा नश्यति वै क्षिप्तं वीजं परपरिग्रहे ॥ खे विद्धमृगस्य घातरन्ध्रे मृगमनुविध्यत इषुर्नश्यति, पूर्व्वहन्तुरेव मृग उक्तः। (5) एतावानेव पुरुषो यज्जायात्मा प्रजेति च। विप्राः प्राहुस्तथा चैतद्भार्य्या भर्त्ता स्मृताङ्गना॥ जाया आत्मा प्रजेति यथा त्रयं पुरुषोऽभिधीयते, तथा भर्त्ता भार्य्येति च द्वयम् अङ्गना। (6) न च क्रीतापि अन्यस्यापि भार्य्या, तेन विक्रीता त्यक्ता वा अन्यस्य भार्य्या भवतीति शङ्कां निराकर्त्तुमाह। न निष्क्रयविसर्गाभ्यां भर्त्तुर्भार्य्या विमुच्यते। निष्क्रयोऽत्र विक्रयः, विसर्गस्त्यागः। (7) तथा। यथा गवोष्ट्रदासीषु अजाविमहिषीषु च। नोत्पादकः प्रजाभागी तथैवान्याङ्गनास्वपि। ये क्षेत्रिणो वीजवन्तः परक्षेत्र-प्रवापिणः। ते वै शस्यस्य जातस्य न लभन्ते फलं क्वचित्। यद्यन्यगोषु वृषभो वत्सानां जनयेच्छतम्। गोमिनामेव ते वत्सा मोघं स्कन्दितमार्षभम्। तथैवाक्षेत्रिणो वीजं परक्षेत्र-प्रवापिणः। करोति क्षेत्रिणामर्थं न वीजी लभते फलम्॥ (8) एतदेव विशेषेण श्रुतमालोकः विशेषयति। फलन्त्वनभिसन्धाय क्षेत्रिणां वीजिनां तथा। प्रत्यक्षं क्षेत्रिणामर्थं वीजाद्योनिर्गरीयसी॥ यत्र क्षेत्रिवीजिनौ न भवतः, तत्र क्षेत्रिण एव, नतु वीजिन इत्यर्थः। (9) एतदेव स्फुटयति। ओघवाताहृतं वीजं यस्य क्षेत्रे प्ररोहति। तज्ज्ञेयं क्षेत्रिकस्यैव न वीजी लभते फलम्॥ तथैव प्रकृतेऽपि क्षेत्रप्राधान्यमित्यर्थः। ओघः प्रवहज्जलं, आहृतं नीतम्। (10) उपसंहरति। एष धर्म्मो गवाश्वस्य दास्युष्ट्राजाविकस्य च। विहङ्गमहिषीणाञ्च विज्ञेयः प्रसवं प्रति॥ एष धर्म्मो न वीजी फलभागिति। (11) शङ्खलिखितौ। क्षेत्रिकस्याविज्ञानेन यद्वीजं प्रकीर्य्यते तत् क्षेत्रिकस्यैव। (12) गौतमः। क्षेत्रियः पारदारिको न विभागमर्हतीति। (13) नियोगविधौ गौतमः। नातिद्वितीयं जनयितुरपत्यं समयादन्यत्र जीवतश्च क्षेत्रे परस्मात्तस्य रक्षणात् भर्त्तुरेव द्वयोर्वा। नातिद्वितीयं नियोगे द्वितीयमपत्यमतिक्रम्य तृतीयादिकमपत्यं नियोक्ता नोत्पादयेत्। यद्युत्पादयेज्जनयितुस्तस्य समयादन्यत्र समयात्सङ्केतात्तदपत्यं सर्व्वमेव भवति। सङ्केतादन्यत्र क्षेत्रिणो भवतीत्यर्थः। जीवतश्च क्षेत्रे जीवतः प्रजनासमर्थस्य पत्युः क्षेत्रे भार्य्यायां यदपत्यमुत्पद्यते, तत्तृतीयमपि क्षेत्रिणो विनापि समयेन परस्मात्तस्य, यदि तु परो वीजी क्षेत्रस्य भरणं कुरुते, तदा प्रथममपत्यं वीजिन एव, रक्षणात् तु भर्त्तुरेव। यदि तु भर्त्तैव भरणं कुरुते तदा क्षेत्रिण एव। द्वयोर्वा यत्र द्वावप्यपत्यार्थिनौ तत्र द्वयोरपत्यमसौ भवतीत्यर्थः। (14) नारदः। न स्यात् क्षेत्रं विना शस्यं न वीजञ्च विनास्ति तत्। अतोऽपत्यं द्वयोर्दृष्टं पितु-

र्मातुश्च धर्म्मतः॥ (15) शङ्खलिखितौ। नियतं क्षेत्रिणामपत्यमिति च वेदवादो मातुरपत्यमित्येके ऋषयो वदन्ति, द्व्यामुष्यायणमनुमन्त्रयतइति। द्व्यामुष्यायणं द्विपितृकमपत्यं अनुमन्त्रयते द्वावपि पितरौ एकत्र पिण्डे अनुकीर्त्तयति। (16) दृष्टान्तमाह। वशिष्ठकश्यपयोर्जलगतयोरुदवासादुत्तीर्य्य एकः प्रजामुत्पादयत्यविज्ञातो लोकानाम्। उदवासाज्जलवासादेकः अन्यतरः अन्यतरस्य क्षेत्रे उत्पादयति। ततः किमित्यत आह। एवं तयोर्द्विधा सन्तानः। (17) विशेषान्तरमाह। यस्मात् कुलधर्म्मपरिग्रहरिक्थपिण्डोदकानि चैकतः कृत्वा परक्षेत्रोत्पन्ना अपि प्रयच्छन्ति। यतः कुलधर्म्माणां परिग्रहो ग्रहणमनुष्ठानमृक्थस्य ग्रहणम्। पिण्डोदकानि च एकत एकस्मै क्षेत्रिकाय दत्त्वा परक्षेत्रेऽपि उत्पन्ना बीजिनेऽपि पिण्डोदकं प्रयच्छन्ति। (18) इति विवादरत्नाकरे पुत्रत्वविचारतरङ्गः।

CHAPTER XXXI.

(1) अथ पुत्रातिदेशः। (2) तत्र मनुः। भ्रातॄणामेकजातानामेकश्चेत्पुत्रवान् भवेत्। सर्व्वे ते तेन पुत्रेण पुत्रिणो मनुरब्रवीत्॥ सर्व्वासामेकपत्नीनामेका चेत् पुत्रिणी भवेत्। सर्व्वास्तास्तेन पुत्रेण प्राह पुत्रवतीर्मनुः॥ (3) बृहस्पतिः। यद्येकजाता बहवो भ्रातरस्तु सहोदराः। एकस्यापि सुते जाते सर्व्वे ते पुत्रिणः स्मृताः॥ बह्वीनामेकपत्नीनामेष एव विधिः स्मृतः। एका चेत् पुत्रिणी तासां सर्व्वासां पिण्डदस्तु सः॥ सर्व्वं तेन पुत्रेण, अत्रासहायेनोक्तं पुंसां सति भ्रातृजे, स्त्रीणां सपत्नीपुत्रे, क्षेत्रजादयः प्रतिनिधयो न कर्त्तव्या इति। पारिजातोऽप्येवमाह। मनुटीकायामुदयकरोऽप्येवम्। (4) इति विवादरत्नाकरे पुत्रातिदेशतरङ्गः।

CHAPTER XXXII.

(1) अथ पुत्रनिरुक्त्यादि। (2) तत्र मनुविष्णू। पुन्नाम्नो नरकाद्यस्मात्पितरं त्रायते सुतः। तस्मात् पुत्र इति प्रोक्तः स्वयमेव स्वयम्भुवा ॥ (3) हारीतः। पुन्नामा निरयः प्रोक्तश्छिन्नतन्तुश्च नैरयः। तत्र वै त्रायते यस्मात्तस्मात् पुत्र इति स्मृतः ॥ (4) बृहस्पतिः। पुन्नाम्नो नरकात् पुत्रः पितरं त्रायते यतः। मुखसन्दर्शनेनापि तदुत्पत्तौ यतेत सः ॥ पौत्रोऽथ पुत्रिकापुत्रः स्वर्गप्राप्तिकरावुभौ। ऋक्‌थपिण्डप्रदानेन समौ सम्परिकीर्त्तितौ ॥ (5) मनुवशिष्ठौ। ऋणमस्मिन् सन्नयति अमृतत्वञ्च विन्दति। पिता पुत्रस्य जातस्य पश्येच्चेज्जीवतो मुखम् ॥ (6) शङ्खलिखितपैठीनसयः। यत्र क्वचन जातेन पिता पुत्रेण नन्दति। तेन चानृणतां याति पितॄणां पिण्डदेन वै ॥ (7) हारीतः। यस्य पुत्रः शुचिर्दक्षः पूर्व्वे वयसि धार्म्मिकः। नियन्ता चात्मदोषाणां स तारयति पूर्व्वजान् ॥ (8) शङ्खलिखितौ। अग्निहोत्रं त्रयो वेदा यज्ञाश्च शतदक्षिणाः। ज्येष्ठपुत्रप्रसूतस्य कलां नार्हन्ति षोड़शीम्। पुत्रपौत्रप्रतिष्ठस्य बहुपुत्रस्य जीवतः। अलुप्तवेदयज्ञस्य हस्तप्राप्तं त्रिपिष्टपम् ॥ अलुप्तवेदयज्ञस्य अलुप्तवेदयज्ञस्य। (9) शङ्खलिखितविष्णुवशिष्ठहारीताः। पुत्रेण लोकाञ्जयति पौत्रेणानन्त्यमश्नुते। अथ पुत्रस्य पौत्रेण ब्रध्नस्याप्नोति पिष्टपम् ॥ ब्रध्नस्य सूर्य्यस्य। (10) याज्ञवल्क्यः। लोकानन्त्यं दिवः प्राप्तिः पुत्रपौत्रप्रपौत्रकैः। यस्मात्तस्मात् स्त्रियः सेव्या कर्त्तव्याश्च सुरक्षिताः ॥ (11) वशिष्ठः। अनन्ताः पुत्रिणो लोका नापुत्रस्य लोकोऽस्तीति श्रूयते, अप्रजाः सन्त्वदनाः ॥ अप्रजा अपुत्राः सन्तु भवन्तु अदनाः अदनशीलाः राक्षसाः। नूनमयं महानपकारो येन राक्षसो नाम गम्यत इति तात्पर्य्यम्। शत्रूणामपुत्रत्वं हि महान् विनाशः, तेनाशास्यिष्यते। (12) अन्यदप्याह। प्रजाभिरग्नेऽमृतत्वमस्यामित्यपि निगमो भवति ॥ प्रजाभिः पुत्रैरमृतत्वमस्यां प्राप्नुयामित्यभिप्रायः। पूर्व्वोऽभिशापः शत्रुविषयः, उत्तरस्त्वाशीःस्वरूपः, आत्मविषय इति प्रकाशकारः। (13) तथा। पौत्रोऽथ पुत्रिकापुत्रः श्रेयःप्राप्तिकरावुभौ। ऋक्‌थपिण्डाम्बुदाने च समौ सम्परिकल्पितौ। अपुत्रेण सुतः कार्य्यो यादृक् तादृक् प्रयत्नतः। पिण्डोदकक्रियाहेतोर्नामसंकीर्त्तनाय च। काङ्क्षन्ति पितरः पुत्रान्नरकापातभीरवः। गयां यास्यति यः कश्चित् सोऽस्मान् सन्तारयिष्यति ॥

वृषोत्सर्गं गयाश्राद्धमिष्टापूर्त्तं तथैव च। पालयिष्यति वार्द्धक्ये श्राद्धं दास्यति चान्वहम्। यथा जलं कुप्लवेन तरन्मज्जति मानवः। तथा पिना कुपुत्रेण तमस्यन्धे निमज्जति॥ (14) इति विवादरत्नाकरे पुत्रनिरूपणादितरङ्गः।

CHAPTER XXXIII.

(1) अथ निन्दिताः। (2) तत्र मनुः। अनियुक्तासुतश्चैव पुत्रिण्याप्तश्च देवरात्। उभौ तौ नार्हतो भागं जारजातककामजौ॥ अनियुक्तासुतो भर्त्तृभावे गुर्व्वननुज्ञातायां यं समुत्पादयति स उच्यते। भागं क्षेत्रियऋक्थादिविभागम्। एतच्च पिण्डदानादेरप्युपलक्षणम्। शुल्कान्वाहृतक्षेत्रोत्पन्नविषयमेतत्, अग्रिमनारदवचनानुसारात्। (3) तथा। नियुक्तायामपि पुमान् नार्य्यां जातोऽविधानतः। नैवार्हः पैतृके ऋक्थे पतितोत्पादितो हि सः॥ अविधानतो नियोगविहितधर्म्माभावेन। (4) गौतमः। देवरवत्यःमन्यजातमभागम्। वर्त्तमानदेवरायामन्यजातमपत्यं न भागभागि। (5) नारदः। जाता ये त्वनियुक्तायामेकेन बहुभिस्तथा। अरिक्थभाजस्ते सर्व्वे वीजिनामेव ते सुताः। दद्युस्ते वीजिने पिण्डं माता चेच्छुल्कतो हृता। अशुल्कोपनतायाञ्च पिण्डदा वोढुरेव ते॥ अनियुक्तायां स्वैरिण्याम्। अरिक्थभाजः क्षेत्रिऋक्थं न लभन्ते, मातृक्षेत्रिकमातामहानां न ऋक्थं भजन्ते इति तु प्रकाशकारः। (6) किमविशेषेण पिण्डदानमित्याह—दद्युस्ते वीजिने पिण्डं माता चेच्छुल्कतो हृता। यदि क्षेत्रिणः शुल्कं मूल्यं दत्त्वा वीजिना माता हृता। अशुल्कोपनतायामित्यादि युक्तम्। (7) पुनः पुनर्भूस्वैरिण्यधिकारे नारदः। अपत्यमुत्पादयितुस्तासां याः शुल्कतो हृताः। अशुल्कोपनतायान्तु क्षेत्रिकस्यैव तत्फलम्॥ (8) मनुः। द्वौ तु यौ विवदेयातां द्वाभ्यां जातौ स्त्रिया धने। तयोर्यद्यस्य पित्र्यं स्यात् स तद्गृह्णीत नेतरः॥ अत्र स्त्री वेश्यापुनर्भूस्वैरिणीतरेति पारिजातः। (9) इति विवादरत्नाकरे निन्दितपुत्रतरङ्गः।

कारित्वम् । एतद्दर्शनाच्च शङ्खलिखितवचनेऽपि व्यवहितकल्पना कार्य्येति देवलवचने अलब्धक्रमे याज्ञवल्क्यविष्णूक्तः क्रमोऽन्वेतीति देवलवचनलिखनानन्तरं याज्ञवल्क्यविष्णुवचने लिखितवतः कल्पतरुकारस्याभिप्रेतम् । वस्तुतस्तु पैठीनसिवाक्ये अपुत्रस्य प्रमीतस्य भ्रातृगामि द्रव्यमिति पितृपितामहाद्यर्जितधनेतरधने, तदभावे मातापितरावित्यपि अन्यत्र खण्डे क्रमादर्शनमेवेति न विरोधः । (14) याज्ञवल्क्यः । पत्नी दुहितरश्चैव पितरौ भ्रातरस्तथा । तत्सुतो गोत्रजो बन्धुः शिष्यः सब्रह्मचारिणः ; एषामभावे पूर्व्वस्य धनभागुत्तरोत्तरः । स्वर्यातस्य ह्यपुत्रस्य सर्व्ववर्णेष्वयं विधिः ॥ एषां पत्नीदुहितृजननीजनकभ्रातृतत्सुतगोत्रजबन्धुशिष्यसब्रह्मचारिणां पूर्व्वस्य पूर्व्वस्य अभावे धनभागुत्तरोत्तरो भवतीत्यर्थः । पत्नी चात्रोत्तमगुणा विवक्षिता । अपुत्रत्वमत्र पौत्रप्रपौत्रशून्यत्वमपि विवक्षितमिति प्रकाशकारेण द्योतितम् । युक्तञ्चैतद्व्यवहारिकत्वात् । यद्यपि पितराविति समुच्चितनिर्देशेन समुच्चिताधिकार आपाततो भाति तथापि भार्य्यासुतविहीनस्य तनयस्य मृतस्य च । माता ऋक्थहरी ज्ञेयेति पितृनैरपेक्ष्येणैव भार्य्यासुताभावे मातुरधिकारबोधनान्मात्रभावे पित्रधिकारबोधनमनेनेति । (15) विष्णुः । अनपत्यस्य धनं पत्न्यभिगामि, तदभावे दुहितृगामि, तदभावे मातृगामि, तदभावे पितृगामि, तदभावे भ्रातृगामि, तदभावे भ्रातृपुत्रगामि, तदभावे बन्धुगामि, तदभावे सकुल्यगामि, तदभावे सहाध्यायिगामि, तदभावे ब्राह्मणधनवर्जं राजगामि ॥ बन्धुरत्र सपिण्डः, सकुल्यः, सगोत्र इति मिश्राः । (16) दुहितृदौहित्रानन्तरं वृहस्पतिः । तदभावे भ्रातरस्तु भ्रातृपुत्राः सनाभयः । सकुल्या बान्धवाः शिष्याः श्रोत्रियाश्च धनार्हकाः । मृतोऽनपत्यभार्य्यश्चेदभ्रातृपितृमातृकः । सर्व्वे सपिण्डास्तद्दायं विभजेरन् यथांशतः । समुत्पन्नाद्धनादर्द्धं तदर्द्धं स्थापयेत् पृथक् । मासषाण्मासिके श्राद्धे वार्षिके वा प्रयत्नतः । बहवो ज्ञातयो यत्र सकुल्या बान्धवास्तथा । यो ह्यासन्नतरस्तेषां सोऽनपत्यधनं हरेत् ॥ मासषाण्मासिके इत्यादौ निमित्तसप्तमी । (17) अनपत्यमुद्दिश्यापस्तम्बः । पुत्राभावे प्रत्यासन्नः सपिण्डस्तदभावे आचार्य्यस्तदभावे अन्तेवासी, हृत्वा तदर्थे चोपयोजयेत्तद्दुहिता वा ॥ (18) बौधायनः । प्रपितामहः पितामहः पिता स्वयं सोदर्य्या भ्रातरः सवर्णायाः पुत्रः पौत्रः प्रपौत्र एतानविभक्तदायादान् सपिण्डानाचक्षते, विभक्तदायादान् सकुल्यानाचक्षते, असत्स्वङ्गजेषु तद्गामी ह्यर्थो भवति, सपिण्डाभावे सकुल्यस्तदभावेऽप्याचार्य्योऽन्तेवासी, ऋत्विग् वा हरेत्, तदभावे राजा ॥ इयञ्च परिभाषा दाय-

विषया नत्वशौचादिविषया तत्र समानपिण्डाः, सपिण्डाः, तेन विभक्तदायादा अपि सपिण्डाः, ते च विभक्तदायादा अत्रासपिण्डाः। अङ्गजेष्वौरसादिषु, तद्गामी सपिण्डादिगामी। (19) नारद.। अभावे तु दुहितॄणां सकुल्या बान्धवास्तथा। ततः सजात्याः सर्व्वेषामभावे राजगामि तत्। अन्यत्र ब्राह्मणात् किन्तु राजा धर्म्मपरायणः। तत्स्त्रीणां जीवनं दद्यादेष दायविधिः स्मृतः॥ सकुल्याः पितृव्यपुत्रादयः, सजात्या एकजातीयाः, किन्त्वित्यादि निर्द्धनब्राह्मणस्त्रीविषयम्। (20) मनुः। सर्व्वेषामप्यभावे तु ब्राह्मणा रिक्थभागिनः। त्रैविद्याः शुचयो दान्तास्तथा धर्म्मो न हीयते। अहार्य्यं ब्राह्मणधनं राज्ञा नित्यमिति स्थितिः। इतरेषान्तु वर्णानां सर्व्वाभावे हरेन्नृपः। सर्व्वत्रादायक राजा हरेद्ब्रह्मस्ववर्ज्जितम्। अदायकञ्च ब्रह्मस्वं श्रोत्रियेभ्यः प्रदापयेत्॥ अदायकं दायादशून्यम्। (21) बौधायनः। ब्रह्मस्वं पुत्रपौत्रघ्नं हन्यादेकाकिनं विषम्। तस्माद्राजा ब्राह्मणस्वं नाददीत कथञ्चन॥ परमं ह्येतद्विषं यद्ब्राह्मणस्वमिति। (22) बृहस्पतिः। येऽपुत्राः क्षत्त्रविट्शूद्राः पत्नीभ्रातृविवर्ज्जिताः। तेषां धनं हरेद्राजा सर्व्वस्याधिपतिर्हि सः॥ (23) शङ्खलिखितौ। परिषद्गामि वा श्रोत्रियद्रव्यं न राजगामि, न हार्य्यं राज्ञा देवब्राह्मणसंस्थितम्। सनिक्षेपोपनिधिक्रमागतं न बालस्त्रीधनानि एवं ह्याह,—न हार्य्यं स्त्रीधनं राज्ञा तथा बालधनानि च। नार्य्याः षड़ागमं वित्तं बालानां पैतृकं धनम्॥ परिषद्ब्राह्मणाः। उपनिधिर्निक्षेपविशेषः। पारिजाते क्रमागतं पितृपरम्परया आगतम्। षड़ागमममध्यग्न्यादिषड़ागमलब्धम्। (24) मनुः। बालदायागतं रिक्थं तावद्राजानुपालयेत्। यावत् स स्यात् समावृत्तो यावद्वातीतशैशवः॥ बालदायागतं बालस्वामिकमनुपालयेद्दायादेभ्यो रक्षयेत्। (25) विष्णुः। बालानाथस्त्रीधनानि राजा परिपालयेत्। (26) शङ्खलिखितौ। रक्षेद्राजा बालानां धनान्यप्राप्तव्यवहाराणां श्रोत्रियवीरपत्नीनां प्रहीणस्वामिकानि राजगामीनि भवन्ति। श्रोत्रियवीरपत्नीनां श्रोत्रिये वीरे प्रोषितेऽपगते वा तत्पत्नीनाम्। (27) पुत्राधिकारे बौधायनः। तेषामप्राप्तव्यवहाराणां सोपचयानंशान् सुगुप्तान् निदध्यादाव्यवहारप्रापणात्। सोपचयान् सवृद्धिकान्, सुगुप्तान् सुरक्षितान्। आङ् अभिविधौ, तेन सप्तदशवर्षात् प्राक्। (28) कात्यायनः। प्रोषितस्य तु यो भागो रक्षेयुः सर्व्व एव तम्। बालपुत्रे मृते रिक्थं रक्ष्यं तत्तन्तुबन्धुभिः। पोगण्डाः परतस्तन्तु विभजेरन्यथांशतः॥ बालपुत्रे बालः पुत्रो यस्य तस्मिन्, पोगण्डोऽतिबालो व्यवहारानभिज्ञः। (29) विष्णुः। यश्चांशहरः स पिण्ड-

दायी ॥ (30) स्मृतिः । यो धनमाददीत, स तस्मै श्राद्धं कुर्य्यात्, पिण्डञ्च त्रिपुरुषं दद्यात् ॥ अत्र श्राद्धशब्देन प्रोषितैकोद्दिष्टान्युच्यन्ते इति प्रकाशकारः । (31) बृहस्पतिः । भ्राता वा भ्रातृपुत्रो वा सपिण्डः शिष्य एव वा । सहपिण्डक्रियां कृत्वा कुर्य्यादभ्युदयं ततः ॥ (32) वशिष्ठः । पुनः पितृवित्तालाभेऽपि पिण्डं दद्यात् ॥ (33) अथ विष्णुः । वानप्रस्थधनमाचार्य्यो गृह्णीयाच्छिष्यो वा ॥ (34) याज्ञवल्क्यः । वानप्रस्थयतिब्रह्मचारिणामृक्थभागिनः । क्रमेणाचार्य्यसच्छिष्यधर्म्मभ्रात्रेकतीर्थिनः ॥ क्रमेण प्रतिलोमक्रमेण, तेन ब्रह्मचारिणो नैष्ठिकस्य धनमाचार्य्यो गृह्णीयात्, यतेर्धनं सच्छिष्योऽध्यात्मशास्त्रश्रवणधारणतदर्थानुष्ठानदक्षः । वानप्रस्थधनं धर्म्मभ्रात्रेकतीर्थी गृह्णाति, धर्म्मभ्राता भ्रातृत्वेन प्रतिपन्नः, एकतीर्थी एकाश्रमी । यद्यप्येवं नाश्रमानन्तर इति वशिष्ठवचनेन विरोधः तथापि यथाकथञ्चिद्वनवस्त्वमादाय समाधेयमिदम् । (35) इति विवादरत्नाकरे अपुत्रधनविभागतरङ्गः ।

CHAPTER XXXV.

(1) अथ संसृष्टिविभागः । (2) तत्र मनुः । विभक्ताः सह जीवन्तो विभजेयुः पुनर्यदि । समस्तत्र विभागः स्याज्ज्यैष्ठं तत्र न विद्यते ॥ सह जीवन्तः संसृज्य जीवन्तः, समस्तत्र विभागो ज्येष्ठोद्धारादिकं न स्यादित्यर्थः । (3) तथा । येषां ज्येष्ठः कनिष्ठो वा हीयेतांशप्रदानतः । म्रियेतान्यतरो वापि तस्य भागो न लुप्यते ॥ संसृष्टानां भ्रातॄणां मध्ये यदि कश्चित् प्रव्रज्यादिना हीयेत म्रियेत वा, तदा तस्य भागो न लुप्यते । (4) कस्तर्हि तं गृह्णीयादित्यत आह । सोदर्य्या विभजेरंस्तं समेत्य सहिताः समम् । भ्रातरो ये च संसृष्टा भगिन्यश्च सनाभयः ॥ सोदर्य्या भ्रातर इत्यन्वयः । तेन भ्रातॄणामेव मध्ये संसृष्टाः सोदरत्वसंसृष्टत्वरूपोभयप्रयोजकविशेषणवन्तस्तमंशं गृह्णीयुरित्यर्थः । भगिन्यश्च सनाभयः, सनाभयः सोदराः ताश्चाप्रदत्ताः, प्रदत्ताः पुनः पतिगोत्रमासादयन्तीति प्रकाशः । (5) बृहस्पतिः । संसृष्टौ यौ पुनः प्रीत्या तौ परस्परभागिनौ । (6) तथा । विभक्ता भ्रातरो ये तु सम्प्रीत्यैकत्र संस्थिताः । पुनर्विभागकरणे ज्यैष्ठं तेषां न विद्यते । कदाचिद्वा प्रमीयेत प्रव्रजेद्वा कथञ्चन । न लुप्यते तस्य भागः

सोदरस्य विधीयते। या तस्य भगिनी सा तु ततोऽंशं लब्धुमर्हति। अनपत्यस्य धर्म्मोऽयमभार्य्यापितृकस्य च। संसृष्टानान्तु यः कश्चिद्विद्याशौर्य्यादिनाधिकम्। धनं प्राप्नोति तत्रास्य हंग्रशः शेषाः समांशिनः॥ विद्याशौर्य्यादिना असाधारणप्रयोजकरूपवदन्येन। (7) नारदः। संसृष्टानान्तु यो भागस्तेषामेव स इष्यते। अतोऽन्यथांशभाजस्तु निर्वीजेष्वितरानियात्॥ अतोऽन्यथा संसृष्टिनामभावे, निर्वीजेषु सन्तानरहितेषु, इतराननंशभाजोऽसंसृष्टिनो भाग इयाद्गच्छेत्। प्रकाशकारस्तु अतोऽन्यथा पुत्रवत्त्वेऽपि त एवांशभाजः। निर्वीजेषु सन्तानरहितेषु भ्रातॄन् भाग इयाद्गच्छेदित्याह। पारिजाते तु अतोऽन्यथा अनंशभाज इति पठितं, तत्तु बहुग्रन्थविसंवादात्त्यक्तम्। (8) शङ्खः। भ्रातॄणामप्रजाः प्रेयात्कश्चिच्चेत् प्रव्रजेत वा। विभजेरन् धनं तस्य शेषास्ते स्त्रीधनं विना। भरणञ्चास्य कुर्व्वीरन् स्त्रीणामाजीवनक्षयात्। रक्षन्ति शय्यां भर्त्तुश्चेदाच्छिन्द्युरितरासु तत्। या तस्य दुहिता तस्याः पित्रंशो भरणे मतः। आसंस्कारात् हरेत् भागं परतो बिभृयात् पतिः॥ स्त्रियोऽत्र वैधव्यव्रतादिसहिताव्यभिचारिण्यः। अभार्य्यापितृकस्य चेत्यत्र भार्य्याशब्दो वैधव्यव्रतादिसहिताव्यभिचारिणीपरः। पारिजाते तु स्त्रियोऽत्र सवर्णा इत्युक्तम्। तेन तन्मते भार्य्याशब्दः पूर्व्वसवर्णभार्य्यापर इति लक्ष्यते। इतरासु शय्यामरक्षन्तीषु। आसंस्काराद्विवाहमभिव्याप्य तावन्तं भागं हरेद्यावता विवाहस्य निष्पत्तिरिति कल्पतरुः। (9) याज्ञवल्क्यः। संसृष्टिनस्तु संसृष्टी सोदरस्य तु सोदरः। दद्यादपहरेद्भागं जातस्य च मृतस्य च॥ संसृष्टिनो मृतस्य तु धनं संसृष्टी हरेत् नत्वंशहरः सोदरस्य तु सोदरः। सोदरासोदरसंसर्गे सोदर एव गृह्णीयादित्यर्थः। (10) इदानीं सोदरस्यासंसृष्टस्य वैमात्रेयस्य संसृष्टस्य सद्भावे संसृष्टिनि मृते यद्भवति तदाह। अन्योदर्य्यस्तु संसृष्टी नान्योदर्य्यो धनं हरेत्। असंसृष्ट्यपि चादद्यात् संसृष्टो नान्यमातृजः॥ नान्योदर्य्यो धनं हरेदसंसृष्टीति श्लोकच्छेदः। अनेनान्वयव्यतिरेकतोऽन्योदर्य्यसंसृष्टित्वं धनहरणकारणमित्युक्तं न तु संसृष्टीति परेणापि सम्बध्यते तेनासंसृष्ट्यपि धनमाददीत, कोऽसावित्याकाङ्क्षायामुक्तं, संसृष्टः एकशुक्रशोणितसम्भवः सोदर इति यावत्, अनेन चासंसृष्टस्यापि धनग्रहणे सोदरत्वमपि हेतुरुक्तः। तेनोभयोरेव धनग्रहणहेतुमत्त्वादुभयोरपि धनग्राहकत्वमुक्तम्। यस्तु कल्पतरौ नान्योदर्य्यधनं हरेदिति पाठस्तत्रापि स एवार्थः। अन्योदर्य्यस्य धनं अन्योदर्य्यधनं तेन अन्योदर्य्यस्य संसृष्टिनो धनमन्योदर्य्यः संसृष्टी न हरेदित्यर्थः। अन्ये तु

अन्योदर्य्यस्तु संसृष्टी नान्योदर्य्यधनं हरेदिति ऋजुमेवार्थमनुमन्यन्ते । (11) कात्यायनः । संसृष्टानान्तु संसृष्टाः पृथक्स्थानां पृथक्स्थिताः । अभावेऽंशहरा ज्ञेया निर्वीजान्योन्यभागिनः ॥ संसृष्टानां मृतानां संसृष्टा अंशहराः, पृथक्स्थानां मृतानां पृथक्स्थिता अंशहरा ज्ञेयाः, अभावे भार्य्याद्यभावे । निर्वीजान्यन्यभागिन इति द्वन्द्वसमासः । (12) बृहस्पतिः । विभक्तो यः पुनः पित्रा भ्रात्रा वैकत्र संस्थितः । पितृव्येनाथवा प्रीत्या स तु संसृष्ट उच्यते । अनास्थायां वाकारः, तेन पितृव्यजेनाप्यंशिना कृतविभाग एकत्रस्थितः संसृष्टः सर्व्वलोके परिगृहीतो लभ्यते । प्रकाशे तु वचनबलेन नियम एवात्रेत्युक्तम् । (13) इति विवादरत्नाकरे संसृष्टिविभागतरङ्गः ।

CHAPTER XXXVI.

(1) अथ विभागनिर्णयः । (2) तत्र नारदः । विभागधर्म्मसन्देहे दायादानां विनिर्णयः । ज्ञातिभिर्भागलेख्येन पृथक्कार्य्यप्रवर्त्तनात् । भ्रातॄणामविभक्तानामेको धर्म्मः प्रवर्त्तते । विभागे सति धर्म्मोऽयं भवेत्तेषां पृथक् पृथक् । दानग्रहणपश्वन्नगृहक्षेत्रपरिग्रहाः । विभक्तानां पृथग्ज्ञेयाः पाकधर्म्मागमव्ययाः । साक्षित्वं प्रातिभाव्यञ्च दानं ग्रहणमेव वा । विभक्ता भ्रातरः कुर्य्युर्नाविभक्ताः परस्परम् । येषामेताः क्रिया लोके प्रवर्त्तन्ते स्वरिक्थतः । विभक्तानवगच्छेयुर्लेख्यमप्यन्तरेण तान् ॥ विभागरूपो धर्म्मः विभागधर्म्मः तस्य संशये जातो न वेत्याकारे दायादानां ज्ञातिभिः निर्णयः कर्त्तव्यः । भागलेख्यं विभागज्ञापकं लेख्यं, पृथक्कार्य्यप्रवर्त्तनात् पृथगायव्ययादिकार्य्यप्रवृत्तिदर्शनात् । धर्म्मो वैश्वदेवादिक्रियाकलापः । आगमोऽर्थप्राप्तिः, व्ययस्त्यागः, अनन्यथासिद्धौ तात्पर्य्यम् । (3) याज्ञवल्क्यः । विभागनिह्नवे ज्ञातिबन्धुसाक्ष्यभिलेखितैः । विभागभावना ज्ञेया गृहक्षेत्रैश्च यौतकैः ॥ यौतकैः पृथग्भूतैः यु मिश्रणे अमिश्रणे च इति धात्वनुसारात् । (4) तथा । भ्रातॄणामथ दम्पत्योः पितुः पुत्रस्य चैव हि । प्रातिभाव्यमृणं साक्ष्यमविभक्ते न तु स्मृतम् ॥ परस्परमिति शेषः । यद्यपि जायापत्योर्विभागो न विद्यते इत्यापस्तम्बः, तथापि यदि कुर्य्यात्समानंशान् पत्न्यः कार्य्याः समांशिका इति वचनाद्याज्ञवल्क्येन पत्न्या अपि स्वामिना सह क्वापि विभागो

बोधित इति, तदभिप्रायेण दम्पत्योरिति याज्ञवल्क्यवचनं नेतव्यमित्यविरोधः । (5) बृहस्पतिः । पृथगायव्ययधनाः कुसीदञ्च परस्परम् । वणिक्पथञ्च ये कुर्य्युस्ते विभक्ताः परस्परम् ॥ परस्परं साहित्यं विना अन्योन्यनैरपेक्ष्येति यावत् । पृथगायव्ययधना इति पृथक्पदमुत्तरत्रापि सम्बध्यते । (6) इति विवादरत्नाकरे विभागनिर्णयतरङ्गः ।

CHPTER XXXVII.

(1) अथ विभक्तकृत्यम् । (2) तत्र नारदः । यद्येकजाता बहवः पृथग्धर्म्माः पृथक्क्रियाः । पृथक् कर्म्मगुणोपेता न चेत् कृत्येषु सङ्गताः ॥ एकवीर्य्यजातत्वम् विवक्षितम् । पृथग्धर्म्माः भिन्नभिन्नमहायज्ञादियुक्ताः । पृथक्क्रियाः पृथक्कुसीदादिवृत्तिमन्तः । पृथक्कर्म्मगुणोपेताः पृथक्प्रजारक्षणकृषिशुश्रूषादियुक्ताः । न चेत् कृत्येषु सङ्गताः न चेत् सम्भूयकारिण इत्यर्थः । (3) अस्योक्तस्य फलमाह । स्वभागान्यदि ते दद्युर्विक्रीणीयुरथापि वा । कुर्य्युर्यथेष्टं तत्सर्व्वमीशास्ते स्वधनस्य वै ॥ अत्र वाक्यान्तरपरामर्षात् सर्व्वपदं सङ्कोच्यम् । सङ्कोचकानि च दत्ताप्रदानिकप्रकरणस्थबृहस्पत्यादिबहुवाक्यानि विभक्ता अविभक्ता वेत्यादीनि तत्रैवानुसन्धेयानि । (4) बृहस्पतिः । येनांशो यादृशो भुक्तस्तस्य तन्न विचालयेत् । स्वेच्छाकृतविभागो यः पुनरेव विसंवदेत् । स राज्ञांशे स्वके स्थाप्यः शासनीयोऽनुबन्धकृत् ॥ स्वेच्छाकृतविभागेन येनांशो यादृशो भुक्तस्तस्य स एव भागः, न तु विचालयेदिति स्थैर्य्यार्थमुक्तं स्वेच्छाकृतविभाग इत्यादिनानुबन्धकृदित्यन्तेन । (5) इति विवादरत्नाकरे विभक्तकृत्यतरङ्गः ।

INDEX.

INDEX.

A.

B.

Page

C

D.

E.

F.

K.

L.

M.

R.